Inside the Foreign Office

John Dickie, a graduate of Glasgow University, worked with the *Sheffield Telegraph*, Reuters and the *News Chronicle*, before joining the *Daily Mail* as the Diplomatic Correspondent in 1960. For thirty years he covered all the major events in international affairs; he knew every Foreign Secretary from Lord Home to Douglas Hurd and acquired unrivalled contacts within the Diplomatic Service. A keen rhabdopholist, he has built up a collection of 87 prized examples during his travels. He was awarded the OBE in June 1991.

'Illuminating insights into what happened behind the scenes at the Foreign Office'
Financial Times

'Full of splendid stories'
Mail on Sunday

'Scores of mini-scoops'
Guardian

'Dickie is a master of the word'
Glasgow Herald

'He has almost ended up by becoming a mandarin himself'
Daily Telegraph

'An entertaining description of how the Foreign Office works'
Gerald Kaufman, *Manchester Evening News*

Inside the Foreign Office

JOHN DICKIE

CHAPMANS

Chapmans Publishers
141–143 Drury Lane
London WC2B 5TB

First published by Chapmans 1992
This paperback edition first published by Chapmans 1992

© John Dickie 1992

The right of John Dickie to be identified as the author
of this work has been asserted by him in accordance with
the Copyright, Designs and Patents Act, 1988

ISBN 1 85592 618 0

Printed and bound in Great Britain by
Clays Ltd, St Ives plc

For Inez
for waiting . . . for ever

Contents

Preface

It is an extraordinary paradox that opposite the most famous open door in Whitehall is the most secretive Department of the Government. The Foreign Office has eschewed the limelight which a cavalcade of prime ministers has enjoyed on the other side of the road at No. 10 Downing Street. The two sides of Downing Street illustrate the basic contrast between party politics and diplomacy. Arrivals at and departures from No. 10 are recorded on television almost every day while the mandarins go in and out of the Foreign Office unnoticed. Cameras and microphones catch every gesture, every word spoken outside No. 10. None is allowed across the threshold into the Foreign Office quadrangle on the other side.

What goes on inside the Foreign Office has stayed secret for a number of reasons. Those on the inside are bound by a code of confidentiality which inhibits the disclosure of affairs of state in any detail that might be damaging to the best interests of the country. Ministers and ambassadors have signed away their right (via the Official Secrets Act) to set down on paper what really went on inside the Foreign Office when they were there. Those on the outside are not allowed the freedom to move at will inside. They are not normally trusted to have access to anything or anyone in the Foreign Office which could result in the outside world getting to know what is really going on inside.

In these circumstances it may seem presumptuous to embark upon an enterprise designed to cast aside the mystique and give an account of what has been happening inside the Foreign Office during the past three decades. The reason for doing so is that it was suggested to me that as the Diplomatic Correspondent of the *Daily Mail* from 1960 until 1990 I was in a position to have a unique insight into the conduct of foreign policy during that period. Travelling round the world with every foreign secretary from Lord Home to Douglas Hurd and attending all the major summit conferences, I had the opportunity to observe the Foreign Office in operation across the entire spectrum of international affairs. The actions and reactions of governments, their ministers and officials formed a fascinating tapestry of evolving trends on which to judge how well the Foreign Office has met the challenge of change.

This book, however, is not a history of foreign affairs during the past thirty years. That is the task of historians detached from the deadlines which determine how far the search for truth can go at any one time. Instead, this is an examination of how the Foreign Office has been handling the affairs of the nation abroad, with illustrations from various events in the past three decades. It describes the system, how it works, who makes it work, when it has worked well, and when it has not done so. As objectively as possible, it sets out to show how the politicians used the system, where they succeeded, and where they failed.

In getting the inside story I have been greatly helped by a large number of people whose trust I have enjoyed over the years and who have spoken in confidence to me with complete frankness. During the research I have had lengthy conversations on tape with over 150 ambassadors and senior members of the Diplomatic Service, past and present, politicians involved with foreign policy, ministers and diplomats of other governments, and international civil servants. These interviews were conducted off-the-record with the assurance that no one who took part would be identified. I am very grateful for their assistance – and for their friendship. Accounts of events compiled from talking to key participants may not have come out as certain contributors expected, but the touchline view is often sharper than the players'.

One apology to the purists. I am perfectly aware that the proper title of the Department is the Foreign and Commonwealth Office, but as people throughout the diplomatic world still refer to it as the FO I have retained the title 'Foreign Office' throughout the book.

Diplomatic colleagues have been generous with their help, particularly David Adamson who took great pains checking every page in the manuscript and tendering advice. David Spanier, who also read some chapters, was perceptive on questions of balance. Mohsin Ali in Washington and Gordon Martin in Geneva offered insights and encouragement. The helpfulness of Gordon McKenzie, Literary Editor of the *Daily Mail*, in getting the project started was much appreciated. I am greatly indebted to the staff of the Daily Mail Library for their endless patience in looking up references. Research assistance from the Royal Institute of International Affairs, the Reference Library of the US Embassy in London, and the Commonwealth Secretariat was prompt and efficient. Despite all their efforts, errors may still be found in the text, in which case the fault lies entirely with me.

One final debt of gratitude is due to my wife, Inez, who has borne the burdens of isolation and neglect during the long stretches of travelling and writing with inimitable grace.

John Dickie,
Brooklands, Oxshott,
November 1991

I

The March of the Mandarins

*Foreign policy would be OK except for the
bloody foreigners.*

Lord (Herbert) Morrison: March 1951

At 10.29 every morning the sound of hurried footsteps on the
gleaming brown marble tiles along the ground floor of the Foreign
Office echoes round the corridors of power. It is the march of the
mandarins. They are on their way to the Meeting. No one ever
needs to ask: 'Which one?' It is the one meeting of the day which
sets the wheels of the Foreign Office in motion. Britain's place in
the world in the light of events round the globe within the previous
twenty-four hours is being determined to the best ability of Her
Majesty's Diplomatic Service. It is the daily review of Britain's
foreign policy and how the foreigners are reacting to it. With the
precision of a military parade, the Meeting is called to order at
exactly 10.30 a.m. by the Permanent Under-Secretary of State –
the grandest of the diplomatic grandees, always addressed by the
initials PUS – in his own room, directly beneath that of the Foreign
Secretary. Neither the Foreign Secretary nor any of his junior
ministers is present. It is an occasion where the elite meet in the
exclusive atmosphere of a Senior Common Room.

This assessment of affairs of state by the combined talents of the
Diplomatic Service became a daily occurrence almost by accident.
Until the general election in October 1964, the PUS's meeting
was not a regular item on the list of engagements each day. Its
establishment as a daily priority was the result of the predicament

created by the strange situation of Patrick Gordon Walker. He was appointed Foreign Secretary in the Wilson Government in 1964 after losing his seat at Smethwick and had to divide his time between contesting a by-election at Leyton and attending to foreign affairs.

In the three months that Patrick Gordon Walker held the office, until his second electoral defeat in 1965, it was considered essential that while he was campaigning he should be kept up-to-date with a daily account of international developments. The system devised by Lord Caccia, then Permanent Under-Secretary of State, was to have a *tour d'horizon* every morning with senior officials and an account of it conveyed to the candidate at the hustings. That mission was usually undertaken by Sir Nicholas Henderson, then Principal Private Secretary, or by Sir Nicholas Fenn, the Assistant Private Secretary. One of them would sit in the gloom of a spartan room near the mayor's parlour in Leyton Town Hall going through the report of the PUS's meeting and the contents of the diplomatic boxes at the lunchtime break while Patrick Gordon Walker munched his way mournfully through a plate of spaghetti. It may not have helped his campaign, but it proved so useful at the Foreign Office in setting out the agenda of the day that the march of the mandarins has become an institution in Whitehall like the Changing of the Guard.

Being at the Meeting is an indication that you are one of the chosen few, a candidate capable of going right to the top of the Diplomatic Service. Who is invited to attend is decided by the PUS. Everyone present realizes that one's performance in this highly competitive brains' trust could well determine how far one's career will go. The number of mandarins present depends on how many are out of the country on the day, but usually it is between twenty-five and thirty. An even more significant indicator of your status is where you take your seat. There is an Inner Circle of twelve at the top of the table. The rest are seated in the Outer Circle, not quite restricted to speaking only when they are spoken to by the PUS but with less chance of direct intervention than those at the top table. The two diplomats next in seniority to the PUS, the Chief Clerk and the Political Director, occupy pride of place alongside the chairman. Around them are the rest of the top echelon, the Deputy Under-Secretaries of State. At the next level most of the fifteen Assistant Under-Secretaries have seats in the Outer Circle.

Two key figures, however, who are well below the others in rank, have places in the Inner Circle. It marks the importance of public relations nowadays that a seat is reserved there for the Head of News Department. He is the Foreign Secretary's chief spokesman, always at his side at home and abroad, and he is listened to with close attention since he has to set out each day the issues on which he will require to state Foreign Office policy both on-the-record and on a background-only (that is to say, not to be quoted) basis. Next to him at the top table is the Foreign Secretary's Principal Private Secretary, the man who walks one pace behind the Minister. As he has to attend meetings with the Foreign Secretary and often be the official note-taker he has to be aware of the preparations being made to handle whatever problems are to be faced.

Three other heads of department are admitted to this inner sanctum on the Outer Circle: the Head of Information, who is responsible for sending guidance on policy to embassies, the Head of Policy Planning, and the Head of Research Department. Extra places were introduced by Sir Patrick Wright who was PUS from 1986 until 1991. He invited the private secretaries to the ministers of state to attend every day and the Foreign Secretary's parliamentary private secretary to come once a week.

Everyone attending the Meeting will have gone through all the telegrams from ambassadors on the priority issues of the day. They are also expected to have read their newspapers or at least the summary page of the Press Cuttings Service, which is circulated round the office, on all matters of international concern. With the background fresh in everyone's mind, the PUS counts on short, sharp assessments so that he can close the Meeting at 11.00 a.m. with the same precision as he started it. No solemn pronouncements are handed down in Churchillian style for 'Action this day'. One of the great values of assembling the expertise of the mandarins round the table at one time is that it provides an early-warning mechanism to alert the rest of the Foreign Office to the prospect of trouble ahead from certain issues which at that moment seem no more than a vague cloud on the horizon. Another advantage is that it collates all elements of a challenging situation so that the administrative aspect can be evaluated along with the political and economic factors. It also enables an overview to be taken so that other departments in Whitehall – Defence, Trade, Treasury or Transport – can be given advance notice of problems.

The same pattern of assessing situations is now followed at British embassies round the world where ambassadors summon key members of their staff each day for what is irreverently called 'Morning Prayers'. Sometimes it is almost on Presbyterian terms of 'two or three gathered together'. Elsewhere it is on a grand scale, such as at the mini-Foreign Office in Washington, where there are 114 UK-based diplomats and as many from other Whitehall departments, or at the High Commission in New Delhi where there are 75 members of the Diplomatic Service and at least half as many from the Home Civil Service.

Inside the Foreign Office the march of the mandarins is the only time of the day when the hushed ambience of the cloisters is disturbed. Unlike any other Whitehall department, the Foreign Office retains the atmosphere created by the architect Sir Gilbert Scott when he built what Beresford Hope described in 1868 as 'a kind of national palace or drawing room for the nation, with working rooms hung onto it for foreign business of the country'. The grandeur is symbolized by the high ceilings in the style of an Italian *palazzo*. Diplomats summoned from posts abroad to see the Foreign Secretary walk up the Grand Staircase with a superb view rising 60 feet to the crown of the gilded dome. Office ceilings signify the importance of the occupant. In the Foreign Secretary's room on the first floor the ceiling is 21 feet high. On the ground floor the ceilings are 17 feet high while on less important floors the ceilings are a modest 13 feet on the second floor and a mere 12 feet on the third floor.

This quiet, pensive environment reflects the origins of the Foreign Office in 1782 when Charles James Fox became the first Foreign Secretary, with the playwright Richard Brinsley Sheridan as his deputy, and Britain's global interests were conducted from a private house in Cleveland Row known as 'Mr Fox's Office'.

After the transfer to Downing Street, life inside the Foreign Office remained virtually the same, apart from an increase in the number of staff, until a revolutionary change was disclosed on 25 January 1924 by the Diplomatic Correspondent of the *Daily Telegraph*.

The report, which sent shock waves from Downing Street to the haunt of the mandarins in the Travellers' Club, stated: 'The Prime Minister yesterday morning established a notable departure from tradition by starting work at the Foreign Office before ten o'clock.' Making sure that the impact of the disclosure was fully appreciated, the correspondent explained:

To realize the importance of this step regard must be had to the fact that, for generations past, the working hours at the Foreign Office have been different from those of other departments, beginning, for certain categories of officials, an hour or an hour and a half later. Of course, it should be remembered that many of the higher officials, more particularly in times of stress, are frequently to be found at the office long after the regulation hours. In his capacity as Foreign Secretary, Mr Ramsay MacDonald is evidently determined to introduce administrative innovations like Signor Mussolini and General Primo de Rivera. He is equally determined, by combining the Foreign Secretaryship with the Premiership, to spare neither himself nor his subordinates, taking the view that abnormal times require abnormal efforts.

Working conditions steadily deteriorated over the next forty years to the point where the Minister of Public Building and Works, Geoffrey Rippon, told the Commons on 13 November 1963 that it was time for radical action.

It has become apparent, after further study, that any attempt to retain the present building, even with such modernization as would be possible structurally, would be uneconomic and would fail to provide accommodation suitable for present-day conditions, let alone future requirements. I have therefore decided to demolish the existing building in due course and to construct on the same site an entirely new building.

The Opposition spokesman, Charles Pannell, Labour MP for Leeds West, gave his complete approval, saying: 'The present accommodation of the Foreign Office is a tawdry slum which would not be tolerated outside.'

The announcement provoked so many angry letters to *The Times* from all over Britain and the United States that a special headline, 'Battle of the Foreign Office', was reserved for the protests. One correspondent, Stella Margetson, gave a clarion call for the campaign to save the national palace: 'We must fight to keep a part of our dear heritage that Hitler failed to destroy and a view that is unique in the world.' Lord Harrowby was outraged: 'It stands magnificently British as seen from St James's Park and embodies all that was, and I hope still is, the British character.' An American historian, Professor D. Emerson from the University of Washington, DC, wrote to deplore the 'baffling stupidity' of the demolition plans and quoted Sir Osbert Sitwell's description from *Great Morning* of the 'view across the length of water from Whitehall and the Foreign Office, as spectacular as any in Venice and Pera' in his appeal to save it.

There were discordant voices, however. One person who knew what it was really like inside the Foreign Office, W. G. Hayter of New College, Oxford, stated: 'It is, in fact, a terrible building to work in. The rooms for senior members of the staff have a certain heavy dignity. But those unfortunate juniors are obliged to work herded together in large, high, cold rooms where five or more telephone conversations and five or more dictating processes make concentration impossible.' His criticism was supported by a plea from Diana Richmond: 'Writing as a stenographer and the wife of a Foreign Service Officer, I suggest that a building should be designed for efficiency and for the comfort of those who use it.' The election of the first Wilson Government caused the demolition plans to be shelved. The cramped working conditions were eased slightly when the Commonwealth Relations Office on the Whitehall side of the quadrangle, which swallowed up the last vestiges of the Colonial Office in August 1966, was merged with the Foreign Office on 17 October 1968. A further easing occurred in 1978 when the Home Office building, which had its front on Whitehall, was handed over to the Foreign Office. But the prevarication of successive governments over the cost of modernization continued until 1979 when the Fire Service Inspectorate warned that the buildings would be denied fire insurance certificates unless they were brought up to date with the requisite safety standards. As the cost of maintenance just to keep the buildings from further deterioration was then running at £1.4m a year, the resistance of the Treasury crumbled. The Government authorized total refurbishment, sector by sector. A twelve-year programme with a budget of £92m was started in 1984.

One of the most ingenious operations of the restoration was undertaken in the largest room in the Foreign Office, which was styled the Cabinet Room by Sir Gilbert Scott although it was never used as such. This magnificent salon, measuring 72 feet by 38 feet, was the reception suite where the Treaty of Locarno was signed on 1 December 1925 by Aristide Briand, Gustav Stresemann, and Austen Chamberlain settling the long-disputed frontiers of France and Germany with the optimistic comment by Briand which has yet to be completely fulfilled in the European Community today: '*A Locarno nous avons parlé européen. C'est une langue nouvelle qu'il faudra bien que l'on apprenne.*' Ironically, the room was also the scene of a minor diplomatic incident which temporarily clouded relations between Britain and her oldest ally. During a reception hosted by Lord Curzon for the King and Queen of Portugal, an overzealous waiter leapt forward to light the Queen's cigarette and set the veil of her hat on fire.

After the Second World War a surge of artistic revulsion against all Victoriana resulted in the salon being divided into drab cubicles for offices. The famous barrel-vaulted ceiling 40 feet high was blocked off with a false ceiling 15 feet from the floor, thus obscuring the fine paintings of satyrs with lyres. White emulsion had been daubed over the gold-patterned walls and the artistic medallions had been scraped off. But forty years later the restorers retrieved the former glory, helped by photographs taken by flashlight which revealed the shape of the hidden patterns. Young craftsmen worked for almost twelve months carefully colouring the walls in the original designs. In the adjacent large conference room they restored the brilliant gold-squared ceiling and the majolica plaques displaying the emblems of the twenty countries with which Britain had diplomatic relations in 1867. It was completed in time to be used by delegates to the NATO summit in London in June 1990.

The showpiece of the restoration is the transformation of the Durbar Court alongside the old India Office. It was opened with a State ball in honour of the Sultan of Turkey on 19 July 1867 and had been neglected after March 1939 when King George VI and Queen Elizabeth entertained President Lebrun of France. Despite the dilapidation in the course of forty years, with busts of Indian viceroys gathering grime beside Corinthian columns of Aberdeen granite, the Court was carefully brought back to the opulent style of its heyday. Instead of the music of the Life Guards band, which played at diplomatic tea parties in the nineteenth century, the Durbar Court resounded after its renovation to the voices of Foreign Secretary Douglas Hurd and members of the Diplomatic Service singing carols round an illuminated tree at Christmas time in 1990.

To mark the completion of the main part of the refurbishment, a bust of Ernest Bevin, presented by one of his private secretaries, Patrick Kinna, was given pride of place at the foot of the Grand Staircase. It was unveiled on 4 October 1991 by Douglas Hurd at the prominent site originally occupied by a bust of Cromwell then later by a showcase of medals awarded to Queen's Messengers, the couriers who bring diplomatic bags from embassies to the Foreign Office.

Mandarins walking up the Grand Staircase in need of inspiration have an inscription at the top from Psalm 67: 'Let the people praise thee O God. Yea let the people praise thee. O let the nations rejoice and be glad for thou shalt judge the folk righteously and govern nations upon the earth.' Eight muses along the corridor of the old India Office embody the virtues which are thought to be appropriate for the conduct of Britain's policy overseas: Prudence, Justice, Honour, Wisdom, Charity, Faith, Courage, and Truth – not necessarily, however, in that order of precedence.

Outside the Ambassadors' Waiting Room, which has a gloomy painting called *The Tower of Babel* by the seventeenth-century artist Christian Micker for envoys to contemplate as they wait to be summoned next door to the Foreign Secretary, there are five huge murals. They are the work of Sir Sigismund Goetze who completed them after the First World War at his own expense. Portraying the various aspects of Britannia's labours, they show her as the devoted mother rearing her children and teaching them the Arts of Peace while in another corner encouraging her sons to prepare themselves in the Arts of War. The message left by Sir Sigismund in 1919 for future policy-makers was symbolized in the 'hands-across-the-sea' image of Britannia linked to what he described as 'America, wearing the cap of Liberty, as the greatest of Republics'. Whether that will be appropriate for mandarins coming to terms with European Union remains to be seen.

The refurbishing required Sir Geoffrey Howe to leave the Foreign Secretary's room in 1987. Sadly for him, the Prime Minister's Cabinet reshuffle in July 1989 meant that he never returned to it. Instead, it was Douglas Hurd who moved back from temporary accommodation across the quadrangle in the former room of the Home Secretary and became the first minister to enjoy the restored splendour of the largest working room in the Foreign Office. As a former member of the Diplomatic Service before turning politician, he had known the room from the time Lord Home first entered it as Foreign Secretary on 28 July 1960. In those days it was dominated by a large imposing picture over the fireplace of King George III, who probably caused more havoc to Britain's overseas relations than any other monarch. Certainly, that was the view of George Brown. The first thing he did on his appointment as Foreign Secretary on 12 August 1966 was to have the portrait of George III taken down and replaced by a painting of a statesman whom he wanted to emulate, Palmerston.

One innovation by Lord Home won the approval of the mandarins – the removal of the coal fire which often belched smoke across the room into the faces of his visitors. He had a gas fire installed, although elsewhere in the building coal fires and even antiquated Victorian coal lifts remained until the final phase of the modernization programme. Above the gas fire the portrait facing foreign secretaries nowadays is a painting of the first oriental prince to visit Britain, Jung Bahadur, the Prime Minister and Commander-in-Chief of Nepal who was royally entertained in 1877.

For the conduct of foreign affairs there is an almost ecclesiastical calm along the corridor outside Room 52 where the Foreign Secretary wrestles with the problems of the world. Hush-hush diplomacy is enjoined by the painted figure on the wall overhead – a maiden with a forefinger to her lips and the admonition in a word underneath: 'Silence'. Inside the room, which is plainly furnished like a headmaster's study with a schoolboy's globe of the world at one end and at the other bookshelves with leather-bound volumes of Hansard from 1964 onwards, the Foreign Secretary has the best views in Whitehall from his five windows. Two of them scan Horse Guards Parade while the others look on to St James's Park, the view Sir Edward Grey gazed at in 1914 as he reflected on the lamps going out all over Europe. From his large desk the Foreign Secretary can press a button to summon expertise on any subject he requires for decisions on foreign policy from the mandarins, the professionals of the Diplomatic Service.

II

The Professionals

My first impression of the Foreign Office, and my very last, was of its quite extraordinary professionalism.

Lord George-Brown,
Sunday Times,
7 April 1968

I admired the men and women of the Foreign Office and felt it a privilege to work with them – they were outstanding, and in my experience their quality exceeds that of any other Department – and any other Foreign Office.

Lord Carrington,
Reflect on Things Past,
1988

Ever since the Foreign Office came into being over two centuries ago, much of its activity has been shrouded in secrecy. That, in turn, has given rise to a certain mystique about those engaged in the conduct of foreign policy, the professionals of the Diplomatic Service. Although they usually ridicule many of the myths that have proliferated around them, most diplomats secretly delight in their reputation as illuminati, the gifted mandarins of our time. By tradition, members of the Diplomatic Service have been set apart from those in other branches of government service as the elite.

Regardless of the radical social changes in Britain over the last fifty years, the Diplomatic Service has remained elitist. The majority of those serving in it not only feel superior to other members of the Civil Service but they often behave – with just a flick of arrogance – as if they actually were so. More than any other department in Whitehall, the Foreign Office engenders an *esprit de corps* which imbues everyone in the Service from the newest third secretary to the most senior ambassador with a sense of mission unparalleled in any other branch of government. They are the *crème de la crème*: they know it, and rarely let an opportunity slip to ensure that other lesser beings realize it.

This sense of superiority is buttressed by the style in which a senior diplomat is sent forth from the Court of St James's to represent Her Majesty the Queen in a foreign capital. It is hard for an envoy not to step out feeling very proud when he leaves Buckingham Palace with a large, red, royal seal on his credentials which send him forth in such glowing terms as these:

> Elizabeth the Second, by the Grace of God of the United Kingdom of Great Britain and Northern Ireland and Her other Realms and Territories Queen, Head of the Commonwealth, Defender of the Faith.
>
> To all and singular to whom these Presents shall come, Greeting!
>
> Whereas it appears to Us expedient to nominate some person of approved Wisdom, Loyalty, Diligence and Circumspection to represent Us in the Character of Our Ambassador Extraordinary and Plenipotentiary,
>
> Now Know Ye that We, reposing especial trust and confidence in the discretion and faithfulness of Our Trusty and Well-beloved Sir Joseph Bloggs have nominated, constituted and appointed, as We do by these Presents nominate, constitute and appoint him, the said Sir Joseph Bloggs to be Our Ambassador Extraordinary and Plenipotentiary to Ruritania aforesaid. Giving and granting to him in that character all power and authority to do and perform all proper acts, matters and things which may be desirable or necessary for the promotion of relations of friendship, good understanding and harmonious intercourse between Our Said Realm and Ruritania and for the protection and furtherance of the interests confided to his care;

by the diligent and discreet accomplishment of which acts, matters and things aforementioned he shall gain Our approval and show himself worthy of Our high confidence.

And We therefore request all those whom it may concern to receive and acknowledge Our said Sir Joseph Bloggs as such Ambassador Extraordinary and Plenipotentiary as aforesaid, and freely to communicate with him on all matters which may appertain to the objects of the high mission whereto he is hereby appointed.

Given at Our Court of St James's, the 31st day of December, and in the 39th year of Our Reign.

The definition originally given in 1604 by Sir Henry Wotton of an ambassador as 'an honest man sent to lie abroad for the good of the state' has long been consigned to the history books. The qualities of an ideal ambassador as set down by Sir Harold Nicolson in his definitive work *Diplomacy*, and thereafter termed the 'Nicolson test', are truth, accuracy, calm, patience, good temper, modesty, and loyalty. Then he added: 'But the reader may object, "You have forgotten intelligence, knowledge, discernment, prudence, hospitality, charm, industry, courage, and even tact". I have not forgotten them. I have taken them for granted.'

The ambassador's role has had to be adapted to the demands of the high-technology age and it is perhaps best described by one of Britain's most gifted ambassadors, Lord Trevelyan, in his memoirs *Diplomatic Channels* in the following terms.

He must regard himself as an economist, a commercial traveller, an advertising agent for his country; he wields the weapon of culture for political ends; he promotes scientific and technical exchanges and administers development aid. He cannot wholly detach himself from the technicalities and personal inconveniences which accompany the battle for intelligence. He must concern himself with the relations not only of governments, but also of politicians, scientists, musicians, dancers, actors, authors, footballers, trade unionists and even women and youth, these two new technical professions in the modern world. But he continues to have a basic political job to negotiate with the other government and to keep his own government informed about anything in the country to which he is accredited which affects his country's interests.

While Lord Trevelyan, with distinguished service in the Middle East, China, and the Soviet Union, amusingly alluded to the notion among the Press that an ambassador is 'there to provide information for the correspondents' copy and a good story out of anything that happens in the embassy', he was also generous enough to acknowledge that 'co-operation between the embassy and the Press correspondent is useful to both'.

Under the codification of immunities and privileges in the Vienna Convention on Diplomatic Relations in 1961, the envoy arriving in a foreign capital with his credentials is, in theory at least, assured of a certain amount of protection. Diplomatic privileges entitle a person to freedom from arrest and detention, immunity from criminal and, in many cases, civil jurisdiction, and the inviolability of his embassy and residence. The diplomat is guaranteed the right of free communication for all official purposes and exemption in the country where he is accredited from all public service and any military obligations such as requisitioning of supplies or billeting of personnel. His most valued privilege is exemption from paying taxes in the state to which he is accredited.

When presenting his credentials, the envoy sent by the Queen to represent her abroad is usually required to wear full dress diplomatic uniform. The regalia, as officially described, starts with a coatee of dark blue cloth, single-breasted with a stand-up collar. 'The collar and gauntlet cuffs are of black velvet, and the pocket flaps of blue cloth. Nine buttons up the front (to button), two at the waist behind and two at the bottom of the back skirts. Pocket flaps buttoned with three buttons. Black silk linings. A white collar may be worn inside the coat.' Rank is indicated on the cuffs, with a first-class envoy having one inch of lace and two rows of Russian braid, and on the collar with half an inch of lace and scaled down embroidery. The trousers in dark blue cloth have gold leaf lace two and a half inches wide down the side seams. He wears a white web belt to carry his ceremonial sword. His sartorial elegance is crowned with a black-beaver cocked hat with 'black silk cockade,

treble gold bullion loop and tassels'. After presenting his credentials, an envoy is entitled to a nineteen-gun salute whenever he
steps aboard a warship of the Royal Navy.

At least when an ambassador establishes himself nowadays in
his mission, he is provided with funds and allowances to help cover
the cost of carrying out his functions. These *frais de représentation*
vary according to the cost and range of entertainment calculated
to be necessary in each country. Ambassadors' allowances as fixed
in 1990 were authorized at £47,000 a year in Moscow and Rome,
£109,000 in Washington, and £120,000 in Paris. Entertaining by
diplomats is justified in R. G. Feltham's *Diplomatic Handbook* on
the grounds that it helps to 'improve the public image of their
country' but even more importantly because 'it enables heads and
senior members of missions informally to "sound out" members
of the Ministry of Foreign Affairs (and to a lesser extent politicians,
businessmen and other diplomats) regarding proposals they would
like to make, but would rather not put in writing or raise officially
lest the result should be a definite, and possibly irreversible, negative'. In former times the cost of conducting the business – and
the entertaining – of a mission had to be met by the envoy's own
financial resources. Until 1919 new members of the Diplomatic
Service were required to have a personal income of at least £400
a year in order to qualify for an appointment abroad.

The tradition of elitism stems from the very beginning of the
Foreign Office when it was established as a socially exclusive preserve. Upper-class families supplied generation after generation
of diplomats. Names appearing in the *Foreign Office List* of 1869
such as Rumbold, Russell, and Elliot are to be found again in the
diplomatic biographies in the 1969 *List*. In the mid-nineteenth
century, Lord Clarendon selected only candidates who were
known personally by him and who were nominated as young men
of repute with good health and the ability to 'write a good bold
hand forming each letter distinctly, to write quickly and correctly
either in English or French from dictation, to understand French
well and to be able to make an accurate and good translation of
any French paper, and also to make a clear and correct précis or
abstract of any set of papers placed in his hands'.

Entrants for places today in Grades 8 and 7D – the fast stream of the Diplomatic Service and the route normally reserved for those expected to reach the level of deputy under-secretary of state and senior ambassadors – are still hand-picked. Civil Service Commission figures for admissions in 1989 showed that fewer than 1 per cent of the people who applied actually secured places. Out of 1,630 applicants, all with first or second class university degrees, only 14 obtained appointments. There was a slight improvement in the 1990 recruitment figures issued by the Civil Service Commission in July 1991. The Open examination produced 27 successful candidates out of 1,411 applicants – but that was still less than 2 per cent. To win through they had to pass a written examination lasting a day and a half with a variety of papers, some of which were in diagrammatic form for applicants whose background was in mathematics or science. Then they were among 227 out of the original 1,411 chosen for the final selection system which is described by the Civil Service Selection Board as an assessment involving 'a blend of job simulation exercises, interviews and objective cognitive tests'. The panel, which includes a psychologist, seeks to gauge the potential of the candidate's ability and personality.

The assessment used to take place in a rambling old country house near Oxshott in Surrey where candidates spent two days feeling that the eagle eyes of the psychologist were always on them even when they picked up a newspaper at breakfast and wondered which would give the wrong impression. Much the same tension was sustained when the CSSB was transferred to London where the examiners studied the candidates in discussions and group exercises organized for tackling imaginary international problems. Although leadership qualities are rated as important, the over-eager 'follow me' types are usually marked down. The main emphasis is on the ability to work well in a team – either as a leader encouraging others or as a member ready to make a useful contribution or undertake tasks whose outcome is unpredictable. What can often be finally decisive is the reaction of the psychologist at a one-on-one session when the aspiring diplomat is casually asked some such question as 'What sort of person would you most like to talk to on a long train journey?'

Here, again, the elitism shines through the statistics. Of the 22 candidates recommended in 1989 for appointments in the Diplomatic Service all but 6 came from Oxford or Cambridge universities, that is nearly 73 per cent. In 1990, when 27 graduates were admitted to the fast stream, 18 were Oxbridge candidates – nearly 67 per cent. The figures show no substantial change from the previous generation. In 1966, for example, 16 of the 19 successful candidates for the administrative grade were Oxbridge applicants, that is 84 per cent. The recommendation for an appointment is not an automatic guarantee of a place in the Diplomatic Service. Two further hurdles have to be overcome: a medical examination and a security test. Sir Andrew Gilchrist revealed that he secured a place as a result of a last-minute fluke. He explained:

> In 1933 I sat an examination in which I came thirteenth and only twelve candidates were to be taken. Would someone fall under a bus, I wondered? No one did, but a man high up on the list was found, on being medically examined, to have only one kidney. Thereupon, having been certified as possessing the correct number, I duly took his place. Later I learned that the regulation was based upon the severe strain imposed upon Foreign Service staff, stationed abroad, by the pressure of the social round of representational life to which their kidneys are regularly and inevitably exposed.

The security check known as PV (TS) – positive vetting (top secret) – covers two aspects of a candidate's profile. Applicants are advised that they will face enquiries 'concerned not only with their political sympathies or associations but also with revealing any characteristics which may be a potential risk to security'. The first barrier is defined in these terms: 'The Government have decided that no one may be employed in the Civil Service in connection with work which is vital to the security of the State if he or she is or has recently been a member of the British Communist Party or of a Fascist organization; or has been sympathetic to Communism or Fascism in such a way as to raise doubts about his or her reliability.' Until 1991 the second barrier was equally emphatic: 'Homosexuality, even if acknowledged, is a bar to employment in the Diplomatic Service.'

Although public attitudes to homosexuality changed radically after the Swinging Sixties it took a long time for the new liberalism to reach the authorities monitoring entrants to the Diplomatic Service. It reflected concern that the Foreign Office was suspect as a haven for clandestine homosexuality. The stern line taken by those responsible for vetting standards was defended on two grounds. First, diplomats were regarded as at risk of being compromised when they served in a Communist country and, secondly, it was considered to be potentially embarrassing to send a diplomat, known not to be heterosexual, to a country where homosexuality is not accepted legally or socially.

After a review by John Major as Prime Minister changes were announced on 23 July 1991 'in the light of changing social attitudes towards homosexuality in this country and abroad, and the correspondingly greater willingness on the part of homosexuals to be open about their sexuality, their life-style and their relationships'. He decreed that homosexuality would no longer be 'an automatic bar to security clearance'. However, being a homosexual remains a handicap for anyone with ambitions to reach the upper echelons of the Diplomatic Service. The Prime Minister put it this way: 'The susceptibility of the subject to blackmail or pressure by a foreign intelligence service will continue to be a factor in the vetting of all candidates for posts involving access to highly classified information.'

An attempt was made to broaden the trawl for new entrants in 1968 when Michael Stewart, a former schoolteacher, was Foreign Secretary. He invited university vice-chancellors from provincial universities and from the ancient Scottish universities of Glasgow, Edinburgh, Aberdeen and St Andrews – all of them more than 500 years old and senior to many Oxbridge colleges – to a day-long seminar at the Foreign Office to discuss ways of encouraging a wider catchment area for recruiting future ambassadors. But the conclusion was that graduates from these universities were not likely to be convinced that they could beat the system when the final selection process after the written examination seemed to them weighted in favour of the Oxbridge candidates. Nonetheless, there are continuing efforts made to attract candidates from provincial universities and polytechnics.

When accusations of elitism were raised in the House of Commons in 1977 by the Defence and External Affairs Sub-Committee of the Expenditure Committee, senior diplomats argued vehemently that questioning someone's social background amounted to inverted snobbery. One of them, Sir Mark Heath, claimed that recruitment to the Diplomatic Service was wide open, to which Mr Neville Sandelson, Labour MP for Hillingdon, retorted: 'Like the Ritz.' He made the point often stressed when the statistics are examined in Parliament: 'We want a Service which represents the mass of the people of this country – and I don't think it does.'

The response from the Establishment is usually to point to the track record of the successful Oxbridge entrants in the fast stream. They substantiate their case by citing as examples the 'Golden Boys' of the intake into the administrative grade in 1966. They pick out high flyers such as Paul Lever (Queen's, Oxford), who distinguished himself from the start in Helsinki, then spiralled up from Brussels to be Head of the United Nations Department and afterwards Head of Security Co-ordination Department, before being promoted in 1990 to be Head of the UK Delegation to the Conventional Forces in Europe conference in Vienna. Other successes from that vintage year were Bernard Everett (Lincoln, Oxford) who became Ambassador to Guatemala at the age of forty-four and Robert Flower (Magdalene, Cambridge) who impressed in Zomba, Kuala Lumpur, and Bonn and was made Deputy Head of Mission in Stockholm in 1990. Another of their contemporaries, David Wright (Peterhouse, Cambridge), made his mark in Tokyo, was seconded to Buckingham Palace as Deputy Private Secretary to the Prince of Wales, and then promoted to be Ambassador to South Korea. Two other rising stars were handpicked to serve with Sir Geoffrey Howe: Russian-speaking Christopher Meyer (Peterhouse, Cambridge) who was outstanding as the Foreign Secretary's chief spokesman, and then went on to become Minister (Commercial) in Washington on his way up the ladder, and Chinese-speaking Anthony Galsworthy (Corpus Christi, Cambridge) who was highly praised as Principal Private Secretary to the Foreign Secretary and was appointed Senior British Representative of the Joint Liaison Group working with the Chinese on the implementation of the Hong Kong agreement.

The Establishment has no 'Golden Girls' of 1966 to cite in support of their case. In that year there was only one woman in the nineteen successful candidates for the administrative grade and she opted out of the Foreign Office in 1985 to transfer to the Department of the Environment. Ever since 1889, when the first woman was admitted to the staff of the Foreign Office and described as a 'lady typewriter', the prejudices and obstacles to be overcome have made it doubly difficult for women to make their way up the ladder. The attitudes of mind which were widespread until relatively recently were exemplified by Mrs Mollie Ashworth in a letter to *The Times* on 13 May 1989: 'When I first joined the Foreign Office the lavatory doors were marked "Gentlemen" and "Women". One assumed that no "lady" would demean herself by earning a living – and that was less than thirty years ago.'

Statistics on the recruitment of women to the Diplomatic Service Grades 8 and 7D make dispiriting reading for female graduates aspiring to have a career in government service abroad. The figures for 1989 showed that 690 of the 1,630 applications for administrative grade appointments came from women with first or second class university degrees. Of the 545 who were invited to the written examination, only 77 survived to the interview stage. Only 3 of the 22 candidates recommended for appointment were women and only 2 were admitted in the end. The proportion was higher in 1990 with 8 of the 27 places going to women – almost 30 per cent. Women fare better in applying for places in the equivalent grade of the Home Civil Service. Of the 54 university graduates who secured appointments in 1990 to Grade 7 posts, 23 were women. The success rate for women seeking entry into the Diplomatic Service in 1990 worked out at 1.4 per cent compared with that of 5.2 per cent for women applying for the administrative grade of the Home Civil Service.

The record of ethnic minorities trying to obtain places in the Diplomatic Service at the lower level of Grade 9 in the executive class is even more discouraging. Out of 1,524 applications in 1990 only 51 came from ethnic minorities – 3.3 per cent. When they were whittled down at tests and interviews to 273, there were only 5 non-white candidates left. One of them was among the 70 given appointments by the final selection board – a success rate of 2 per cent. Although more members of the ethnic minorities applied for places in the administrative grade of the Home Civil Service, the results were more dispiriting. There were 124 applications out of a total of 1,872 in 1990 – that is 6.6 per cent – but only one was successful. Their performance was much better in the competition for posts as executive officers in the Home Civil Service. There were 2,272 applicants out of a total of 18,089 in 1990 and 113 of the 2,802 successful candidates were from the ethnic minorities, giving a success rate of 5 per cent.

In the United States, where the Foreign Service Act of 1980 requires that it should be 'representative of the American people', the proportion of minorities is still low compared with the percentage of those employed in the private sector. Although the appointment of minorities to the Foreign Service was increased between 1981 and 1987 from 7 to 11 per cent that was partly the result of 'positive discrimination' which in some cases amounted to rigging the examinations in their favour. When it was realized that the written examination was proving an enormous hurdle with only 5 per cent of the minority candidates passing compared to 20 per cent of the other candidates, the rules were bent. A substantial number of the minority candidates who were deemed to have 'almost passed' the written examination were allowed through to the next phase, the oral test. That meant that 28 per cent of the minority candidates were invited to the oral examination instead of only the 5 per cent who had actually passed the written examination – and the oral examiners were similarly considerate to them. Nonetheless, the increasing number of minorities obtaining employment generally in the United States has not enabled the State Department to record a significant improvement as an employer of minorities in comparison with the private sector.

One of the arguments frequently employed in Britain to explain why so few women have reached ambassadorial level is that until relatively recently women were obliged to leave the Diplomatic Service on marriage. But the regulations were changed in 1972, enabling women to stay in the Service after marriage or have up to five years' absence on special unpaid leave before deciding to return or resign. There has been ample time, therefore, to enable suitably qualified women to be considered for senior posts.

Another reason given is that it would not be 'appropriate' to appoint a woman as ambassador to an Arab country. No such consideration has been a restriction on women in the United States Foreign Service.

Ms April Glaspie, a career diplomat, was appointed US Ambassador to Iraq in 1987 at the age of forty-five after serving in Egypt, Tunisia and Syria. She achieved such fluency in Arabic that she was in charge of the State Department's language school in Tunis. Dr Kissinger singled her out for high praise during his Middle East shuttle diplomacy in 1973 not only for her Arabic but for being his 'laundry officer', ensuring that his shirts were not over-starched by Egyptians in Aswan. She was at the centre of controversy over comments which she was alleged to have made to President Saddam Hussein one week before he invaded Kuwait in August 1990. She was quoted as saying to him: 'My assessment after twenty-five years' service in this area is that your objective must have strong backing from your Arab brothers.' But in March 1991 she told the Senate Foreign Relations Committee that the Iraqis had edited out a warning against the use of violence when they quoted her as saying: 'We have no opinion on Arab–Arab conflicts like your border disagreement with Kuwait.' Some of her female colleagues, who admired her performance before the Committee, wondered whether their cause was advanced by the disclosure that she insisted that her mother accompany her to Baghdad as she had done to other Arab capitals.

The record of the Foreign Office in promoting women is a lamentable reflection of its failure to move with the times, particularly when the impact of the Equal Opportunities Commission set up in 1975 after the passing of the Sex Discrimination Act has had an important influence in other occupations. Until now no woman has reached the senior mandarin level of the six deputy under-secretaries of state working with the Head of the Diplomatic Service, the Permanent Under-Secretary of State. The highest rank any woman has attained has been assistant under-secretary of state, which Miss Catherine Pestell achieved in May 1987 after serving as Minister (Economic) in Bonn, where she was awarded the CMG. Only two of the fifteen assistant under-secretaries in the 1991 list were women. With 170 British missions around the world headed by an ambassador or a high commissioner, the Foreign Office has appointed only eight women so far to be in charge of a mission. No woman has been appointed yet as ambassador to any country in Eastern Europe. On only two occasions so far has the Queen been asked to present credentials to a woman to represent her as ambassador in a Western European capital – to Dame Anne Warburton in April 1976 to Copenhagen and to Mrs Juliet Campbell in February 1988 to Luxembourg.

Africa has been considered the most appropriate continent for the talents of women to be employed as head of a mission – to countries such as Botswana, Burkina Faso (formerly Upper Volta), Chad, Côte d'Ivoire, Mozambique, and Niger. In fact, when Miss Maeve Fort arrived as Ambassador in Mozambique in September 1989 half the eight-member mission were women. One woman, Susan Rogerson, whose posting to Africa was cancelled, won an apology in November 1986 for the first time in the history of the Diplomatic Service. She took her case to an industrial tribunal, alleging that sex discrimination had resulted in her promotion to deputy high commissioner in Zambia being withdrawn. Although the 44-year-old high flyer had served in Africa previously and had got on well with Africans at the United Nations, the Foreign Office claimed there would have been problems in Lusaka since her presence there would have made the political section at the High Commission all-women. But forty-eight hours before her case was due to be heard the Foreign Office backed down, expressing regret for 'the distress' she had suffered. It was admitted that 'while acting in good faith, their decision to abandon Mrs Rogerson's proposed posting to Lusaka was mistaken'.

No woman has ever been sent as ambassador east of Suez and only one woman until now – Mrs Margaret Bryan – has ever been in charge of a British Embassy in Latin America. The latest figures for the highest grade so far reached by women, that is fifth from the top at SP5, show that there are only six women in that bracket. The next grade down the scale, DS4, has only ten women in the list. One major advance since the regulations were changed in 1972 is that there are now ninety married couples working together in the Service, forty of them in joint postings abroad.

Despite the temporary toe-hold gained by April Glaspie in the male-dominated world of diplomacy in the Middle East, the record of advancement of women in the US Foreign Service is almost as bleak as in the British Service. Although there were fanfares for the achievements of Mrs Anne Armstrong, who became the first American woman accredited to the Court of St James's in 1976, and of Mrs Shirley Temple Black, who won almost as much praise in diplomatic circles as she formerly did in Hollywood, when George Bush became US President in 1989 only six of America's ambassadors were women. He acted quickly to improve the record by putting forward twelve women among his first nominations for ambassadors. But there was still widespread dissatisfaction at only 9 of the 135 deputy chief of mission jobs being held by women in a service where 24 per cent of the staff at that time were women. That figure caused particular resentment since there were about 320 women who had the qualifications for the 30 to 40 posts of deputy chief of mission which became available in 1989. As in Britain, women in the US Foreign Service had to resign on marriage until 1971. Yet even with a master's degree in government and fluency in eight languages it was not until 1989 that Mrs Julia Chang Bloch became the first Asian American ambassador when she was appointed to Nepal.

Demand for change became a major public issue in America when a US District Court Judge, Aubrey E. Robinson Jr, ruled in 1989 that the State Department had discriminated against women in appointments abroad. Because his ruling on discrimination also applied to the process of selecting 250 entrants from the 20,000 applying for admission to the Foreign Service, the 150-question general background section of the general examination was scrapped. As a result the State Department was ordered to offer places at the penultimate oral examination to the 400 women candidates who had the best results in the written examination which had been judged as discriminatory. One immediate consequence was that the number of women among the new entrants rose to 35 per cent in the following year.

All entrants in Britain to the Diplomatic Service at whatever grade – administrative Grades 8 or 7D, executive at Grade 9 for applicants up to forty-five years of age with at least two A levels, and clerical at Grade 10 for candidates between seventeen and twenty with at least five O levels including one in a foreign language – are trained from their first day to be professionals. Their first lesson is never to knock on any door inside the Foreign Office but to walk straight in, head high, and never to address anyone as 'Sir' except the Foreign Secretary, and he normally prefers to be addressed as 'Secretary of State'. The first year is usually spent in a department at the Foreign Office in what is termed the Third Room, where the lowliest members work, so that they can absorb a basic knowledge of the system and its techniques before being sent abroad.

This in-house training to enable the newcomer to settle down quickly into an embassy on a first posting as a useful member of the staff puts great emphasis on learning languages. In contrast with the laughable reputation of the average Englishman in a foreign language, members of Britain's Diplomatic Service enjoy tremendous esteem as linguists, particularly in the so-called 'hard languages' – Arabic, Russian, Japanese, and Chinese. The high standard of Arabic spoken by diplomats is traditional in the Service. It used to be the pride of Sir Donald Maitland in his days as Director of the Middle East Centre for Arab Studies (MECAS) at Shemlan, a village twenty miles from Beirut, until the fighting in Lebanon forced it to be closed. That reputation is fully maintained today at the Diplomatic Service Language Centre in London under John Moore. It was demonstrated to the amazement of Saudi Arabian ministers when Lord Carrington visited that country in November 1981 and made four speeches. Each time his address was translated into faultlessly pronounced Arabic by different members of the British Embassy staff under the watchful eye of the distinguished Arabist who was Ambassador, Sir James Craig. There are 185 serving diplomats who are able to speak Arabic.

The lack of equivalent expertise in Hebrew – although obviously not expected on the same scale – angered Foreign Secretary Douglas Hurd during a Middle East tour in October 1990, since it was one of the factors that made his visit to Israel a diplomatic shambles. At the end of a difficult first day he was told to mind his own business after urging the Israelis to co-operate with a proposed United Nations inquiry into the killing of twenty-one

Arabs during shooting by security troops at the Temple Mount in Jerusalem. Then came a leak from a meeting he held with MPs at the Knesset which claimed that he said the British Government 'firmly opposes the idea of a separate state for Palestinians'. Although the report of the leak, with all its damaging implications for the Foreign Secretary's status as an even-handed statesman on the Arab–Israeli dispute, was carried on the main evening television news bulletin in Israel, Hurd remained in the dark about it. There was no one available at the British Embassy with a knowledge of Hebrew monitoring television to alert him to the danger of leaving the report unchallenged.

The Foreign Secretary was furious at not being informed about it until the next morning. Alarm bells rang when the Arabists at the British Consulate-General in East Jerusalem reported the furore among Palestinians caused by the leak which was published in the English-language *Jerusalem Post*. Hurd, who was handicapped by not having his main Arab expert, the Hon. David Gore-Booth, another distinguished graduate from MECAS, in his delegation, sent his newly appointed Deputy Under-Secretary of State, Patrick Fairweather, on an immediate damage-limitation mission. But by the time Fairweather tried to argue that the Foreign Secretary had been misquoted, the Palestinians had lost patience after waiting over fifteen hours for an explanation. The thirty leading Palestinians from the Occupied Territories, who had been invited to lunch with Hurd, much to the annoyance of his Israeli hosts, rebuffed the Foreign Secretary by calling off the meeting with him forty-five minutes before it was due to start. While Hurd said he was 'too well trained to be angry' – at least in public – it was particularly galling to him as a politician with an exceptional talent for languages. Only a few weeks before his Middle East visit, he demonstrated linguistic skills unmatched in a foreign secretary since the days of Sir Anthony Eden. He went to Paris where he delivered an address and answered questions afterwards in French and then ten days later gave a similarly impressive performance at Rome in Italian.

The gaffe in Israel was a rare occurrence. The Diplomatic Service sets so much store on languages that there are courses in more than fifty languages provided under a budget of £1m. Instruction is geared to four standards: survival, which is merely to enable a person to handle everyday situations; functional, which is to meet the requirements of straightforward work in a foreign country; operational, which is to ensure that a person can deal with substantive business; and extensive, which is an in-depth knowledge making a person capable of coping with complex negotiations. Each new entrant in the administrative and executive grades normally spends three months on full-time language training during the first year of service. Everyone in the Diplomatic Service – and spouses as well – can have up to 100 hours of free tuition in French, German and Spanish, irrespective of whether the language is required for the current posting.

Diplomatic posts are classified in terms of the level of language proficiency needed for them. Diplomats appointed to a post without a language requirement are allowed to take time off-duty for a course of up to 100 hours in the language of the country. Courses for 'hard languages' last much longer. The ten students usually taking the long Arabic course at any one time spend seven months under intensive instruction at the Language Centre and then a further eleven months in an Arab country. More than 120 diplomats are proficient in Russian, about 60 speak Chinese, and 70 speak Japanese. There are five diplomats fluent in Lao and three in Mongolian. In the latest examination results two candidates passed with proficiency in Tagalog, the principal language of the Philippines. Even when English is in widespread use in an East African country such as Tanzania, diplomats posted there usually take a course in Swahili before they arrive.

Emergency arrangements had to be made for crash courses in Czech, Polish, Bulgarian, and Hungarian to train the extra staff who were drafted into Eastern Europe in 1990 when the shackles of the Communist regimes were thrown off and governments looked to Western countries for help in democratizing their systems. As embassies were able to have vastly greater contact with people in Eastern Europe – particularly in helping to administer the 'Know-How Funds' set up by the British Government – diplomats who had previously been treated with suspicion in the Cold War era suddenly found themselves face to face with a much wider variety of people. Full-time training in Eastern European languages was increased to 5,272 student working days in 1990–91, almost double that of the previous year. Despite a scaling down of embassy staff in South America, there was an increase in the number of diplomats with proficiency in Spanish – a total of 511 in 1991 compared with 459 in 1985.

There are, of course, incentives for young diplomats to acquire proficiency in languages – financial rewards as well as extra qualifications to press claims for career advancement. Everyone passing the preliminary examination in French receives £115 extra each year; in Arabic, Chinese, or Japanese the payment is £255. Spouses who pass the examinations are given half the rate of the serving officer. For passing examinations in Lower French the payment is £420, in Intermediate French it is £840, and in Higher French it is £1,259. In Arabic, Chinese, and Japanese there is a further examination for Advanced Level with passes carrying a payment of £2,940. All allowances are increased each year in accordance with pay increases, but to ensure that people continue to qualify they are tested every five years. One diplomat receives allowances for proficiency in six languages – Arabic, French, German, Hungarian, Italian, and Spanish.

Refresher courses are arranged for senior diplomats to brush up their knowledge before a posting. For ambassadors going to a French-speaking country arrangements are made for them to spend a month with a family in France. Ambassadors take pride in retaining some degree of fluency in a language learned in the early days of their service. Visitors to the British Embassy compound in Addis Ababa are shown the bungalow where Sir Ewen Fergusson learned Amharic and are informed that when he became Ambassador to South Africa and later to France he still kept his knowledge of the language in a serviceable state in case he met an Ethiopian minister.

Training ranges extensively, far beyond linguistic expertise, to promote a high level of professionalism in specialized subjects. One area of skills which has been given great emphasis in the past two decades is the work of the commercial counsellor and his attachés in assisting British exporters in their 'Buy British' campaigns. Each year sixty UK-based diplomats attend the five-week courses run five times a year by the Training Department under Terence Curran. Diplomats are then assigned for a fortnight to a major

British company which operates in the country to which they are being posted. With a vastly expanding volume of work involved in handling applications at embassies for entry certificates to Britain, there is also a steadily increasing requirement for training more consuls in the complexities of issuing visas.

The establishment of the Single Market in the European Community in 1992 has already put fresh emphasis on diplomats' expertise in economics, finance, and Community affairs in general. A five-day EC seminar for young diplomats leads to a further five-day seminar at the Community headquarters in Brussels. Techniques for negotiation in the EC are studied at a three-day course and there is an intensive course, cynically nicknamed by some as 'Know Your Enemy', on France and the European Community which takes eleven days, ten of them spent in Europe. To equip diplomats to face all the problems of pollution, the Training Department runs courses five times a year on the economics of energy and the environment. Human rights issues which loom large at the United Nations and in Third World countries are tackled in a special two-day course which has lectures from Amnesty International.

Surprisingly, the diplomats assigned to work in the News Department and deal with journalists from the Press, radio and television were often plunged in at the deep end until relatively recently. They usually arrived without any advance knowledge of what happens inside a newspaper office or television newsroom, how a journalist has to operate, or what the competitiveness of news gathering requires journalists to do. Now that presentation of foreign policy and reaction to the policies of others are given such a high profile, there are media courses to train diplomats on the techniques of handling journalists' questions on television, radio and the telephone. The Foreign Office has its own workshop for teaching the use of word processors and facsimile machines. It has its own studio to instruct diplomats in interview techniques and test them in a series of playbacks. Even experienced senior ambassadors call in for refresher courses. In the short period between transferring from Ambassador to the European Community in Brussels to become Ambassador at the United Nations in New York in 1990, Sir David Hannay, a highly skilled exponent in Press briefings, took three days in London to brush up on techniques for facing the media in the United States.

Training is accorded such high priority that every entrant to the executive grade as well as the administrative fast stream is given an individual training plan designed to make each new diplomat develop his or her talents to their fullest potential. A twelve-page booklet beomes a logbook of obligatory and optional programmes shaping the progress of the newcomer in acquiring all the necessary skills for a career in the Service. The essential elements at the outset are a two-week introductory course followed by a one-week policy-drafting course. Alongside the language course in French – with the option of German, Spanish, or Italian for those proficient in French – there are compulsory courses in economics, international affairs, and keyboard skills for word processors. Because of the special emphasis now being put on cost-effective diplomacy, diplomats are started early in their career on learning management techniques, beginning with a five-day residential course, then moving on later to intermediate level and ultimately to studies in senior management systems.

This sort of expertise which provides the professionalism throughout the Diplomatic Service has discouraged political appointments, which are so widespread in many other countries. In South America ambassadorial appointments are used as a reward for services to the regime or sometimes as a means of keeping political opponents out of the country. Occasionally Australian and New Zealand Governments have made an appointment to their High Commission in London the consolation prize for not getting a seat in the Cabinet. The most widespread use of patronage in diplomacy is in the United States where at times one out of every three ambassadors comes from outside the ranks of career diplomats. During the Reagan administration the number of political appointees in the Foreign Service went up to 40 per cent when there were more than 100 senior American diplomats consigned to be 'corridor walkers' – officers left without assignment – at the State Department.

It reached such controversial proportions that Senator Claiborne Pell, Chairman of the Senate Foreign Relations Committee, condemned the system as beyond a joke after hearing that the undiplomatic Ambassador in Rome, Peter Secchia, a wealthy timber merchant who contributed substantially to the Republican campaign, outraged other diplomats by posing the question 'Why do Italian warships have glass bottoms?' and answering: 'So they can see the previous Italian fleet.' Another envoy, former Nevada Senator Chic Hecht, listed as his qualifications for becoming Ambassador in the Bahamas the fact that he played a good game of golf and came from a state noted for its gambling facilities.

Only on rare occasions have there been special reasons for Downing Street selecting someone outside the Diplomatic Service for a particular appointment. It happened in 1961 when Lord Harlech was sent by Prime Minister Harold Macmillan to be Ambassador in Washington for his closeness to President Kennedy, and in 1968 when Sir Christopher Soames, the former Conservative Cabinet minister, was sent by Prime Minister Harold Wilson to be Ambassador in Paris with the intention of impressing President de Gaulle. These appointments were accepted without demur in the upper echelons. But the imposition of politicians in senior ambassadorial roles can cause resentment in the Diplomatic Service. That happened when Sir Donald Maitland, a much admired ambassador, was suddenly recalled after eight months in New York to make way for the former Labour politician, Sir Ivor Richard, who was given the post by Prime Minister Harold Wilson as compensation after losing his parliamentary seat in the 1974 general election. There was a much greater uproar over the peremptory dismissal of the Hon. Sir Peter Ramsbotham as Ambassador in Washington by Foreign Secretary David Owen in July 1977 and his replacement by Mr Peter Jay, the journalist son-in-law of Prime Minister James Callaghan. The way the change was announced and explained in Downing Street caused such a furore at Westminster that thereafter prime ministers and foreign secretaries have thought twice before considering political appointments to senior embassies.

Because the traditional public concept of a British diplomat as a person in striped trousers, black jacket, and a rolled umbrella is not one easily abandoned, it is often assumed that the diplomat's salary is as inflated as his image. 'If only it were so' is the *cri de coeur* heard in British embassies all round the world. Although the running costs of the Diplomatic Wing were put at £467m for 1991–92 out of a total Foreign Office budget of £2,932 m – including £1,911m for aid programmes – it is completely misguided to assume that diplomats are paid on anything like the scale of the City or big business. The Head of the Diplomatic Service, who is the Permanent Under-Secretary of State responsible for the worldwide operations of 6,605 UK-based staff – about 2,700 of them abroad at any one time – and 7,000 locally engaged staff, earns a salary which was set on 1 January 1991 at £98,000 a year. That may look impressive against the salary of the Prime Minister at £72,533 or of the Foreign Secretary at £59,950. Compared with salaries in the private sector, however, the earnings of the PUS and of the Political Director, who is paid £60,100, make them look poorly rewarded. Glaxo's chairman Sir Paul Girolami was given a pay increase of £388,000 in June 1991 to bring his salary up to £1,080,000. British Telecom chairman Iain Vallance was earning £450,000 in 1991, British American Tobacco chairman Sir Patrick Sheehy was getting £529,335 while his financial director Brian Garraway was on £414,234. Sir Denys Henderson was receiving £440,000 as chairman of Imperial Chemical Industries with his deputy Frank Whiteley getting £278,500. British Airways chairman Lord King took a cut of 21 per cent in 1991 to bring his salary down to £407,650 while Sir Colin Marshall received £350,000 as chief executive and deputy chairman. In many cases there are substantial bonus payments, share options sometimes worth over £1m, and the use of a company helicopter or executive jet.

Diplomats in charge of major embassies rarely complain about the rewards of thirty years in the Service which amount to a salary of £84,250 for the most senior ambassadors, to £74,000 for middle-ranking ambassadors, and to £60,100 for SP3 grade. It is those on their way to the top in the Foreign Office who often feel inadequately rewarded. The grade which is the highest so far attained by a woman diplomat, SP5, carries a salary of £51,300. Beneath that level the so-called workhorses of the Diplomatic Service are the counsellors at Grade DS4 earning between £35,720 and £46,746, depending on length of service and performance points, and the first secretaries at DS5 on a scale of between £24,641 and £34,301. For the upper reaches of the executive officers in Grade DS7E, the salaries vary from £14,630 to £20,326. The young high flyers entering the Service are paid £12,867 in Grade DS8 at the age of twenty-two or £15,891 in Grade DS7D at the age of twenty-six – not the sort of magnet which on its own is calculated to draw graduates into the Diplomatic Service instead of the City.

It used to be thought that honours were conferred on diplomats not just to recognize meritorious service but to compensate for the low salary scales. But the distribution of honours has been curtailed over the past two decades. In the Diplomatic Service List of 1971 there were 55 knights and 188 diplomats holding the award of Companion of St Michael and St George. In the 1991 list there were 31 knights and 118 CMGs. Over the last ten years there has been an average of 7 knighthoods and 23 CMGs awarded each year to diplomats.

Extra incentives are provided in the form of a Boarding School Allowance, which helps defray the cost of educating children in Britain while parents are abroad and enables them to be flown out to posts during holidays, a Climatic Clothing Allowance which is a one-off payment for tropical wear, and a Transfer Grant to ease the cost of changing posts. There is an Enhanced Diplomatic Service Allowance to compensate for living in a hardship post with a different climate, and an Indirect Representational Supplement which goes some way to meet the burden of extra entertaining. Duty-free liquor and tobacco cushion the rigours of watching the sun go down in a Third World post where the only excitement is the arrival of the diplomatic bag with letters from home once a week. On top of all that is the provision of accommodation abroad free of charge – sometimes, as head of mission in a post such as Singapore, in the fine colonial style of Eden Hall with a large rambling garden and swimming pool; sometimes, lower down the scale, in the cramped conditions of a compound, or struggling for survival in the ghetto atmosphere of a block of diplomatic apartments in Eastern Europe. One administrative assistant on arrival at his first posting in Nigeria complained to the deputy head of mission that the furniture in the accommodation was not up to the standard to which he and his wife had been accustomed in their semi-detached house in Surbiton.

The main allowance for covering the additional expenses of living abroad is worked out separately for each post on quaint calculations of the differential above what it costs for Bromley Man to live at home. It is measured on a scale of purchases like a cost of living index. So if the cost of a cabbage in the market at Moscow is four times the cost of one in the market at Bromley, the local allowance takes account of that. It covers buying shirts and socks as well as food and makes provision for the extra travelling required when serving abroad. But it often calls for hard negotiating, as when it was argued that a young clerk in Grade DS10 would probably not be able to buy a new car if he lived in Bromley and therefore could not expect his allowance to reflect the cost of a car on being posted to India. Then it had to be pointed out that no young officer could be expected to do his job properly travelling in India by bus.

Entertaining abroad by Bromley Man is sometimes assumed to be a gourmet's delight at the taxpayer's expense. In fact, all entertainment by diplomats is subject to a strict budget under the hawk eyes of the Diplomatic Service inspectors. An up-and-coming first secretary cannot use half his allowance entertaining his old chums from school or his cousins swanning round the world on holidays. Every item of expenditure on entertainment has to be accountable. Each guest for lunch or dinner has to be listed by name, and checked by the head or deputy head of mission to ensure that there is no unnecessary duplication in entertaining members of ministries in the government. There are often quotas for the number of lunches, dinners, and receptions for each department in an embassy. Wives, whose services as hostesses are free and usually taken for granted, have to supply inspectors with a typical menu for twenty people, costed in detail down to the number of after-dinner mints. Sometimes the costing has to account for the extra electricity used for a barbecue supper out of doors, the overtime payments for serving staff, and even the candles used in a power cut.

Senior ambassadors are subject to the same detailed scrutiny of their entertaining as young diplomats on their first posting. The biggest auditing operation occurs at the magnificent Lutyens mansion in Washington's Massachusetts Avenue, where the British

Ambassador's invitation is one of the most sought-after in the American capital. During his five years there from 1986 to 1991 Sir Antony Acland, the most influential envoy since Lord Harlech in Kennedy's Camelot days, had to account for entertaining 24,000 people to receptions, 9,000 to dinner, 3,700 to lunch, and 6,500 to afternoon tea. Every expense in accommodating 1,700 overnight guests, even when they were members of the royal family or Cabinet ministers, had to be costed to the nearest pound.

Whitehall's parsimonious bookkeeping sometimes goes to ridiculous lengths, as John Sankey discovered in 1984 when he was High Commissioner in Tanzania. He sent seven of his ten salt-cellars to be re-silvered in London because they looked so shabby when he was entertaining guests to dinner. The cautious book-keepers in Whitehall checked their records and informed him that originally the High Commission's entitlement had been fixed at six salt-cellars but that in a new economy drive the figure had been reduced to three. So only three salt-cellars were sent back re-silvered to Dar-es-Salaam, regardless of protests from the High Commissioner that it was 'sometimes farcical and always embarrassing' to have only three to pass round dinner guests at ten separate tables.

Despite the excitement at times of service abroad, the satisfaction of keeping Britain's diplomatic reputation burnished bright in the capitals of the world, and the perks that go with it in terms of foreign allowances, ambassadors became aware in the 1980s of a growing sense of frustration among diplomats between the ages of thirty-five and forty-five. These professionals, who included most of those taking the biggest burdens of the diplomatic workload, were becoming more and more dissatisfied. They were irked by the slowness of promotion – and the financial hardship accentuated by delayed access to the higher-paid ranks – the lack of flexibility in using talents, and the sheer inefficiency of resource management. One voice spoke out for them in a remarkable way – that of Sir Hamilton Whyte, known affectionately throughout the Service as 'Ham' and always something of a maverick even to the extent of having enormous murals, painted by his artist wife Sheila, of nude figures amorously intertwined, hung behind his desk wherever he went.

His valedictory dispatch to the Foreign Secretary on 13 May 1987 on retiring as High Commissioner in Singapore was not the traditional ritual review of Britain's place in the sun as seen from South-East Asia. 'Ham' Whyte used the occasion to jolt Sir Geoffrey Howe into re-examining what could be done to restore some of the *joie de vivre* to the frustrated ranks of the Service. It was not a sour farewell. The dispatch, which was marked 'In Confidence' but was smuggled out of the dusty Foreign Office files, began on a happy note: 'I have had a good run, thanks to good luck, good jobs, rarely a dully moment. No complaints on my own account.' He went straight to the heart of the trouble:

In the FO we are skilful (mostly) at moving people to the top. But below the top we create frustration and inefficiency by being unable to retire decently those we could do without. This impairs promotion prospects for the middle ranks where the pressure of work is greatest and increases the temptation among those we can least spare to peel off for higher salaries. Let those who prefer the security of the Home Civil Service or the fast track in the City go their separate ways. For those with a taste and a flair for government service overseas and a career very different from that of the Whitehall commuter or the business whiz-kid, greater upward mobility and more scope to get round pegs in round holes should offset the prospect of having to find a new niche in middle age.

'Ham' Whyte's plan was simple: 'We need to change the terms on which we recruit. To take on people in their twenties with tenure to sixty (short of defection, sexual aberration or senility) is in this day and age plain crazy. How do we know what they, or the world, or our requirements will be like in thirty years' time? We need a regime more like that of the Royal Navy: over the years, Up or Out, depending on individual performance, number of ships and number of hands and variety of skills required.' One of his arguments for a more flexible career structure by filling gaps through 'in-and-out' arrangements with industry and the academic world did find favour at the Foreign Office. In 1991 there were twelve diplomats on secondment to City firms and industrial management while five senior staff from the private sector were seconded to the Foreign Office. Outsiders joining the Service for even a short period are required to be bound by the Official Secrets Act. Another of his suggestions for more flexibility towards the 7,000 locally engaged staff at missions fell on sympathetic ears. 'Our missions are dotted with loyal servants of long standing, many worth their weight in yen but some long dormant and virtually irremovable, more than a match for us who come and go. Consistent with local law and practice, we should move towards contract terms, say five or seven years, terminable either way.' That policy of short-term contracts is being implemented as fast as possible throughout all posts.

The 'Up or Out' suggestion found little support, largely because of financial considerations. It was argued that if a senior ambassador were moved from Europe at the age of fifty-five to a minor embassy in South America to make way for a high flyer kicking his heels waiting for promotion, the downgraded envoy would suffer financially in terms of a pension calculated on his earnings over his last three years before retirement. If, however, the senior ambassador were retired at the age of fifty-five on full pension, it was estimated that it would cost the Treasury – and ultimately the taxpayer – up to £200,000 more than if he stayed until normal retirement at sixty.

While 'Ham' Whyte's solution was consigned to the pending tray indefinitely, the statistics kept underlining the problem even more forcefully. Between 1979 and 1989 there were almost 300 early retirements. In the lower ranks of the frustrated administrative grade the number of disenchanted diplomats who left the Service increased in five years from just under 1 per cent to 6 per cent in 1988. Above them there were significant signs of disillusionment in the DS5 grade with the number of people becoming fed up and leaving after ten or twelve years' service doubling to 2.75 per cent. This 'wastage factor' was highlighted when Sir Patrick Wright was questioned as Permanent Under-Secretary of State by the Foreign Affairs Committee of the House of Commons in 1988. He acknowledged that allied to the pay factor was what he called 'the problem of the professional spouse'. Because an increasing number of wives of diplomats pursue a professional career, a posting can mean the wife – or husband of a woman member of the Service – giving up a job and losing the extra salary.

Sir Patrick told the Committee: 'It is very often the strain on the family, which comes from the need to choose, which coincides with the point at which you have to decide whether your children are going to remain with you and follow a fairly uncertain and sometimes quite questionable educational system, or whether you are going to take the hard decision to send your children to boarding school. It is really around the ages of late thirties and early forties when all these circumstances tend to come together.' The PUS admitted: 'Bright, well-qualified members of the Service very often find they can earn very much higher sums in the private sector.' He cited as an example a high flyer in Grade DS4 who left 'first because his wife could not pursue her profession if she went abroad, secondly because his language specialization meant that he was likely to go a long way away, and thirdly because his children would have to be moved after quite a long spell at home'. This dissatisfaction and disillusionment aroused so much concern that the Foreign Office took the unprecedented step of calling in one of the most prestigious – and expensive – firms of consultants, Coopers & Lybrand Deloitte, to undertake a full-scale investigation of the management problems of the Foreign Office in 1989.

The responses from disgruntled diplomats, which the Foreign Office intended to keep out of the public domain but which can now be revealed, disclosed a deterioration of morale on a much more alarming scale than had ever been imagined in the top echelons. What emerged in the report, which was delivered by the consultants and the FO's Management Review Staff in March 1990, was described as 'not only a rare insight into the morale of the staff but also a view of staff perceptions of the effectiveness and efficiency in the management of the Service's primary resource'. Such an assessment of the Foreign Office's efficiency in management was acknowledged to have a direct bearing upon its effectiveness in executing foreign policy decisions and meeting the multifarious demands on the Diplomatic Service.

After analysing more than 1,000 responses from members of the Diplomatic Service who filled in – anonymously – long and highly detailed questionnaires, the investigators pronounced a devastating verdict on the system: 'There is a widespread belief that the Foreign Office–Diplomatic Service fails to provide all its staff with good careers and more than half of the sample population said they would leave the Service if a comparable job were available.' The breakdown of the figures disclosing that 55 per cent would quit if they had the chance showed that 62 per cent of the 'workhorse' age group between thirty and thirty-nine had reached a stage of frustration. It was not a question of loyalty. A large majority – 73 per cent – affirmed that they were proud to work for the Foreign Office: the highest proportion was among the research and legal staff at 92 per cent, with the senior members of the Diplomatic Service in Grades 1 to 4 close behind at 86 per cent. But one of the recurrent themes discovered in the investigations was what the report termed 'the disparity between expectation and reality'.

The consultants anticipated that some of those in the hierarchy would be dismissive of the finding that more than half the staff were prepared to leave. They were prepared for the argument that there is no real alternative since the Foreign Office has 'no direct competitors' able to offer comparable employment. Nonetheless, the consultants issued an ominous warning: 'Something is clearly wrong in an organization when its personnel service is found to be staffed by dedicated individuals working very hard over long hours and seeking to achieve high levels of fairness and objectivity in its processes and when the recipients of that service have so little confidence in it.' The report highlighted the fact that people felt that their working lives were 'driven by decisions made in the dark by strangers' and added: 'There was for too many a "cloud of unknowing" over the whole process.'

Some of the less pleasant aspects of the elitist nature of the Diplomatic Service, which are so often brushed aside as misconceptions of the ill-informed looking in from the outside, were exposed by the findings of the attitude survey, showing that it was not a unified organization. 'It is one in which there are two distinct cultures,' the report stated, emphasizing the 'Oxbridge–other university split' and what it described as the 'most overt of all', the divide between the administrative grade and the executive class. The general discontent was greater in the executive class, with the level of pride in working for the Service at its lowest – a mere 51 per cent – among the cipher and signals staff.

While the positive aspects of working in the Diplomatic Service were still acknowledged – the biggest attractions being the opportunity to travel (90 per cent) and the chance to meet interesting people (76 per cent) – there was heavy emphasis on the negative aspects. The most serious complaint was over pay. In the responses poor pay was highlighted as the most negative aspect by 88 per cent, with the greatest resentment among the senior diplomats in Grades 1 to 4. Not far behind as serious causes of dissatisfaction were the long hours of work and the key question on the basic issue of management, that of career prospects. Most of the wrath was directed at the working of the Personnel Operations Department which was established to deal with career planning, postings, and promotions. A large number of those questioned about their contacts with the department – 72 per cent – said it had failed to give them regularly a clear picture of their future career prospects and 61 per cent thought their career development had been badly managed by the department.

The report found that the almost obsessional emphasis inside the Foreign Office on secrecy towards the general public had increasingly pervaded operations involving personnel management within the Diplomatic Service. Among the persistent criticisms encountered by the investigators was that the Personnel Operations Department was too secretive, reluctant to give information, and – most damning of all – was 'not always straightforward with staff'. The system of an annual job appraisal with an assessment of an individual's performance was strongly criticized, with 84 per cent arguing that they should be allowed to see the entire report. This criticism was linked to the fact that 74 per cent regarded the promotion system as unfair and that 58 per cent believed it sometimes appeared biased, some of them cynically observing that the department existed 'to advance the careers of the favoured few'. The final accusation that Personnel Operations Department was not considered flexible enough to keep pace with changes in society and had failed to keep up-to-date with current thinking on personnel management was tantamount to a call for a complete reappraisal of the entire management system inside the Foreign Office.

This drastic demand for the Foreign Office to gear itself to meet the management requirements of the next decade could not be ignored. The Establishment had to face the basic challenge spelled out in the report as 'the tension between evident pride in, and commitment to, the Service and disillusionment about what the Service actually "delivers" to its employees'. After long – and at times highly controversial – deliberations over many months the Foreign Office hierarchy decided on a fresh start. The highly unpopular Personnel Operations Department was abolished. A completely different approach was launched with the establishment of a new department called Personnel Management Department in June 1991. It gave rise to great expectations that there would be a new surge of enthusiasm throughout the Diplomatic Service to ensure that the Foreign Office machine would be run with much more dynamism into the twenty-first century.

III

How the Foreign Office is Run

We have no eternal allies, and we have no perpetual enemies. Our interests are eternal and perpetual, and those interests it is our duty to follow.

Lord Palmerston, 1848

Cynics at Westminster are apt to regard the Foreign Office in much the same light as the Brussels bureaucrats – 'more against us than for us'. Sceptical MPs belittle the work of diplomats by resort to the aphorism: 'The Home Office looks after people here at home while the Foreign Office looks after foreigners.' Experienced diplomats, however, see no contradiction between understanding a foreigner's point of view – even, on occasion, actually liking foreigners – and being effective in upholding and advancing Britain's interests round the world. Their attitude was passionately upheld by Lord Carrington who summed up their subtlety in this way: 'They are periodically objects of suspicion to their more belligerent countrymen, who too easily forget that the aim of diplomacy is to make friends, advance peace and commerce, and influence people; and that is the way to promote British interests.'

In Palmerston's day the Foreign Office had a staff of only sixty people to look after British interests. When George Brown took over his responsibilities a hundred years later it had increased by more than a hundred times that figure. Since then the Diplomatic Service has been severely streamlined while the area covered and the volume of work undertaken have greatly increased. In 1968 Britain had diplomats in 136 countries. At present there are British embassies in 168 countries – an increase of over 23 per cent – the latest additions being in the Baltic with diplomatic recognition having been accorded to Lithuania, Latvia and Estonia in September 1991 after they regained their independence from the Soviet Union. The UK-based staff at embassies numbered 8,140 in 1968. By 1991 it had been reduced to 6,605 – a cut of 19 per cent. Nowadays there are only 2,700 abroad at any one time and only 1,920 are diplomats. Alongside these are 7,000 locally engaged staff.

The distribution of diplomats indicates Britain's priorities. The largest proportion, 27.4 per cent, are based in Western Europe. The next five most important areas demonstrated by the percentage of the British diplomatic staff are Asia with 14.5 per cent, Sub-Saharan Africa with 13.3 per cent, North America and the Caribbean with 11.3 per cent, the Middle East with 10.2 per cent, and Eastern Europe and the Soviet Union with 8.2 per cent.

Inside the Foreign Office in London there is a staff of 3,805. Of these 1,500 are diplomats. Working with them are 1,700 members of the Home Civil Service – researchers, legal experts, computer technicians, and all the support staff. The remaining 605 are secretaries, clerks, telephonists, drivers, and electricians. The diplomats' activities fall into two main categories: geographical and functional. Gradually, the geographical work, which was predominant until the Second World War, has been reduced to 13 per cent. Functional departments are concerned with international aspects of issues such as aviation, energy, and environment. They are supported by the administrative sector which covers financial, estate, and personnel management. Foreign Office staffing is only 1 per cent of the total manpower of the Civil Service. It is dwarfed by other departments like Social Services with over 90,000 and the Inland Revenue with 70,000. In the words of one PUS: 'We are slightly smaller than Stockport Borough Council.' The running costs of the Diplomatic Wing, however, are substantially larger at £467m for 1991–92.

How the staff are organized in departments has undergone

radical changes in the past twenty-five years. In 1965 there were 44 departments inside the Foreign Office. Today there are 65. Some were created in the 1960s for a purely temporary situation such as the Joint Malaysia–Indonesia Department to handle the crisis of confrontation in South-East Asia. In those days there was no Training Department, which today is regarded as one of the important departments in meeting the ever-increasing demands for higher management skills. The requirements of a new generation of issues and problems dictated much of the expansion such as the Narcotics Control and AIDS Department, the Environment, Science and Energy Department, the Information Systems Divisions, and the Technical Security Department for protecting embassies. Britain's entry into the European Community with the Treaty of Accession in January 1972 resulted in a major reorganization of departments to deal with the political and economic consequences. Demands for more modern techniques in planning proper use of resources led to drastic changes in departments handling personnel and resource management. All departments operate under the scrutiny of superintending under-secretaries of state, including some, such as Policy Planning, under the scrutiny of the PUS. Supervision of the Permanent Under-Secretary of State's own department, which is responsible for liaison with the Cabinet Office and other government departments in Whitehall, is undertaken by one of the deputy under-secretaries.

Foreign Office departments have as their working guidelines two main objectives which are officially described as: 'to enhance the security and prosperity of the United Kingdom and Dependent Territories; and to promote and protect British interests overseas, including the interests of individual British citizens'. In an elaboration of these objectives there is an eleven-point programme of objectives which they are committed to work towards with other government departments. These set out lofty aims in such pompous terms as 'strengthening democracy and stability throughout the world, encouraging respect for human rights, putting across a positive image of British society and values', and even 'promoting greater understanding of Britain through our culture'. But they also include the one major activity of British diplomacy which has been given a greater boost by successive governments in the past three decades than any other aspect: 'to promote Britain's commercial and financial interests overseas by assisting British business in the generation of visible and invisible exports, including defence sales, the promotion of inward investment and the protection of British investments abroad'. That has reached such a level of priority that commercial work accounts for the largest single element in the operations of the Diplomatic Service at 29 per cent, which is double the resources devoted to political work.

This development has required ambassadors to acquire extra talents as market analysts. Knowing the right person in a government ministry or a company and having the latest run-down on the economic indicators can enable an ambassador to secure an advantage for a British company against the competition of rivals from other countries. It is not just a question of using influence to help land the big deals such as the Tornado aircraft contract with Saudi Arabia in 1988 worth £15bn, the Harrier aircraft contract with India in 1985 worth £140m, or the £67m contract in 1989 by a consortium headed by Tarmac for a new sewerage system in Cairo. Ambassadors harness their know-how to special market drives such as the 'Focus Germany' campaign. That operation resulted a year later in 1989 in a 10 per cent increase in British firms' share of global German imports, which meant £400m worth of extra British exports. For the small and medium-sized British companies, there is a vast network of commercial services available through embassies working in conjunction with the British Overseas Trade Board (established in 1972 with members mainly from industry and commerce).

Any manufacturer wishing to explore the prospects of a market abroad for his product can tap into the expertise of an embassy through the Export Initiative Scheme promoted by the Department of Trade and Industry. It is not a facility offered free to exporters at the British taxpayer's expense. Charges are made for information supplied or special undertakings carried out by commercial attachés ranging from a country profile at £10 to investigative operations costing £600. Sector reports enabling a manufacturer, for example, to size up the potential of the confectionery market in a country can be provided by the British Embassy for as little as £30. Status reports on the reliability of a company with which a British firm may wish to do business are compiled at a cost between £60 and £180.

For a small company without the means of finding a suitable agent or distributor overseas, there is the Export Representative Service undertaken by embassies. A comprehensive study which normally takes eight weeks to prepare will provide a short-list of experienced and reliable business people with a detailed assessment of the scope of their activities, the area they cover effectively, warehouse and distribution facilities and after-sales service. That costs between £300 and £600 depending on the length of investigation, but it is still only a small fraction of the air fare and hotel costs of sending an investigator from Britain. On-the-spot help is provided for exporters wanting to hire premises for exhibits or conferences, for any of the 7,000 participants at overseas trade fairs supported by the Department of Trade and Industry, and for visiting groups sponsored by chambers of commerce or trade associations. Enquiries to embassies about market opportunities increased from 84,500 in 1982 to 120,500 in 1990 – a rise of 43 per cent.

One important aspect of promoting Great Britain Ltd which the Foreign Office is reluctant to acknowledge publicly is the way royal visits are fitted into the scheme of things. Here again, the inside knowledge of an ambassador on how a visit by a member of the royal family could be most appropriately timed for Britain's best interests is often of great value. Such information is fed into the deliberations of the small committee which meets regularly in Downing Street to consider proposals for royal visits abroad and state visits to Britain. Its key members are the Queen's Private Secretary, the FO's Permanent Under-Secretary of State, and the Cabinet Secretary. Naturally, if it appears that a royal visit to country X would be more beneficial for Britain's immediate and medium-term interests than a visit to country Y, then that opinion from the Foreign Office would carry substantial weight in the advice which is presented for the consideration of the Queen. The final recommendation on visits to foreign countries is made by the Foreign Secretary who is clearly well aware of the factors to which the Permanent Under-Secretary of State attaches importance.

Ultimately, it is the Queen's own decision, so a certain amount of circumspection is necessary to avoid the suspicion of undue pressure. Two occasions when the velvet touch of the Foreign Office was not involved in the discussions about a royal visit ended in acrimony. Despite a public furore over the risks for the Queen in flying to Zambia in July 1979 for the Commonwealth Heads of Government meeting in Lusaka, it was made clear from Buckingham Palace that since her visit was to a Commonwealth country, not a foreign country, it was not a matter for a recommendation from the British Government. Nor was there any disposition to give much weight to the highly publicized views of New Zealand's Prime Minister Sir Robert Muldoon on the dangers of the Queen being surrounded by African nationalists.

In April 1989, the Queen ignored strong suggestions peddled in Downing Street that Prime Minister Margaret Thatcher would not be happy about a state visit to the Soviet Union until there was a better record there on respect for human rights. At the end of President Gorbachev's visit to Windsor Castle – where he was shown a portrait of Alexander I, an ancestor of Tsar Nicholas, the victim of the Bolshevik Revolution who was a cousin of the Queen's grandfather – it was made clear that the Queen was delighted to accept a formal invitation.

Next to the promotion of commercial interests, the fastest-growing sector of the Diplomatic Service's activities is immigration and visa work. That accounts for 14 per cent of the workload overseas while consular duties take up 10 per cent. Entry clearance work at posts abroad is on a steadily rising curve. Visas are required by citizens of sixty-nine countries, entry certificates for certain Commonwealth citizens, and letters of consent for some foreigners travelling to Britain. The sudden introduction of visa regimes for Turkey, Ghana, Nigeria, and the Indian sub-continent required an extra 244 staff. Latest figures show that 742 people were employed in this work alone, some 250 of them UK-based including 64 Immigration officers seconded from the Home Office. The total cost of processing applications exceeded £30m, with the average cost of £35 in 1989 when 1,065,000 applications were received. The 1994 estimate is put at 2,010,000 applications.

Consuls in the Diplomatic Service are a bulldog breed ready to cope with any emergency as a combination of lawyer, travel agent, nanny, banker, agony aunt, and mediator with the local police. They have to attend to any SOS from the six million Britons resident abroad and the ever-increasing number of travelling Britons whose visits abroad total more than 30 million a year. Their ingenuity is legendary. Once the consul in Moscow received a desperate plea from a British woman in a Soviet hospital who wanted a change of underwear. There was nothing like Marks and Spencer in Moscow, so he took her a present of two pairs of his own boxer shorts. When a student knocked on the British Embassy door in Luxembourg with no money for a hotel room and nowhere to pitch his tent, he was taken into the garden of the residence where the Ambassador, Mrs Juliet Campbell, rolled up her sleeves, helped him put up his tent, and gave him some hot food.

The 530 members of the consular staff are usually tolerant with awkward customers, but when Timothy Eggar was a Foreign Office minister in 1988 he issued instructions to them to give short shrift to the 'nasties' who cause trouble. He listed the trouble-makers as the Scrounger, the Comedian, the Freeloader, the Artful Dodger, and the Hooligan. Typical of the Scrounger type was the tourist who expected the consul in Athens to track down a brand of laxative toffee and buy it for him. Another demanded that the consul take him to someone to cure his baldness. But most aud-acious of all was the woman in New York who wanted the consul to arrange for her dogs to be flown back to Britain – all forty of them. Those who qualify as Comedians deserving the response 'You must be joking' included the Briton who telephoned in the middle of a furious matrimonial row and insisted that the consul in Lisbon translate what his angry Portuguese wife was saying. Another was the tourist who complained that he was not welcomed personally by the consul at Palma Airport. The Freeloader is the traveller who imagines that the consul should pay his bills when he runs out of money. In 1988 half the 140 Britons who were given small loans by a consul failed to repay the amount within six months. The Artful Dodger is the sort of traveller who thinks he can get away with defraying the cost of his holiday by a little bit of theft on the side. Over 1,600 Britons were in foreign prisons in 1988. The worst of the 'nasties' are the young Hooligans who go on the rampage at holiday resorts after drinking too much. Mr

Eggar gave his full support to local police at resorts to take stern action, saying: 'Our consuls have got better things to do than clear up after kids who have not grown up.'

The consul's main duty as defined by Article 5 of the Vienna Convention on Consular Relations is 'protecting in the receiving State the interests of the sending State and of its nationals, both individuals and bodies corporate, within the limits permitted by international law'. On average, consuls deal with the registration of over 12,000 births and deaths each year, register around 600 marriages, and issue over 270,000 passports to Britons abroad. Top of the league table for the speed in issuing passports is the consulate-general in Istanbul. Normally it takes only one day there. The next quickest is at Vienna where the average is two days, followed by Athens and Oslo which take three days. The places to avoid unless you are in no hurry for a passport are Canberra which takes 60 days in high season to deal with an application, with Ottawa next taking 40 days and Wellington averaging 20 days. Where the consuls are most appreciated is in helping relatives of Britons in prison, and visiting people arrested or held in detention. It is often the consul who is the first to help stranded travellers or visitors involved in accidents. They are pitched into relief work after natural disasters, such as evacuating Britons after the San Francisco earthquake and Hurricane Hugo in the Caribbean in 1989. Consuls as career diplomats have the same immunities and privileges as any other member of the Service. At a maritime post, however, they are entitled to only a 7-gun salute compared to an ambassador's 19-gun salute from a Royal Navy warship. On some occasions the Briton in need will find himself in the hands of an honorary consul who handles the responsibilities on a part-time basis, often as a shipping agent at a port, and who is not necessarily British.

In its traditional role of providing an informed basis for policy-making, the way the Foreign Office machine runs today is vastly different from what it was a generation ago. In those more leisurely days when a telegram arrived at the Foreign Office it was not instantly photocopied and sent all round the building. It would go directly to the Desk Officer in the department responsible for the area from which the telegram originated. According to the jargon of the time the telegram was 'entered', that is registered on a file – a file of its own. Next, the Desk Officer would assess the import of the dispatch and 'minute' it, in other words write a submission adding some observations and recommendations which would go up to the Assistant in the department, who would sign it and pass it on to the Head of the department. This was the decisive stage. If the minute was approved by the Head of the department, it would proceed smoothly onwards and upwards until it landed on the Foreign Secretary's desk where, if it received the nod, the minute would become official policy on paper marked in the left-hand margin with one of the five security categories – Top Secret, Secret, Confidential, Restricted, or Unclassified.

Since the merger of the Commonwealth Relations Office with the Foreign Office in 1968, the role of the Desk Officer and in some cases the Head of the department has been much less influential. The main reason is that the next layer upwards occupied by the assistant under-secretaries has become steadily more important. On the eve of the merger, the Foreign Office had 6 deputy under-secretaries of state and 10 assistant under-secretaries of state. At the Commonwealth Relations Office there were 4 deputies and 10 assistant under-secretaries. A year later at the newly combined Office, there were 10 deputy under-secretaries of state and 15 assistant under-secretaries of state. Since then, the deputy under-secretaries have been scaled down to 6 but the assistant under-secretaries remain at 15. Usually it is an assistant under-secretary who travels with the Foreign Secretary to conferences or important visits abroad where policy has to be reviewed. Until his appointment as Ambassador to the European Community in 1990, Sir John Kerr as Assistant Under-Secretary was the overlord on the conduct of policy towards the European Community. At the same time John Goulden as the Superintending Under-Secretary over the Arms Control and Disarmament Department and the Security Department had the most powerful role on defence decisions taken by the Foreign Secretary.

With the rise in the influence of assistant under-secretaries, there has been a significant decline in the role of the Permanent Under-Secretary of State in the policy-making process. In the time of Lord Greenhill as PUS from 1969 to 1973, the Foreign

Secretary always had him at his side when travelling abroad even on extended visits such as that of Lord Home to China and Hong Kong. Prime Minister Harold Wilson insisted on having Lord Greenhill as his main adviser when he went to Moscow. As PUS he was present at all major meetings so that he had a direct assessment of policy positions presented to British ministers by statesmen in other countries. Subsequently the PUS has been edged into a different role of 'minding the shop' while the Foreign Secretary is out of the country, including the task of keeping an eye on junior ministers who might otherwise overstep the mark and create a diplomatic headache which could cause problems in Cabinet. In recent years the PUS has only travelled with the Foreign Secretary to Commonwealth Heads of Government meetings or on a special visit to the United States. When the Foreign Secretary wants specialist advice he usually turns to one of the under-secretaries of state.

Each PUS has his own style of operating and his own sense of priorities. Lord Gore-Booth had an Olympian view of his role – and a sharp sense of humour in defining it. When asked how he ensured that he had control over foreign policy and its implementation he confided: 'Largely by silence.' For him it was essential to have proper delegation of authority and trust in the abilities of well-chosen assistants. That explains his reactions to two sudden developments which occurred when he was abroad. In August 1966 when he was at a camping site in France he made a check call to the British Embassy in Paris which caused him to abandon his holiday and return to the Foreign Office at once. He felt it was his duty to be back in charge when Prime Minister Harold Wilson appointed a new Foreign Secretary – George Brown. Two years later he was on holiday in Italy when President Leonid Brezhnev moved Soviet tanks to crush the Czech uprising led by Alexander Dubček. Instead of rushing back to London he watched the drama on Italian television, confident that the preparations for making a stand at the United Nations were well in hand without any need for him to be fussing about at the Foreign Office supervising their implementation.

It was that ability of knowing when to intervene and when to devolve authority – having a 'good head' – which impressed

Douglas Hurd as Foreign Secretary in selecting Sir David Gillmore to take over as PUS in June 1991. His appointment broke the mould. He came to the Diplomatic Service as a late entrant at the age of thirty-five with experience of the real world outside the Foreign Office cloisters. After graduating from King's College, Cambridge, he became a journalist with all the discipline required for checking facts and statements at Reuters news agency. Two years later he abandoned journalism to work in Paris for five years but returned to writing during four years as a teacher in the Inner London Education Authority with the publication of a novel, *A Way from Exile*. Unusually for a person of his rank, Sir David spent only ten years of his time abroad after joining the Service in 1970, including only one posting as head of mission – High Commissioner to Malaysia. But he was recognized as a man who operated best on the inside track in Whitehall, knew the power game there, and wanted to be on hand for decision-making in Downing Street.

Whatever the individual talents of the PUS, however, three factors have emerged to bring about changes to the job and the way it is carried out. First was the emergence of a new *éminence grise* in the Foreign Office hierarchy with the creation of the post of Political Director as a consequence of Britain's membership of the European Community. Initially, the opportunities of the role were developed quietly without much high-profile activity. But, as the holder of the post from April 1982 until July 1984, Sir Julian Bullard, who was one of the intellectual giants in the Foreign Office once favoured to be appointed Permanent Under-Secretary of State, carried substantial weight in shaping the policies of ministers. The mandate was left flexible enough to allow scope for John Weston to be what colleagues described a 'firecracker of ideas' over a wide range of issues in that job until his posting to be Ambassador to NATO in July 1991.

Attending meetings of the European Community at political co-operation sessions, NATO, the Western European Union, and the seven major industrialized nations in G7 usually means that the Political Director is out of the country at policy-making occasions one day in four. It was John Weston's skills that Douglas Hurd relied upon in the complex 'Two Plus Four' negotiations over the external problems to be resolved by the Quadripartite

Powers – the United States, the Soviet Union, Britain, and France – in the unification of the two Germanies in 1990. It is the Political Director who has the key responsibility of the 'nexus relationship' – the interaction of Britain's interests across the whole spectrum with the United States, Japan, Europe, China, and the Soviet Union.

One unexpected advantage of having a Political Director as a free-ranging senior mandarin was discovered by Sir Geoffrey Howe when he wanted to obtain a secret assessment from the dissidents in Czechoslovakia during a visit to Prague in April 1985. The Foreign Secretary hoodwinked his hosts by dispatching his Political Director, Sir Derek Thomas, from his delegation to undertake a special mission while he was being entertained at a nightclub called the Seven Angels. As Sir Geoffrey sat carousing with the Czech Foreign Minister, Bohuslav Chnoupek, to the music of violins, his Political Director was driven to the home of the Embassy's Third Secretary for a clandestine meeting set up by Ambassador Stephen Barrett with five members of the Charter 77 movement founded to monitor human rights. It had been carefully planned in advance to give a boost to those defying the regime. Sir Geoffrey knew he could not invite members of Charter 77 to an official Embassy reception, otherwise the Czechs would cancel the programme. Nor could the top echelon of Charter 77 be seen going into a British diplomat's home since they were closely watched. So Sir Derek Thomas had to make contact with the second ranks of the movement.

To divert his hosts from noticing that his Political Director was absent, Sir Geoffrey moved around the room at the Seven Angels persuading everyone to join him in a singsong. With Lady Howe taking her turn in spinning out the singing, he got the Czechs to sing a version of 'Good King Wenceslas' and 'It's a Long Way to Tipperary'. They even hummed along with him as he sang the Welsh anthem 'Cwm Rhondda'. He kept the musical evening going until 1 a.m. when the Political Director slipped in with a 'Thumbs Up' sign, passing a note to the Foreign Secretary saying 'Mission accomplished'. The Czechs were furious the next morning when they realized that their security system had been circumvented by the enterprising Political Director. But by then Sir

Geoffrey was on his plane to Warsaw with a detailed account of how repressive life was for dissidents in Czechoslovakia.

Political priorities in the agenda of the PUS have been overtaken in recent years by his managerial responsibilities as Head of the Diplomatic Service which had previously been undertaken by the Chief Clerk. Sir Michael Palliser, who was Ambassador to the European Community before taking over as PUS from 1975 to 1982, strove hard to retain a considerable influence in the development of economic and political policies in Europe. He travelled with the Prime Minister and often had a key role at economic summits. But by 1990, when serious issues of morale in the Diplomatic Service and the cost-effectiveness of Foreign Office operations were raised, the PUS was spending at least 40 per cent of his time on matters which had nothing to do with the formulation of foreign policy. Although the PUS sees the Foreign Secretary regularly – including a session alone with him every week – and chairs the Board of Directors comprising all the deputy undersecretaries of state in a monthly review of issues liable to command the serious attention of ministers, he has been obliged to concern himself more and more with internal housekeeping and the demands of the Top Management Round in Whitehall.

The PUS's presence is required at the House of Commons to appear before MPs in the Foreign Affairs Committee to answer their questions on Foreign Office expenditure, recruitment, and the use of manpower. By virtue of his accountability on management resources, the PUS travels much more extensively on his own than in previous decades in order to find out for himself how the Service and diplomats operate on the spot. That gives him an opportunity to assess morale at first hand and to discover how well diplomats – and their spouses – think the Foreign Office machine is being run. Other duties at the Court of St James's take him away from supervising policy-making. The PUS has to attend at Buckingham Palace when an ambassador presents his credentials – which at certain times of the year can be three times a week, lasting up to forty-five minutes. But one of Sir Antony Acland's boasts as PUS from 1982 to 1986 was that his skill as a quick-change artist enabled him to get into the ceremonial dress uniform in his room in four minutes.

The third, and perhaps most decisive, factor making it difficult for the PUS to have the dominant role as political adviser in the Foreign Office which his predecessors enjoyed a generation ago is the communications revolution. It is hard for someone with global responsibility to keep pace with the flow of information inward and outward at the Foreign Office on all the issues of major importance. Lord Home tried to control the tide when he returned for his second term as Foreign Secretary in 1972 by instructing all posts to curb their output of words by 20 per cent. It resulted in a 10 per cent reduction in the following twelve months, but as Britain's membership of the European Community sucked British diplomats more and more into what they term the 'Brussels word factory' the steadily mounting flow defied all attempts to keep it in check. During the intense diplomatic activity after the Argentine invasion of the Falkland Islands in April 1982, the flow of telegrams reached a peak of 2,000 a day. That figure was swept aside in the record books by the deluge of telegrams in the Gulf crisis following Iraq's invasion of Kuwait in August 1990 when there were 10,000 telegrams a day making a total of 3 million words.

What used to be quaintly called the Diplomatic Wireless Service has been transformed into the Information Systems Division of the Foreign Office employing a staff of over 1,000 at home and overseas, that is one in every six people in the Diplomatic Service. In the early days of the DWS it could sometimes take twenty-four hours for a dispatch sent from a post abroad to reach the Foreign Secretary's desk in London. At the other end it could take someone ten hours with a code book at his side to get the dispatch ready for transmission, then the operator would be transmitting by Morse for up to four hours, and when it reached the Foreign Office there could be a further ten hours having it deciphered. Nowadays a 'Flash' telegram can be in London in seconds. There are hotlines not just between Downing Street, the White House, and Moscow, but for quick action in an emergency at the United Nations in New York.

During the Falklands crisis, Britain's Ambassador to the United Nations, Sir Anthony Parsons, was faced on occasion with a fresh amendment to the draft resolution at eleven o'clock at night. When put under pressure to vote, Sir Anthony would stall for five minutes, race upstairs to his delegation room, and use the hotline to the Prime Minister at four o'clock in the morning in London to get instructions. It is not the sort of intervention even a highly trusted ambassador can make every other night. But when there is a critical decision to be made at the United Nations Security Council which requires an instant political judgement, it can only be taken on the word of the Prime Minister or Foreign Secretary directly assessing the situation with the ambassador.

Normally, however, the Foreign Office is not run by dramatic decisions taken by telephone while the rest of the country is asleep. Even in the high-tech age of satellite communications and sophisticated word processors, the Foreign Office remains what mandarins call 'a paper-based organization'. Information pouring into the Foreign Office has to be put down on paper – sometimes as many as 300 copies circulate inside the Foreign Office and other government departments – so that it can be studied by various people before a recommendation on policy is made to ministers. Inward and outward communication takes place at the operations centre of the Information Systems Division at Hanslope Park near Milton Keynes, but it still depends on the atmospheric elements which can cause difficulties during the winter solstice with signals disrupted by sunspots. For security reasons more than 50 per cent of the entire wordage is in cipher.

One innovation which has accelerated the diplomatic process more than anything else is the introduction of fax machines. Half of the communications between the Foreign Office and Britain's EC delegation in Brussels is by fax. It has proved of great value in many other posts when texts of documents which are not confidential have to be transmitted, especially if they are in Chinese, Japanese, or Arabic. It is a slower system than telex since it does not make instantly available the large number of copies needed in the Foreign Office. There are limitations to its use by certain departments of the Foreign Office since even with a special line which provides the necessary level of privacy there is not the requisite guarantee of security for classified material. That security requirement has limited the use of computer technology in the Foreign Office because a high proportion of the material being circulated throughout the building is classified. Safeguards against unauthorized access to materials, which might be stored in computers and brought on to a large number of screens, have not been devised so far to the satisfaction of the security authorities at the Foreign Office.

High-tech experts, however, are critical of the slowness of the Foreign Office in adapting to the new technology and its old-fashioned attitude in trying to 'muddle through' compared with major international businesses which have to be equally vigilant about the confidentiality of their work and the accuracy of their financial accounting. Some of that criticism was corroborated in an extraordinary report in February 1991 by the National Audit Office which highlighted chaos in the Foreign Office's computer system, lack of adequate financial control, and unreliable records. Faced at one stage with discrepancies of £485m between the money allocated and the Foreign Office's records, the Comptroller and Auditor-General, John Bourn, reported that he could not verify the accounts which dealt with embassies, the British Council, the BBC World Service, NATO, and the UN. The Foreign Office came out badly in the sorry story of how it had tried to cope with a new computer system which did not work. The National Audit Office report stated: 'The company providing the software went into liquidation while the system was under trial. Shortly thereafter the old system broke down irreparably, forcing the Foreign Office to rely on the new one, even though it had known – and probably unknown – faults.' A consultant from the bankrupt software company had to be called in by the Foreign Office to work on sorting out the muddle at a salary of £53,000 – more than what some ambassadors are paid.

One successful communications innovation introduced by George Brown when he was Foreign Secretary in 1966 changed the style of reporting from missions. Because he did not want to have to plough through several pages until the end of a telegram to discover what the conclusions were, George Brown instituted the time-saving device of having what he called 'the guts of the message' right at the start so that if the matter interested him he would read on and if it did not he would be able to pass on to the next telegram. Accordingly, the 'Brown formula' means that telegrams appear on the Foreign Secretary's desk in this manner:

Confidential

Fm Ruritania
To Priority FCO
Telno 123
Of 311100oz December 99
Info Priority Washington, UKmis New York UKdel NATO,
Info Priority UKdis Geneva, CSCE Vienna
Info Saving Moscow, Paris, Rome

Ruritania Seminar on Human Rights and the Disarmament
Process

Summary

1. Delegates from 34 countries emphasized the need for
social progress to be achieved step by step with
disarmament. Even the Soviet delegate admitted
mistakes had been made and the leadership would have
to improve its record before it could win the trust of
the West. Papers circulated by Soviet Academician
Bloggsatov went far beyond what had been expected by
US delegates.

Detail
2......
3......
4......
5. Copies of main papers presented at seminar will be
sent by bag.

Bloggs

Distribution 151

Two quaint features of the communications system have defied
modernization for decades. Down in the basement of the building
is the Tube Room where messengers deal with telegrams in the
same way as they did when Sir Edward Grey awaited dispatches
on the last moves leading to the outbreak of the First World War.
Advance copies of telegrams are put into tubular metal containers
like a larger version of the bobbins which used to be sent zooming

to the cash desk in haberdashers' shops along a network of wire ropes above the customers' heads with their payment for ribbons. From a battery of thirty-six outlets in the bowels of the Foreign Office the telegram containers go 'whining like Scud missiles', according to the messengers, on their way along tubes to No. 10 Downing Street and the Ministry of Defence. Inside the Office the Lamson tubes, as the containers are called, are trundled round the corridors in trolleys with wicker baskets. Senior diplomats on the special delivery list have their own keys for opening the locks on the base of the Lamson tubes to extract their advance copies of telegrams. Others not in such urgent need of the information receive printed copies which are sorted into bundles by hand and locked in blue dispatch boxes which are also wheeled by messengers round the departments in trolleys.

Another relic of the past is the system of having diplomatic bags ferried round the world by Queen's Messengers. These couriers, mainly ex-Army officers, claim their descent from the seventeenth-century body of loyalists used by King Charles II from his exile in Holland during the Civil War to send messages to his supporters in England. They carry a medallion featuring a small greyhound which was the badge of loyalty identifying the King's couriers. Their duties make them the most seasoned air travellers in the world, logging on average 250,000 miles a year in first class seats in charge of white canvas bags, made in eight different sizes by inmates of Her Majesty's prisons. Under the Vienna Convention on Consular Relations, the bags are intended to contain only diplomatic documents and items or equipment solely for diplomatic use.

Sometimes for diplomats in difficult circumstances this definition can be stretched to cover special requirements. There was an arrangement for a beleaguered British diplomat in Hanoi, who could only travel on foot or by bicycle, to include his shoes in the diplomatic bag when they needed repair. Once a British naval attaché in Moscow had special dispensation to have his uniform dress shirt collars sent back in the diplomatic bag to London to be laundered. Other countries use the diplomatic bag – which can be any container up to the size of a 10-ton truck – for a variety of strange purposes. Drugs, weapons, or, in one case, 2,000 watches

59

which a courier for the Italian Embassy in Paris tried to smuggle into Britain, have been discovered. Occasionally, attempts have been made to ship kidnap victims under the guise of diplomatic baggage as happened in the notorious incident of the Nigerians trying to take a former minister, Umaru Dikko, back to Lagos in a box from Stansted Airport in July 1984 (see pages 160–3).

One other strange feature of how the Foreign Office operates is the night watchman system. A team of bright young first secretaries keep the wheels of diplomacy turning at the Foreign Office while the Foreign Secretary is asleep at his official residence at No. 1 Carlton Gardens, or, if it is a weekend, at the ministerial retreat at Chevening in Kent where Sir Geoffrey Howe dearly loved playing the country squire. Ensconced in an eyrie, modestly furnished but usually discreetly supplied with good claret, these nocturnal diplomats known as Resident Clerks keep watch over the world from six o'clock at night until the morning when the mandarins return to their offices. They have to judge when it is necessary to alert a head of department to a sudden development affecting British interests or a British citizen. The Resident Clerk is often the first person in London to know when there has been a *coup d'état*, an earthquake, or a hurricane disaster in some remote part of the world. When he receives 'Flash' telegrams he has to decide whether to wake the Foreign Secretary or rouse his principal private secretary and leave that delicate decision to him. One nonchalant member of the nocturnal team who received a Flash telegram from the Persian Gulf in the 1960s saying 'Ruler died suddenly. Please advise' sent back the reply: 'Hesitate to be dogmatic but suggest burial.'

Flash telegrams about natural disasters activate the emergency services of the Aid wing of the Foreign Office which manages to do good works all round the world despite its ever-changing semi-detached status. Having grown out of arrangements made under the Colonial Development Act of 1929, which limited the aid budget to £1m in any one year for the first ten years, the Government's overseas aid programme expanded over the years to an allocation of £1,721m for 1991–92 rising each year to £1,860m for 1993–94. In the past three decades the department has been in and out of the Foreign Office with seventeen changes of ministers and several titles. In the Labour Government of 1964 Harold Wilson made it a separate ministry with Barbara Castle at its head having a seat in the Cabinet. It had six different ministers until 1970 when the Conservatives demoted it to be the Overseas Development Administration. On Labour's return to power in 1974 the Ministry of Overseas Development was restored with Dame Judith Hart as minister. But Mrs Thatcher turned it back to the ODA in 1979 with a minister of state heading it under the overall authority of the Foreign Secretary. The ODA staff of 1,600 operating from headquarters in London and East Kilbride in Scotland are recruited separately from the Foreign Office and are not members of the Diplomatic Service.

Conservative governments have related their aid programmes more directly to foreign policy objectives in the past few years. Countries claiming priority for aid are required to meet certain criteria in terms of efficient government, free-market economies, and human rights. Douglas Hurd set them out clearly in a warning issued at the Overseas Development Institute in June 1990: 'Governments who persist with repressive policies, with corrupt management, or with wasteful and discredited economic systems should not expect us to support their folly with scarce aid which could be used better elsewhere.' Sixty per cent of Britain's aid is sent directly to the country needing it and 40 per cent is channelled through the European Community, the World Bank, the United Nations, and other agencies. Commonwealth countries get 75 per cent of all Britain's bilateral aid. One of the largest single items is the allocation of over £100m a year to support 15,000 overseas students in Britain, mostly on post-graduate courses not available in their own countries.

Although 54 per cent of the bilateral aid goes to Sub-Saharan Africa, there is concern among diplomatic missions that political interest in helping Africa is waning in Downing Street. Veteran observers put it down to a combination of decolonization fatigue and compassion fatigue. Certain countries have been favoured, such as the Front Line states. To help maintain stability in Zimbabwe, funds were made available not just for the Mayfair and Claw Dams but for a substantial military training programme under British officers to make the Zimbabwean forces the best small army in black Africa. But elsewhere in Africa there has been a feeling that in Downing Street the focus is being switched to Eastern Europe now that capitalist enterprise is being encouraged there. Warnings from West Africa about the danger of Britain turning its back on African problems caused so much embarrassment at the Foreign Office in 1991 that the issue was ruled out of the agenda for a Heads of Mission conference convened by the Minister, Lynda Chalker.

There has never been any shortage of suggestions from outside the Foreign Office as to how it could be run more efficiently or more cheaply. No other department in Whitehall has been subjected to so much scrutiny, not just in Parliament and the Press, but by official committees of investigation. In the past three decades the Foreign Office has been deluged by proposals for changes in its structure, its objectives, the scale of its operations, the size of its staff, and even how it treats foreigners. That the Diplomatic Service managed to concentrate on doing its job while visiting committees of inquiry and inspectors probed into its operations and life-style – sometimes to the extent of surreptitiously lifting the carpets in the ambassador's residence to check the dust on the underlay – surprised even its critics.

The first major inquiry after the Second World War, which was appointed by Prime Minister Harold Macmillan in July 1962 under the chairmanship of Lord Plowden, provoked the most radical changes and the least controversy. Its mandate was: 'To review the purpose, structure and operation of the services representing the interests of the United Kingdom Government overseas, both in Commonwealth and foreign countries; and to make recommendations, having regard to the changes in political, social and economic circumstances in this country and overseas'. The Plowden Report delivered in February 1964 was responsible for a fundamental structural change: the creation of a unified service known as Her Majesty's Diplomatic Service. Although the Report accepted that a separate Commonwealth Relations Office should be retained for the time being, it pointed to the inevitability of a merger with the Foreign Office four years later.

Lord Plowden's assessment of Britain's role in the world carrying 'a high degree of worldwide influence' was well received by diplomats. They glowed when they read the Report, which said: 'We believe that the British people wish to sustain that influence and share Sir Winston Churchill's view that Britain should not be content to be "relegated to a tame and minor role in the world". If our influence is not felt, not only national but international interests and objectives will suffer.' Defying the trend towards retrenchment, the Report recommended better conditions of service and better amenities for staff in hardship posts. Although they were never implemented, the Report set down staffing proposals which the Diplomatic Service has yearned for subsequently despite all the streamlining: a margin of 10 per cent above basic requirements to cover training, travel, leave, and sick leave.

After Plowden the Foreign Office had its back to the wall against a series of assaults. First came the Review Committee on Overseas Representation appointed by Foreign Secretary Michael Stewart, with Sir Val Duncan as chairman, which operated under the shadow of Treasury demands for substantial expenditure cuts following the major shift in Britain's overseas commitments with the withdrawal of forces from East of Suez. The Duncan Report, which was delivered in July 1969, set out propositions for a cost-effective Diplomatic Service intended to produce savings of between 5 and 10 per cent of the current expenditure. These ideas required the Foreign Office to roll up the map of the world with all Britain's historic interests marked on it and adopt a totally new perspective which was highly insular with extremely narrow horizons.

Its radical proposals included dividing Britain's diplomatic operations into two categories: an Area of Concentration involving 'about a dozen or so countries in Western Europe plus North America' and an Outer Area comprising 'the rest of the world'. It was acknowledged that there were some industrially advanced countries outside the Area of Concentration such as Australia and Japan with which Britain's interests would be very close for other reasons. But with an astonishing lack of awareness of the Japanese potential for industrial domination in the high-tech era, the Duncan Report opined: 'There is not the immediate prospect here of the mutual commitment in the day-to-day process of government that there is in Europe.'

Equally surprising from a high-powered committee which

included the eminent economist Andrew Shonfield and a former Ambassador in Moscow and Bonn, Sir Frank Roberts, was the failure to realize the appalling damage to Britain's interests in the Middle East, the Caribbean, West and Southern Africa, South-East Asia, and the Pacific which would occur by dismissing them as second-rate or third-rate. Although there was a patronizing reference to a continuing concern for the 'welfare' of the Commonwealth, which commands considerable attention from the Queen as Head of the Commonwealth, the Duncan Report relegated links with it to 'a form appropriate to contemporary requirements'. Apparently oblivious to the concern of the Commonwealth countries in resolving the problems of Rhodesia and South Africa, the Duncan Committee reached the conclusion that mature Commonwealth relations 'should be marked by a depth of social affinity between peoples combined with a significant diminution in the depth of political contact between governments'.

These ideas, when translated into scaling down the size of missions, were even more bewildering to the Service. The Duncan Report was coldly clinical: 'Throughout the Area of Concentration political influence will remain of major importance to us. In the Outer Area, on the other hand, our need (and ability) to exert political influence will in some (though not all) cases virtually disappear.' It involved dividing missions into Comprehensive Posts, which would continue to be staffed with the customary numbers, and Selective Posts, which were to be consigned to the level of a village store with only three UK-based officers. The Committee saw no need for an officer to handle the conduct of intergovernmental relations in a selective post: 'Any residual work of this kind would fall naturally to the Head of Mission but it would not be expected to take up much of his time.' A number of capitals might not be worth even a selective post, according to the Committee. 'If it is felt in any particular instance that the benefit to Britain of having an Embassy in the country concerned falls short of the basic figure of expenditure [which the Committee put at around £30,000 a year], then the logical step would be to remove the resident representation altogether.'

One of the traditional requirements of the Diplomatic Service, its duty to keep the Foreign Secretary well informed of developments around the world, was threatened by the Duncan Committee's call for substantial reductions in political reporting. It admitted that there would be opposition at Westminster, stating somewhat condescendingly, 'It may not be altogether easy to break the habit of assuming (in Parliament and elsewhere) that the Government are and should be fully and currently informed on the latest developments anywhere in the world.' In one respect the 'New Diplomacy' as defined in the Report won approval from practitioners in the field: 'The Diplomatic Service should consist neither of experts nor of amateurs but of "professional generalists"' – a phrase which gained increasing currency throughout the Foreign Office. Emphasizing the more complex demands on diplomats, it stated: 'Career planning should therefore avoid trying to give everyone a little experience of everything; the aim should be to encourage the acquisition of a relevant depth of knowledge on particular areas and subjects.' The main emphasis was to be on commercial work aimed at promoting exports.

Shock waves reverberated for many months throughout Whitehall and missions abroad – especially those earmarked to be downgraded as selective posts in the Outer Area. A typical stiff-upper-lip performance by Sir Oliver Wright as Chief Clerk before the House of Commons Expenditure Committee assured MPs that the Duncan Report's division of the world into two areas of diplomacy had been 'useful in concentrating our minds on the problem'. But he left them in no doubt that the Foreign Office rejected its 'rigidity'. However, as so often happens in Whitehall, delaying tactics paid off. After the general election in June 1970 brought a change of party and foreign secretary with the return of Lord Home to the Foreign Office, the Duncan Report was shelved.

Seven years later the Foreign Office was again the target of radical reappraisal. This time it was undertaken by the Central Policy Review Staff, known as Whitehall's Think Tank, under Sir Kenneth Berrill, the former Cambridge don who became Chief Economic Adviser to the Treasury. The instructions from the Foreign Secretary, then James Callaghan, went far beyond those given to Lord Plowden or Sir Val Duncan on Britain's overseas interests. The Think Tank was asked to make recommendations 'on the most suitable, effective and economic means of representing and promoting those interests both at home and overseas'. Thus the investigation ranged over the activities of some 35,000 people in various departments in Whitehall working on matters affecting Britain's overseas interests, only one in seven being members of the Diplomatic Service. It resulted in a number of political bombshells being dropped in Whitehall when Sir Kenneth Berrill delivered his report in August 1977 after visiting 44 posts in 27 countries.

One of his basic criticisms of diplomats was that their work was often done to 'an unjustifiably high standard' because the Diplomatic Service 'tends to err on the side of perfectionism in work whose importance is not always commensurate with the human and material resources'. Following the Duncan Report which led to 30 posts being closed, the Berrill Report went further with the recommendation that 55 posts should be closed with a reduction of 365 to 500 jobs at Executive Officer level and above, almost all of them abroad. It was scathing in its attack on the life-style of diplomats as hosts at dinner parties. Berrill claimed that very little information was obtained at them which could not just as easily be acquired by 'calling on people in their offices, reading newspapers, journals, Government publications and books, attending lectures, monitoring TV and radio, etc.'. The Think Tank's recommendations were spartan: 'We welcome the demise of the large cocktail party and we would also welcome the demise of the large formal dinner party in most posts.' Small business lunches for two or three people in restaurants or evening drinks in local bars were recommended as the main way of entertaining except for certain unspecified African countries 'where lunches at restaurants are not practical'.

The blockbuster from the Report was that in many specialist sectors of the work connected with Britain's interests – economic work, export promotion, aid administration, and immigration – members of the Home Civil Service would be better than diplomats. In negotiations abroad on highly technical matters it was proposed that emissaries from the Home Civil Service should take over from diplomats. While the Think Tank acknowledged the case for greater interchange between the Home Civil Service and the Diplomatic Service, it came down in favour of a more radical reform. The best way to achieve greater functional specialization and have the same staff doing the job both in London and abroad was, in its view, to have a complete merger of the Diplomatic Service with the Home Civil Service.

With the abolition of the Diplomatic Service there would be the creation of a Foreign Service Group combining talents from both services. Most of the scaling-down would affect the diplomats since the Berrill Report saw 'no alternative to a fairly large programme of compulsory retirement'. Despite a few perfunctory regrets, he took the view that diplomats spent too much of their time abroad and that service overseas tended to lead to a 'blunting of intellectual capacity'. There was also a danger that the much-prized *esprit de corps* could encourage 'an elitist view of "them and us", particularly in relation to the Home Civil Service'.

Predictably, the Think Tank report provoked widespread anguish, from the outposts of Ulan Bator and Kathmandu to the inner sanctum of the Travellers' Club in Pall Mall. Some diplomats threatened direct action never before contemplated, such as working to rule without overtime and even walking out on strike. Their outraged feelings were registered in responses to a confidential questionnaire circulated in the Diplomatic Service Branch of the Society of Civil and Public Servants. Only 14 per cent of the 1,400 diplomats at home and abroad who answered the questionnaire were willing to accept a merger. Almost 300 diplomats stated that they would take early retirement rather than be merged with the Home Civil Service. One angry mandarin told a meeting convened to plan a campaign opposing implementation of the Think Tank report: 'Jim Callaghan once hailed the Foreign Office as the Rolls-Royce Department of Whitehall. Now he is being urged to let a Mini take over the job.' As a result of these rumblings and the skilful damage-limitation operations conducted by Sir Andrew Stark, the Deputy Under-Secretary of State appointed to 'liaise' with the Central Policy Review Staff, James Callaghan, who was by that time Prime Minister, decided that he had enough problems on his hands without having a showdown over the Foreign Office.

Although spared the Berrill axe, the Foreign Office has

remained under constant scrutiny, more so than any other department in Whitehall. It is a sitting target for those who regard anything short of gunboat diplomacy as appeasement. It comes in for frequent criticism in Parliament and the Press when it appears that Britain's interests are not being properly defended at meetings of the European Community or when British diplomacy fails to take a tough stand against actions by some of the authoritarian governments around the world. It is often in the dock at investigations of the Foreign Affairs Committee of the House of Commons.

Under the chairmanship first of Sir Anthony Kershaw, a former Foreign Office minister, and subsequently of David Howell, a former Energy Secretary, the Committee has tried to prod the Foreign Office into changing its priorities over policy and improving the way it uses its resources. The Committee strongly criticized the Foreign Office over its inadequate reaction in 1988 to the commercial challenges in the Pacific rim where the economies of Singapore, South Korea, Taiwan, and Hong Kong were offering 'a huge potential growth in purchasing power'. Sometimes it has acted as a very sharp watchdog over the way the Foreign Office exercises its influence on the BBC External Service by virtue of its financial provision which amounted to £130m in 1991.

On one important issue, however, the Foreign Affairs Committee's strictures were blandly ignored. That was over the Foreign Office response to BBC appeals for funds to launch a world television news service on the model of the radio service which has 130 million listeners in almost 40 languages. The project, which was supported by a motion in the House of Commons signed by 230 MPs, was designed to keep the BBC World Service in the forefront of international broadcasting. It was also recognized throughout the media as a means of enhancing the high reputation Britain enjoys through a broadcasting service which is universally accepted as credible and objective. A plea in 1988 for second thoughts by John Tusa, Managing Director of the BBC External Service, contained a remarkable forecast of what was subsequently to occur during the Gulf crisis in 1991: 'If the challenge is declined this country will find that more and more of the global audience will turn to sources such as Cable News Network of the USA.' In television budgeting terms the £5m sought by the BBC was paltry. Ironically, the BBC was made aware of the decision to leave the world television project to the 'funds of the market place' when Sir Geoffrey Howe attended a dinner hosted by John Tusa to mark the retirement of its distinguished Diplomatic Correspondent, Gordon Martin. Undeterred, however, John Tusa persisted with the project, finding funds for a pilot service launched on 15 April 1991. Initially, it was limited to Europe with a 30-minute newscast from World Service resources once a day in the course of an 18-hour television transmission on weekdays and 12 hours at weekends. After six months it was expanded to a 24-hour service and extended to Asia.

Foreign Office interest in the burgeoning arena of cultural diplomacy remained marginal for a long time while the French promoted their culture with relentless vigour. The British Council, founded in 1934, was given a low priority except when areas for budget cuts were being considered. But in the last few years, under the former BBC executive, Sir Richard Francis, as Director-General, its activities have been greatly extended. The traditional involvement in film festivals and travelling Shakespeare productions accounts for only 5 per cent of the Council's expenditure nowadays. With a billion people all over the world studying to learn English, the Council spends 10 per cent of its budget on teaching and 14 per cent on libraries. Its staff of 4,500, including 2,800 locally engaged personnel, help to run 55 language schools and 116 libraries in 89 countries.

Teaming up with British industry, the Council has become business-oriented with education and training projects boosting its cost-effectiveness. Typical of these was a £40m contract with Kuwait in May 1991 to re-equip schools after the Gulf War. In the first independent audit of its activities, the Council was praised by the National Audit Office in 1991 for its promotion of British interests and trade as 'one of the principal arms of the United Kingdom's overseas diplomacy'. While the Council is largely financed by Foreign Office funds – amounting in 1991 to a direct grant of £78m plus £24m from the Overseas Development Administration – its own revenue from earnings amounted to £55m in 1989–90. Although the Council has changed its image, there is still suspicion at Westminster that too often it is used as an extra arm of propaganda by the Foreign Office.

Regular monitoring of the Foreign Office's use of manpower is undertaken by the National Audit Office. In its assessment in 1990 of the resource bids in the annual Top Management Round, the National Audit Office found fault with the Foreign Office for not expressing them in terms of their impact on objectives and for assessing requirements largely on the basis of existing work and staffing currently available. While acknowledging that the Foreign Office has particular difficulty in predicting trends, the National Audit Office stressed the need for better long-term planning to 'direct their recruitment policy and deal with structural problems'. But one area of activity which is crucial to the way the Foreign Office is run has been carefully shielded from prying eyes seeking means of improving the system. Every Foreign Secretary has preserved his own staff organization, known as the Private Office, in the same way as Ernest Bevin found it on his first day in the Foreign Office in 1945. It stays as it has always been – the power house of the Foreign Office – because it can get things done as no other part of the system can.

IV

The Power House

The Private Office is the place where politics and diplomacy come together; Ministers and the Machine interlock, home and abroad meet, a clearing house for papers, a meeting-point, a bedlam.

Sir Nicholas Henderson,
The Private Office,
1984

Next door to the Foreign Secretary is what is called the Private Office, the nerve centre of the Foreign Office. It is the domain of the person whom some regard as the most influential in the entire Diplomatic Service, known by the initials PPS: the Principal Private Secretary. His importance is not immediately obvious from his office, which looks like a somewhat shabby reading room in a municipal library left undecorated for many years. Apart from the replacement of the dingy flock wallpaper from Ernest Bevin's day, it has stayed virtually the same for the last fifty years. The change of the seasons is marked by the alternating arrangement of dried flowers in the fireplace four times a year. A tall table for reading newspapers standing up has survived for generations. Like a theatre with pictures of stars from past productions, the walls have rows of portraits of every Foreign Secretary since Charles James Fox started the sequence in 1782 – all fifty-five of them. Diplomatic theatrical props are there on a table in the form of piles of dispatch boxes, some blue, others red or black. The sole painting in the room, above the fireplace, shows the thin red line of British troops at the battle of Kirkee near Poona in 1817. It was chosen to symbolize the atmosphere of the Private Office by Stephen Wall, a much-esteemed PPS who served with three foreign secretaries, Sir Geoffrey Howe, John Major, and Douglas Hurd, after a testing apprenticeship with Dr David Owen.

More than anyone else in the Foreign Office the PPS is chosen with extreme care. He has to be one of the high flyers, destined for the top like Sir Nicholas Henderson who served five foreign secretaries – Anthony Eden, Ernest Bevin, R. A. Butler, Patrick Gordon Walker, and Michael Stewart – before becoming Ambassador to France and subsequently to the United States. Besides being someone of sound judgement and discretion with a flair for improvisation when work schedules are overloaded, the PPS has above all to be a person in whom the Minister can have absolute confidence that his own interests will be upheld no matter what happens. It requires a particular talent to be able to interpret the Minister's opinions to the Office and, almost as important, the views of the Office to him.

As the one person spending more time with the Foreign Secretary at home and abroad than any other member of the Diplomatic Service, the PPS knows the Minister's mind better than anyone else. He is trusted to be at the Minister's side at all meetings with other statesmen. Since he is often the note-taker keeping a record, it is his version of the discussions which is circulated to the other senior diplomats who are not present at the meeting. That can be a crucial responsibility at times of crisis. Apart from being the keeper of the secrets, the PPS has one incalculable advantage over everyone else as the person 'who opens the door to the Minister and closes it as well'.

In his dual role as promoter and protector of the Foreign Secretary's position in the Downing Street power game, the PPS has to have a good knowledge of which way the wind is blowing in Whitehall on current issues before the Government. That requires him to have useful contacts in other ministries to be able to judge the support or opposition which policies being developed by the Foreign Secretary will attract. His soundings with the Ministry of Defence or the Department of Trade can be important for decisions on how certain propositions are to be presented at meetings involving various Whitehall departments. During the premiership of Margaret Thatcher it was always important to check in advance of any meeting what her attitude was likely to be. That could amount to around twenty telephone calls a day from the PPS to Sir Charles Powell, the confidant of the Prime Minister as her Private Secretary handling foreign affairs. Usually, Mrs Thatcher's position on matters affecting European Community partners was predictable, but occasionally she could confound even the expectations of her Cabinet colleagues.

One such occasion was an extraordinary Thatcher U-turn over the Channel Tunnel which was never disclosed despite the fact that all the ministers beside her at the time subsequently resigned. On the eve of going to Paris for a meeting with President François Mitterrand on 29 November 1984, Mrs Thatcher convened a briefing session of ministers and officials at No. 10 Downing Street. Shortly beforehand the newly arrived French Ambassador in London, Jacques Viot, telephoned the Foreign Office to say that his President was anxious that the Prime Minister should join him at a Press conference at the end of their talks to endorse the decision of transport ministers to have a fresh look at the Channel Tunnel project. Predictably, Mrs Thatcher showed no enthusiasm when the agenda item was reached at the briefing meeting: 'Channel Tunnel? Not much to be said about that,' she snapped. When it was pointed out that President Mitterrand had domestic political reasons for wanting a joint statement she said: 'The transport ministers have said all there is to be said. I want nothing more to do with it. There's no public money going into it. I shouldn't think it will ever get off the ground. Next item.'

In Paris the following evening she went to dinner at the Elysée Palace and was absolutely charmed by the Socialist President. When she returned for a debriefing meeting late that night at the British Ambassador's residence, the ministers who had been involved in discussions with their French opposite numbers were waiting to know what had transpired at her *tête-à-tête*. None of them – the Foreign Secretary Sir Geoffrey Howe, Chancellor Nigel Lawson and Transport Minister Nicholas Ridley – had evinced much enthusiasm for the Channel Tunnel at that time.

They had assumed that the hard-headed attitude taken by the Prime Minister at Downing Street would have been repeated at the Elysée Palace. Instead they were bowled over by the transformation. They had never seen her glowing with such delight after a *tête-à-tête* with a foreign statesman.

Watching his cigarette smoke curl up to the ceiling, Nicholas Ridley suddenly turned pale when he heard Mrs Thatcher enthuse: 'The Channel Tunnel is a tremendous scheme. No public money in it, of course. President Mitterrand absolutely agrees on that. But it's going to be a wonderful project – perhaps the most dramatic engineering project of the century. Simply marvellous.' She strode off to her room leaving everyone dumbfounded. Next morning, with President Mitterrand beaming at her side, the Prime Minister totally abandoned her Downing Street disdain of the proposition and talked as a convert at the Press conference. The Channel Tunnel scheme, she proclaimed, was 'something very exciting, a project which can show visibly how the technology of this age has moved to link the Continent and Britain closer together'. Once she had given the lead, the other Cabinet ministers concerned, although far from swallowing their doubts, had no option but to go along with the preparations for the project.

No one would blame a PPS for not always knowing other ministries' reactions when even senior Cabinet ministers are sometimes unable to predict what the Prime Minister's attitude will be on a specific issue. Where he would not be forgiven is if he did not alert the Foreign Secretary to a new development in a situation which is before the Cabinet or is likely to cause trouble in Parliament. That means keeping a careful watch on the flow of telegrams into the Private Office. On a normal day when there is no crisis, the PPS is at his desk at 7.30 a.m. studying the first batch of telegrams for the Foreign Secretary at 8 a.m. At least 100 telegrams – sometimes double that number – arrive in three deliveries a day and are sorted out by two assistant private secretaries who divide the world between them. The PPS will check the sifting and read carefully through the twenty-five or so selected for the attention of the Minister. All 'Immediate' or 'Flash' telegrams are handed directly to the Foreign Secretary. There is always close contact with the Head of News Department, who is the Foreign Secretary's spokesman, so that the Minister can be made aware of urgent news agency bulletins and of reports causing enquiries from the media.

Before he leaves the Private Office in the evening – rarely before 9.30 p.m. and often much later if there is a crisis – the PPS will select items for the overnight box sent to the Foreign Secretary's official residence at No. 1 Carlton Gardens. These will include telegrams on matters of current concern, recommendations on policy questions from an under-secretary, and notes on any calls received from the Prime Minister's advisers or ambassadors. By virtue of having a broader knowledge of the background and knowing how the Minister's views have been evolving in the course of the day, the PPS can often add his own comments to the documents. Where he normally draws the line is in becoming involved in long overnight discussions. That was a feature of the sometimes tempestuous relationship when George Brown was Foreign Secretary and Sir Donald Maitland his PPS. After a good dinner George Brown would open the box from the Private Office at 2 a.m. and discover something he did not like. He would rouse Sir Donald at home and order him to send some abusively worded instructions to an ambassador or an under-secretary immediately. When Sir Donald demurred there would be a long harangue culminating in the telephone being slammed down. Next day the Foreign Secretary would appear in the Private Office full of repentance and enquire if he had upset people. He was fortunate in having diplomats around him with long slow-burning fuses to their tempers who would usually assure him that no offence had been taken. Once, however, when there had been a particularly unreasonable outburst from George Brown and he arrived at the Office worried about how his behaviour had been taken, he had his comeuppance. Sir Donald Maitland drew himself up to his full height of 5 feet 4½ inches and delivered a stern observation: 'People of my stature learn early on that to survive they have to know how to deal with bullies.'

There is rarely any escape from the boxes for a Foreign Secretary. Even in the grouse-shooting season Lord Home organized his day to cope with them at Castlemains in Ayrshire in August 1960, a month after he took over the job. His PPS, Sir Oliver

Wright, stayed with the Homes and arranged for one of the beaters to start his day early by going down to the railway station at 7.30 a.m. to collect the boxes sent from the Foreign Office overnight by train. Sir Oliver would sift through the telegrams quickly and set out the ones commanding the greatest priority. At 8.30 a.m. he would have thirty minutes with Lord Home assessing the responses to be made and what points to pursue in telephone consultations with the departments at the Foreign Office. They would meet again during the picnic lunch on the moors when Lord Home enjoyed what his colleagues described as 'reviewing the Cold War over the cold turkey'. Then at the end of the day's shoot, when his guests were discussing their bag, Lord Home returned for another hour and a half on the diplomatic bag so that the telegrams could go back to London overnight with advice for action. These were the days before the fax machines which John Major found so convenient when he took over at the Foreign Office almost thirty years later.

Knowing how to adjust to the moods and pressures is one of the key factors in the relationship between a PPS and the Foreign Secretary. That is often a formidable challenge for a PPS when he finds, as Sir Ewen Fergusson did between 1975 and 1978 in the Private Office, that adjustments had to be made to such diverse personalities as James Callaghan, Anthony Crosland, and Dr David Owen. A large measure of tact is required if a PPS is to keep his Minister on schedule throughout a busy day, guiding him from one meeting to another without causing offence to the people who say: 'I just want a quick word with the Minister.' With each day's engagements worked out between him and the Social Secretary in the Private Office, the PPS takes the opportunity of the presence of all the senior mandarins at the PUS's morning meeting to set out the Foreign Secretary's programme of meetings and the way he sees the priorities of the day. Some ministers are more exacting than others about strict time-keeping. As an ex-Guards officer, Lord Carrington had an obsessive concern for punctuality and would become very testy with his PPS Brian Fall if he were kept waiting for more than thirty seconds. When he was in the chair at NATO meetings, Lord Carrington brought a bell with him so that when a session was convened for nine o'clock he started it precisely on time by ringing the bell to get people into their places.

On the way from one meeting to another, Foreign Secretaries often use the time alone in the car with their PPS to sound him out on the possible reactions inside the Foreign Office to some project under consideration. The inside knowledge of a PPS on the personalities and prejudices of people in the Service is sometimes a very important factor in helping a Foreign Secretary make up his mind. That assessment can be the decisive influence in some appointments made by Foreign Secretaries. It was the advice sought by Sir Geoffrey Howe from his PPS, Len Appleyard, which determined who was chosen as his spokesman in 1984. Recalling Christopher Meyer's skill as a speechwriter in Planning Department, Len Appleyard suggested that he was the ideal person to be Head of News Department and spokesman. When Sir Geoffrey was visiting Moscow in July 1984, he met Christopher Meyer as Head of Chancery in the Embassy and confirmed Len Appleyard's nomination on the spot.

Trying to ensure that the Foreign Secretary's speaking engagements go without a hitch has become an increasing problem for the PPS despite all the advantages of modern communications. One minor drama which befell Canada's Foreign Minister, Paul Martin, at a NATO meeting in Luxembourg has served as a warning to any PPS never to be left without a spare copy of a Minister's speech. The unfortunate Canadian Minister was rehearsing his speech by his hotel window as he dressed for breakfast when a gust of wind sucked two pages of the text out of the room and onto the rooftop. As the hotel staff could not retrieve them, the fire brigade had to be summoned to get someone onto the roof. But the length of time it took to assemble the whole text again meant that Paul Martin missed his turn to speak and had to make his intervention later.

Television coverage of speeches has obliged the PPS to be very conscious of the timing and the opportunities for 'sound bites' in news bulletins. Those who give the final polish to the Minister's speech are under pressure to be brilliant phrasemakers devising passages which will command headlines and provide television and radio extracts. Although politicians are often themselves to blame for the lack of headlines after speeches, there was one significant occasion when it was the fault of the media. When Prime Minister Harold Macmillan decided to make his historic visit to South Africa in January 1960, he chose a special speechwriter to accompany him – Sir David Hunt, an assistant under-secretary who had been Private Secretary to Sir Winston Churchill and Clement Attlee.

For the first speech of the tour delivered at Accra on 9 January in the presence of Ghana's President Kwame Nkrumah, Sir David coined a phrase which Macmillan delivered in his usual sententious style: 'The wind of change is blowing right through Africa.' But despite an advance text being circulated by Press Secretary Sir Harold Evans, it was ignored by the media. Three weeks later, when Sir David was drafting the speech for the climax of the tour in Cape Town, he felt that his phrase was too good to lose so he inserted a slightly modified version. Again, when Macmillan, addressing both houses of the South African legislature, spoke of the growing strength of African national consciousness and said 'The wind of change is blowing through this continent', there was no response from the audience. But this time the Press benches were alert and the 'Wind of Change' not only became headlines round the world but received a place in the history of Africa which even Sir David Hunt never anticipated.

In contrast, a speech a year later by Lord Home as Foreign Secretary made instant headlines worldwide over 'double standards' at the United Nations. No one was more surprised than Lord Home. He had intended to 'stir it up a bit', but the speech was prepared as a carefully drafted balance sheet of pluses and minuses. It was one he had written himself without any speechwriter's help, since he never liked speaking anyone else's words. Weighing the current pessimism about the UN against the optimism, Lord Home stated: 'I come down decidedly on the side of hope.' It was not planned as a great media event. A bitterly cold night on Saturday, 28 December 1961 kept the numbers down to a faithful few at the United Nations Association meeting of the Berwick-on-Tweed branch. But an enterprising night editor on the *Sunday Express* saw an arresting headline to be made out of the contrast cited by Lord Home. New members were trying to impose their views on colonialism instead of focusing on the UN's main purpose, the search for peace and security. Lord Home put it bluntly: 'This concentration on colonialism leads to the adoption of a double standard of behaviour by many of the newly elected countries.' While Russian colonialism had been 'the most ruthless in history', the Foreign Secretary said Britain had freed 600 million people in fifteen years and given them complete independence as equal members in the Commonwealth. He asked the question: 'Is there growing up, almost imperceptibly, a code of behaviour where there is one rule for the Communist countries and another for the democracies?' Lord Home left people to draw their own conclusions. The media had no doubts and the 'double standards' headline stayed to haunt him for years.

The impact of speeches depends on the importance attached by politicians to putting foreign policy across by public address – and their ability on the rostrum. Sometimes a minister's enthusiasm far exceeds his oratorical talents. Michael Stewart found it difficult to grip the attention of an audience except at the Oxford Union debate on Vietnam. Lord Carrington did not regard making speeches as having any great priority in shaping foreign policy. But Sir Geoffrey Howe set greater store on speeches than any other foreign secretary. While he had a talent for 'saying a few words' with gentle wit at an informal gathering, he lacked the ability to make an audience hang on every word – with one memorable exception, his famous 'resignation speech' on 13 November 1990 in the House of Commons which led to the downfall of Mrs Thatcher.

Sir Geoffrey's Private Office, however, had to ensure that a steady stream of policy speeches was prepared. He held regular planning meetings to signpost the themes and occasions for his oratory. Some speeches were acknowledged afterwards to have injected fresh impetus into debatable issues in the Western Alliance such as his provocative 'Star Wars' lecture on 'Defence and Security in the Nuclear Age' to the Royal United Services Institute for Defence Studies in March 1985. But often they fell with a dull thud on the audience despite long hours spent by the PPS, the Head of News Department, and others in trying to improve the fifth or sixth draft with eye-catching phrases. It could sometimes take until two o'clock in the morning poring over revised texts in a hotel room abroad before they could meet the demands of Sir Geoffrey, a perfectionist who was never satisfied until he had the last comma correctly in place.

Labour foreign secretaries have always felt the need to have political weight in the Private Office to balance the advice available to them through the Foreign Office machine. Foreign secretaries, like other government ministers, have had the services of a parliamentary private secretary to keep them in touch with opinion at Westminster. On his arrival at the Foreign Office, George Brown introduced an extra political adviser. William Greig, a highly respected journalist from the *Daily Mirror*, was appointed Special Assistant to the Secretary of State. His role was largely a public relations function, 'protecting George from himself' as one colleague put it. Although Michael Stewart did not add anyone to his staff, Lord Home began his second term at the Foreign Office in 1970 with the appointment of Miles Hudson as Political Secretary. An Oxford graduate with fluent Russian, Miles Hudson had been in charge of Rhodesian Affairs at the Conservative Research Department. As an African expert he was very useful in the Private Office, especially since Lord Home was not always at ease over African issues and had the habit of referring to Tanzania as Tanganyika years after it had become independent.

The biggest political change was made by James Callaghan when he became Foreign Secretary in March 1974. He introduced three experienced political heavyweights. For a start he upgraded the job of parliamentary private secretary by appointing a rising star in the Labour Party, Dr Jack Cunningham. Then he brought in Tom McNally, who had been International Secretary of the Labour Party and his principal adviser during his time as Shadow Foreign Secretary. Thirdly, he broke with tradition by removing a career diplomat, Lord Nicholas Gordon Lennox, as Head of News Department, and replacing him with Tom McCaffrey, who had been his spokesman at the Home Office. The title of Political Adviser, instead of Secretary, for Tom McNally signalled a much greater political emphasis inside the Private Office. To make sure that he was aware of all information coming in from posts, Callaghan insisted that Tom McNally be able to see all telegrams except those dealing with security and intelligence matters.

Although the new Political Adviser had the customary role when Labour is in power of being a 'mine detector', alerting the Minister to possible sources of trouble within the party on certain international questions, he quickly asserted himself on policy issues within the Private Office. Tom McNally became the main speech-writer for James Callaghan on sensitive matters such as the renegotiation of the terms of Britain's membership of the European Community. Sir Michael Butler as assistant under-secretary supervising relations with European Community partners blinked at some of the undiplomatic language in the McNally drafts and wondered how the other ministers in Brussels would take it. Tom McNally knew he had the full backing of the Foreign Secretary and could advise Sir Michael that they would just have to get used to it. The trust placed in him by Callaghan was demonstrated when he sent Tom McNally with Lord Greenhill, former PUS, on a fact-finding mission in February 1976 for talks with the rebel Rhodesian Prime Minister Ian Smith.

What has come to be called 'political spin' became much more noticeable on policy issues under the new monitoring system operated by Tom McNally in the Private Office. While Michael Stewart had given his support at the NATO Foreign Ministers' meeting in Rome in May 1970 to the Soviet proposal for a conference on security and co-operation in Europe, it had been shelved at the Foreign Office until Callaghan authorized Tom McNally to blow the dust off it. In some quarters of the Foreign Office it was treated as a trap devised by Soviet President Brezhnev to ensure that the Communist frontiers in Europe would be set in concrete. But Tom McNally pushed for a reconsideration of the proposition as a means of leverage for greater respect for human rights. Although he made some progress on that issue, his pressures for changes on policy towards Chile and South Africa were not able to produce any substantial reorientation. However, it was not all softly-softly advice. Political pressure from Dr Cunningham and Tom McNally persuaded James Callaghan to take a tough stand over Guatemala's threats to Belize in November 1975. As a result Callaghan was the first minister to send a squadron of RAF Harrier jets on a 'fire brigade mission' abroad to reinforce the British garrison.

One of Callaghan's most significant 'firsts' as Foreign Secretary was to add a new dimension to the Private Office with the establishment of what has become known as the 'Flying Foreign Office'. On 30 December 1974, he flew to Africa in an RAF VC 10 troop-carrying jet transformed into an airborne office taking his Private Office, African experts, secretaries, and journalists on a 20,000-mile tour to six countries. The RAF had previously carried ministers but usually just for a short European visit such as George Brown made to the Soviet Union in November 1966. James Callaghan inaugurated a new style of 'Meet the People' diplomacy with his own plane enabling him to visit several countries on a short tour of eight or ten days. Correspondents flying with him on the RAF VC 10 and paying the equivalent of the commercial fare were able to cover all the events. Trying to keep up with the Foreign Secretary by scheduled flights would have resulted in some of his stops not being covered by the media.

Another of Callaghan's innovations was to use the 'Flying Foreign Office' for a mercy mission to Africa in July 1975. This was a unique occasion. No other Cabinet minister had ever taken such political as well as physical risks. It was the climax to a drama begun when Uganda's President Idi Amin threatened to execute by firing squad a 61-year-old British lecturer, Denis Hills. The offence which caused Hills to be held incommunicado at Bombo barracks was his accusation in the manuscript for a book that Amin ruled 'like a village tyrant'. Attempts to assuage Amin's anger even involved the Queen. The Foreign Office pondered for a long time about whether it would be judicious to recommend that the Queen should send an envoy. Was it wise to send a general alone? Was there a danger he might be locked up? Should he, therefore, take someone with him? If so, whom? All these questions ricocheted back and forward from Buckingham Palace to the Private Office.

There was considerable trepidation when the Queen sent Lieutenant-General Sir Chandos Blair, who had been Commanding Officer of the 4th King's African Rifles when Amin was in the ranks. But he returned empty-handed. The dilemma remained. In the end, after intensive debate between the Foreign Office and No. 10 Downing Street, it was accepted that the only way to get Hills out of Uganda alive was for the Foreign Secretary to fly to

Kampala on a rescue mission. Amin was demanding an end to what he called 'malicious propaganda' from Britain, plus a consignment of spare parts for military equipment he had bought from England, and personal assurances from the Queen or Prime Minister Harold Wilson that these two requirements would be fully met. He made no promises about what he would do in return. Even though he eventually promised clemency, Amin was so unpredictable that no one was sure what would happen. What persuaded James Callaghan that he had a chance of bringing Hills back in the VC 10 was the behind-the-scenes assistance he secured from President Mobutu of Zaire and President Kenyatta of Kenya who both agreed to 'make Amin see sense'. Part of the secret deal was an arrangement for Callaghan to be seen thanking President Mobutu in his own capital with television cameras recording the event.

Watched by the travelling Press, and guarded by six security officers, Callaghan drove from the VC 10 at Kinshasa to pay his respects to President Mobutu at a ceremonial breakfast banquet overlooking the River Congo. Everything on the table was gold – plates, cups, cutlery – except for one item: a plastic tub of margarine for the diet-conscious President. There was no such ceremony in Kampala. After an hour's negotiations in Amin's command post alongside pictures of Libya's Colonel Gaddafi and a copy of the Annigoni portrait of the Queen, Hills was handed over. On his way back to the VC 10, Callaghan had his most frightening experience of the visit – a personally conducted tour of the town in a Mercedes driven in demoniac style by a barefoot Amin in a bemedalled camouflage uniform and a Seaforth Highlanders glengarry.

Since then there have been many improvements and refinements to the way the Private Office organizes the 'Flying Foreign Office'. Sophisticated radio communications installed in the VC 10 make it possible for the Foreign Secretary to keep in touch with the Foreign Office all the time and send messages to the capitals he passes. Sir Geoffrey Howe used the VC 10 for extensive travelling to India, Hong Kong, China, Australia, New Zealand, and Japan. He made so many tours, including one round-the-world trip, that the RAF were considering naming one of the planes after him. And as Sir Geoffrey Howe could manage with only four or five hours' sleep, he liked his PPS to fit as many engagements into the day as possible. A typical programme was the last day of a six-day tour of Pakistan, India, Qatar, and Bahrain on Saturday, 1 April 1989. It made his entourage groan at the prospect of a very exhausting day ahead when they scanned their copy which read as follows:

Saturday 1 April

05.00	Luggage (unlocked for security check) ready for collection by the RAF
06.00	Breakfast
06.30	Car to New Delhi Airport
07.30	Farewell meeting with Minister of State
08.00	Take-off for Qatar
10.40	Arrive Doha airport
11.15	Talks with Ruler and Heir Apparent
12.15	Visit 'Best of Britain' exhibition
13.00	Lunch with Heir Apparent
14.15	Meet Embassy staff
14.40	Car to Doha Airport
15.00	Take-off for Bahrain
16.00	Arrive Bahrain
16.20	Talks with Foreign Minister
17.30	Call on Prime Minister
18.15	Call on Ruler
19.00	Call on Crown Prince
20.00	Dinner with Foreign Minister
22.15	Press conference
23.00	Car to airport
23.30	Take-off for London

Sunday 2 April

05.30 Arrive Heathrow (Southside)

Although the Private Office staff were often on the point of collapse at the end of gruelling tours such as that one, Sir Geoffrey Howe appeared to have endless reserves of stamina. Before leaving the VC 10 he would go through the plane thanking everyone for their part in what he called 'keeping the show on the road'. As he headed back to the official residence to read through the weekend dispatch boxes in preparation for the week ahead, some of his travelling companions wondered why he bothered to spend a Saturday in such small desert sheikhdoms. Sir Geoffrey's view was that being seen at the helm in times of calm waters in distant places usually paid dividends later in times of trouble. Two years after his visit, the attitude of the Gulf states towards Britain following Iraq's invasion of Kuwait was seen in many quarters as justifying the attention paid to them in the past by the helmsmen at the Foreign Office.

V

The Helmsmen

*Search the world over, hunt history from
beginning to end, and you will conclude as the
result of your labours that the great Foreign
Minister is almost the rarest bird that
flies.*

F. S. Oliver, *The Endless Adventure*

*Any Foreign Secretary in any Government
knows that there are always several of his
colleagues who, whatever their personal
goodwill towards him, would like to have
his job.*

Michael Stewart, *Life and Labour*

Being at the helm at the Foreign Office puts the Foreign Secretary
into difficult, sometimes dangerous, waters, which can be unnerv-
ing however much experience he may have had elsewhere in
government or opposition. At most other government departments,
a minister usually takes charge with a programme of policies which
are largely worked out in advance. Except for the broadest outlines,
very little can be translated from party manifestos into foreign
policy. All the Foreign Secretary's Cabinet colleagues, apart from
those at the Treasury and Defence, can conduct their departments
with their attention focused mainly upon the impact of their
decisions within Britain. For him it is sometimes a challenge to
distinguish where to focus with so many trouble spots demanding
attention at one time. As one minister described it: 'The Foreign
Secretary is at the mercy of political currents from A to Z – from

Argentina to Zimbabwe.' Most of his time is spent reacting to situations arising from events outside the country. Often they cannot be dealt with in isolation since they affect several nations simultaneously. No matter how efficiently the Foreign Office experts set out the problem and the options for dealing with it, the Foreign Secretary has the responsibility of deciding what action the Government should take.

For any Foreign Secretary, two main factors largely determine how much he can achieve: the standing of Britain in the eyes of the rest of the world, economically as well as politically, and his own standing in the country, in Parliament, and in the party. The débâcle of the Suez War in 1956 signalled the end of Britain's pretensions to Big Power status. Despite the creation of the Commonwealth from the ashes of Empire, no one after Prime Minister Harold Macmillan could attempt to perpetuate the fiction of imperial power. Foreign policy had to be adjusted to the reality of Britain in the role of what the Duncan Report described as 'a major Power of the second order'. Much of the scope in this new role often depends upon the state of the British economy, company order books, and the strength of the pound. When the Foreign Secretary had to work by candlelight at the Foreign Office, as Lord Home did in 1972 because industrial disputes brought electricity cuts, it was not easy for him to demand attention in an international forum as the spokesman of a nuclear power. Strikes in many sectors of industry, plus high inflation figures and statistics showing over 3 million people unemployed, all combined in the early 1980s to make other governments wonder whether ministers from Britain attending international conferences had a strong enough economic base from which to wield any political clout.

Establishing one's credentials as Foreign Secretary can be as much of an ordeal as entering the international arena with a weak negotiating hand. James Callaghan's surprising choice of a relatively unknown junior minister, Dr David Owen, to take over as Foreign Secretary in February 1977 on the death of Anthony Crosland caused other foreign ministers in European capitals to exclaim: 'Dr Who?' But no one could have had a stormier start than Lord Home when he was first appointed Foreign Secretary by Harold Macmillan in July 1960. There was an extraordinary wave of indignation in public, in Parliament, and in some quarters of the Conservative Party at the choice of someone whom the *Sunday Express* described as 'this unknown and faceless earl'. The Prime Minister was berated in the *Daily Mirror* for a move which would 'reduce the British Foreign Office to a laughing stock in the capitals of the world'. His promotion of Lord Home was condemned as 'the most reckless political appointment since the Roman Emperor Caligula made his favourite horse a consul'.

In Parliament there was an unprecedented step to register disapproval. The Leader of the Opposition, Hugh Gaitskell, forced an adjournment debate to censure the Government. While the main burden of his criticism was the affront to the House of Commons by the appointment of a member of the House of Lords, there was an unusual outburst of venom from the normally mild-mannered Labour leader at the choice of someone 'closely identified' with the Munich Agreement made by Chamberlain with Hitler in September 1938. After listening to the thirty-minute tirade, Macmillan defended his choice as the 'best man for the job' who should not be debarred by being a peer and defeated the censure motion by 332 votes to 220.

Lord Home's skill in establishing himself as a tough negotiator with the Russians quickly silenced his critics. It earned him the sort of admiration at the Foreign Office only accorded in the same affectionate terms to one other minister since the Second World War – Ernest Bevin. His record in handling the Russians at difficult periods during his two terms of office also ensured that there was no repetition of the criticism when Lord Carrington was appointed Foreign Secretary by Margaret Thatcher in 1979. Lord Home had studied books on the Russians when he lay crippled with spinal tuberculosis in 1940–41. It paid off twenty years later when he faced the veteran Soviet Foreign Minister Andrei Gromyko at the testing time which followed the shooting down of the American U-2 spy plane. His handling of the Berlin crisis in March 1962 was firm when the Russians stepped up their war of nerves. He had warned Gromyko not to be provocative over Berlin. 'One false step, one failure in communication, even one failure in comprehension might mean war,' he emphasized.

Lord Home knew the Russians would only take a warning seriously when they were left in no doubt that it would be carried out. However, that did not inhibit Home from making the most of any opportunity to do business with the Russians when it suited the West to reach agreements. One of the most significant achievements was the nuclear test ban treaty which Macmillan regarded as 'one of the great purposes which I had set myself'. While Macmillan sent messages to President Kennedy and Nikita Khrushchev to edge them into concessions, Lord Home did much of the spadework in framing the formulas for meeting the requirements of the two superpowers. Although he was no intellectual, Lord Home was recognized in the Foreign Office as a quick, concise drafter. When the Russians wanted top-level delegations to come to Moscow in July 1963 for the final round of negotiations, it was Lord Home who suggested Lord Hailsham as Minister of Science to impress the Soviet leader alongside America's Averell Harriman. In recognition of his persistence with disarmament negotiations over the years in Geneva, Macmillan sent Lord Home for the signing of the treaty in the Kremlin on 5 August 1963.

It was not always stern confrontation, however, between Lord Home and the Russians. He enjoyed joking with them to break up the tedium of long propaganda speeches. He delighted in rebutting Gromyko's argument that there was no need for on-site inspections to check on an explosion because the Russians would know when it was an earthquake and would say so. With a straight face he would enquire: 'Could it not be Mr Molotov being kicked downstairs?' Lord Home liked stories about Gromyko. One of his favourites illustrated that Gromyko had some of Home's sense of humour. The Soviet Foreign Minister began striding angrily out of the UN Security Council chamber on one occasion when he suddenly turned away from the main exit and left by another door. The reason was that his security officer whispered that his trouser zip was open and he was heading for the television cameras. Gromyko shrugged it off saying: 'The Americans always wanted open diplomacy.' On another occasion Lord Home had Gromyko puzzled by saying that he would be offered the chairmanship of the Conservative Party on his next visit to London. 'Why such an honour?' the Soviet Minister asked. Lord Home, as ever straight-faced, said the views of Gromyko had not changed for decades so he was the most consistent conservative for the job.

Like other ministers, Lord Home had to face demands at home and abroad for action on the problem of Rhodesia. His attempt at a settlement in 1971 sought to avoid the errors made by Prime Minister Harold Wilson in the negotiations with Ian Smith aboard HMS *Tiger* in 1966 and HMS *Fearless* in 1968. The principal flaw in Wilson's approach was the assumption that an agreement reached with the white Rhodesians would have to be accepted by the black majority without a genuine test of its acceptability. Lord Home realized he had to make sure of a 'window of opportunity for the blacks'. He sent out a mission under Lord Goodman to shift the Smith regime from the vague promise of eventual black and white parity to the concept of African majority rule. When that was achieved – somewhat to the surprise of Foreign Office officials – Lord Home went out to Rhodesia for the full-scale negotiations on the terms for independence.

The outcome was an agreement which Lord Home believed was the best that could be realistically wrung from the white Rhodesians. It was well short of bringing majority rule within a reasonable time-scale for the African nationalist leaders. But the crucial element on which Lord Home had insisted was that the terms of the settlement had to be tested by an independent commission to find out whether they were 'acceptable to the people of Rhodesia as a whole' under the terms of the fifth of the famous Six Principles established by the Wilson Government in 1966.

A commission under Lord Pearce, a former Lord of Appeal in Ordinary, delivered its verdict in May 1972 after many months of on-the-spot investigations. That verdict was emphatic: 'We are satisfied on our evidence that the proposals are acceptable to the great majority of Europeans. We are equally satisfied after considering all our evidence, including that of intimidation, that the majority of Africans rejected our proposals. In our opinion the people of Rhodesia as a whole do not regard the proposals as acceptable as a basis for independence.' Lord Home was disappointed since he saw it more as a vote against Ian Smith than against the independence terms. There was, however, one positive outcome. It ensured that future attempts at a settlement had to have the African nationalists directly in the negotiations.

Lord Home was one of the most enthusiastic travellers during both his terms at the Foreign Office. Although his mileage was much less than subsequent Foreign Secretaries who had the 'Flying Foreign Office' at their disposal, he travelled over 148,000 miles in his first three years – more than double Michael Stewart's travels. One country outdid all the others in the red carpet welcome for him – China. Lord Home was delighted to find that he was given a splendid guest house inside Peking's Forbidden City in a road called Anti-Imperialist Street. He was saluted with great enthusiasm for two main reasons: first, as the Foreign Secretary bold enough to expel 105 Russians as spies and secondly, as the minister who the Chinese believed would have the most significant influence in Europe with Britain joining the European Community.

The tribute which touched Lord Home most was in the Great Hall of the Peoples in Peking where Foreign Minister Chi Peng-fei hosted a fourteen-course banquet in his honour. While Lord Home was trying to come to terms with his chopsticks, the band of the Chinese People's Liberation Army saluted him with the Scottish tunes, 'Wi' A Hundred Pipers' and 'Green Grow the Rushes'. But the highlight of the evening came when they played the Eton Boating Song, which the Chinese had discovered always reminded Lord Home of his college days when he first met his wife, Elizabeth, who was the daughter of his Headmaster at Eton, Dr Cyril Alington. Lord Home was so moved that he walked over to the bandstand and stood hand-in-hand with his wife, listening to the music. Although not a person who often showed any emotion he was seen wiping a tear from his cheek. After an encore he raised a glass of Mao Tai to toast the conductor and told him: 'You played that beautifully.' How the conductor obtained the sheet music to rehearse the army band he never disclosed.

Taking over the helm at the Foreign Office in October 1964, when Lord Home crossed to the other side of Downing Street to become Prime Minister, was not an assignment seized with any enthusiasm by R. A. 'Rab' Butler. He had hoped to be at No. 10 Downing Street himself. Many others thought he would be, too. Lord Home's mother, the Dowager Countess of Home, then aged eighty-one, admitted she had not expected her son to succeed Harold Macmillan: 'I am quite amazed – I was sure it was going to be Mr Butler.' So did 'Rab' Butler's wife, Mollie. She was in tears: 'My husband would have made the best Prime Minister in the world – I know he would.' It was only out of loyalty to the Party that 'Rab' Butler accepted the Foreign Secretaryship.

Throughout his year at the Foreign Office he made no secret of his conviction that Lord Home would lose the general election and blurted out his forecast of doom for the Tories in a famously indiscreet interview with George Gale of the *Daily Express* just before polling day. Although he carried out a full programme of engagements at home and abroad, there was no disguising that it was being done perfunctorily. 'Rab' Butler got high marks for his sense of duty, low marks for his lack of commitment. At his first meeting with other foreign ministers in the Western European Union at The Hague in May 1964, they were put off by his waxen smile as he dolefully recited arguments in a familiar Foreign Office draft for using WEU as a bridge between the Common Market Six and Britain. He made only one major foreign policy speech in the House of Commons – on 17 June 1964 – and it did not command much attention. Despite his fondness for mordant humour, most of the time he looked bored.

One other candidate for virtual oblivion was the next to get his picture on the wall, the luckless Patrick Gordon Walker. He had to spend most of his short spell as Foreign Secretary trying to get elected after being defeated in the general election of October 1964. Despite that distraction, he did his best to get to grips with the job. Patrick Gordon Walker had a good command of German and used it talking to the German Foreign Minister Gerhard Schroeder, even though there was no need to do so since Schroeder's English was excellent. When he went to Washington on Harold Wilson's first visit as Prime Minister just after the election, he deployed a very cogently argued case against the American MLF scheme – the proposition for a multilateral force giving the Germans an indirect say in nuclear strategy. The carefully orchestrated opposition from Wilson and Gordon Walker was credited with sinking the project. Where he was less successful was in assuaging the wrath of Britain's partners in the European

Free Trade Association when the new Labour Government imposed a 15 per cent import surcharge. That was just one of many headaches left for his successor when the result of the Leyton by-election announced on 22 January ended Patrick Gordon Walker's term at the Foreign Office.

Coming straight from being Minister of Education to take charge at the Foreign Office at short notice, Michael Stewart was not thought to be the sort of person likely to make his mark as a helmsman. A schoolmaster for ten years, he gave the impression of being pedantic, a man who liked papers more than people. He had a shy, reserved manner. His observations were punctuated by so many pauses that it was hard to know whether he had finished what he intended to say or was merely searching for words. As a politician who was extremely conscientious in mastering his briefs, he was heard with great respect but he attracted little admiration and even less affection. Yet Michael Stewart had one rare quality which made many who worked with him feel he was seriously underrated as a Foreign Secretary: the strong conviction that public affairs must always be conducted on a firm base of principles. He despised any course of action which smacked of expediency. On several occasions in both his terms at the Foreign Office he could have avoided trouble if he had not insisted that his actions had to be 'defended in the realm of morality and justice'.

No one in the 1960s and 1970s had a harder time within his own party over the way foreign policy was conducted than Michael Stewart. The left wing of the Labour Party was particularly agitated over Vietnam. They wanted the Government to dissociate itself from the American policy of President Lyndon Johnson. Less than a month after establishing himself at the Foreign Office, Michael Stewart found his dilemma was intensified by Johnson's decision to authorize air strikes against military targets in North Vietnam. This brought furious demands from the Labour left wing for the Government to condemn the bombing. But Stewart refused to be rushed into one-sided judgements. He made clear in the House of Commons that the United States had a right to counter the invasion of its ally South Vietnam, not just in the territory invaded but in the land from which the invasion was supplied with weapons. An opportunity to state his case to a wider audience arose with an invitation to take part in a day-long seminar on 16 June 1965 which was convened as a 'teach-in' on Vietnam at the Oxford Union and was being televised.

At first the Foreign Office mandarins bristled at the prospect of the mild-mannered Foreign Secretary demeaning himself to take on rowdy students. They feared he would not be able to stand up to the devious arguments of the anti-American lobby. But as a stout opponent of the vociferous supporters of the Campaign for Nuclear Disarmament in his constituency at Fulham, Stewart refused to be browbeaten. Having been President of the Union in 1929, he was eager to prove he had lost none of his old debating skills. All he insisted on was that he would not be required to present the United States case on Vietnam. That had to be put by an American, so Henry Cabot Lodge, just returned as US Ambassador in Vietnam, was flown over from Washington.

Convinced that his case for the British Government's stand on Vietnam was based on sustainable principles, Michael Stewart had no qualms about going into what he regarded as a lion's den – and to ensure that he would be rescued if the mauling turned too nasty, he was accompanied by his PPS from Hertford College, Oxford, Sir Nicholas Henderson. There were the predictable catcalls and jeers as he began in the style of a tutorial with a brief history of the origins of the conflict in Indochina. He silenced most of them by saying how much he enjoyed teach-ins and would rejoice 'when students in China, the Soviet Union and even in North Vietnam would have the same freedom to express their views'. While Cabot Lodge had despairingly appealed for a hearing, saying 'Why do you not listen to me?', Michael Stewart quickly secured a very attentive audience. He undermined the arguments of those who derided the Americans for supporting a 'rotten democracy' in Saigon by pointing out that one million people had fled from the Communist north to South Vietnam. The United States had offered to negotiate. The barrier, he insisted, was the refusal of the governments of North Vietnam, China, and the Soviet Union to negotiate at all.

His speech – and his assurance in answering questions – took the wind out of his opponents' sails. It caught everyone so much by surprise that there was a burst of applause at the end – a very rare occurrence for Michael Stewart. The planned demonstration for left-wing students to stand up and tear up their Labour Party membership cards was abandoned. Even more significant, by shrewdly releasing an advance text of the highlights of his speech to the Press, Michael Stewart saw his reputation soar to unexpected heights in the newspapers the next day. If he had to be remembered for one intervention only as Foreign Secretary, Stewart left no doubt that he was proud to rest his case on his Vietnam performance at the Oxford Union. When he returned in May 1970 to the Oxford Union, he was confronted with a noose hanging from the gallery and shouts of 'Hang him' and 'Stewart, we want you dead.' Chants of 'Ho, Ho, Ho Chi Minh' drowned his attempts to start his address. He walked away an embittered man. In recalling the episode a decade later in his memoirs *Life and Labour*, Stewart observed: 'The chairman appealed to their leader (Mr Christopher Hitchens who now writes for the *New Statesman*) but his reply was that if you know what someone is going to say, and you know that it is wrong, you are entitled to protect the audience from being misled.'

His other main difficulty with the left wing of the Labour Party was over the Government's policy towards Nigeria in the civil war which followed the secession of the eastern region as Biafra under Colonel Chukwuemeka Ojukwu in May 1967. There was strong criticism of his decision to sell arms to the Federal Government of General Jack Gowon. The pro-Biafran lobby, whose case was cleverly presented by Markpress, a public relations company operating from Geneva, had considerable support in Britain from Catholics and Scottish Presbyterians, whose churches had longstanding links with the Ibos. Over twenty MPs were angry because they thought the Government's policy was influenced by British oil interests in Nigeria. Michael Stewart could have argued that if Britain had not agreed to sell arms to Nigeria the Russians would have increased their military supplies. But for him it was a question of principle, not expediency. He took on his critics on the grounds that a fellow member of the Commonwealth was entitled to be given help in time of trouble. To have denied General Gowon arms would have been taken as support for secession which could have inspired other attempts to redraw the boundaries of Africa.

As a methodical politician Michael Stewart always wanted to

know the legalities of any international problem. On his first day as Foreign Secretary he ordered two documents to be available on his desk at all times: a copy of the United Nations Charter and a list of the fifteen members of the UN Security Council. It caused some sniggering in the corridors, but Michael Stewart was a stickler for quoting the legal justification for a proposed course of action at the UN when under attack over Rhodesia, Gibraltar, the Falklands, and Anguilla. On occasion he could put the velvet gloves aside and strike a harsh note which had all the more impact for being so infrequent. In July 1969 he became very angry with the Spanish Government for stopping the ferry service from Algeciras to Gibraltar. Knowing that Spain depended on the British for one in five of their tourists, Michael Stewart suggested that the answer was in the hands of 'every patriotic citizen'. They should think not just twice but many times about having a holiday in Spain and consider Gibraltar instead. Even he was surprised at the boost it produced for Gibraltar's tourist trade.

Velvet gloves were never part of the diplomatic accoutrements which George Brown thought were necessary when he took over at the Foreign Office at the end of Michael Stewart's first term in August 1966. The fact that his first decision was to have a portrait of Palmerston put opposite his desk was a sign of rumbustious times ahead. He began in a vigorous assertive manner with an address to over fifty senior members of the Foreign Office, assuring them: 'I'm in charge.' Regardless of suspicions that Prime Minister Harold Wilson would not be prepared to take a back seat, the new Foreign Secretary was adamant: 'Foreign policy will be run from this building.' But even from the outset there were serious doubts about whether Brown was the right man for the job. Wilson acknowledged afterwards in *The Labour Government: 1964–70* that there were anxieties at the time of the appointment: 'Many members of the Parliamentary Party, and, I soon learnt, leading members of the Cabinet, felt that he had not the precisely right temperament for the Foreign Office.'

George Brown's mind was always bubbling with ideas. Any opposition to them, however, made him abrasive and abusive. His temper was uncertain at the best of times. During the day people summoned to his room never knew whether they would get a friendly slap on the back or a dressing down. In the evening his excitability – especially after a few drinks – made him totally unpredictable. One senior ambassador's wife ran to her room in tears when he upbraided her for not being able to identify one of the 200 guests at a reception held in his honour. In one of his tantrums he publicly announced the dismissal of his spokesman, Sir Robin Haydon, and then laughed it off as a joke the next morning.

Hardly a day passed without some outburst. His impatience was a test of nerves for his staff. On his way to the Soviet Union in November 1966 he had to postpone his journey twice because of fog. On the third day when he went to London Airport at 7 a.m. he was in no mood for further delay and ordered the RAF plane to fly to Copenhagen to await a further weather report. After an hour there he insisted on flying onwards to Moscow despite the fact that fog made landing impossible at Vnukovo Airport. At the point where the RAF commander had to divert to Leningrad, if he decided it was unsafe to go on to Moscow, George Brown used his favourite argument as Her Majesty's Principal Secretary of State for Foreign Affairs: 'I'm in charge.' He ordered the plane to proceed. It took all the persuasiveness of his PPS, Sir Donald Maitland, to calm him down and accept the alternative of the night train from Leningrad to Moscow.

Brown's impulsiveness alarmed the Ambassador, Sir Geoffrey Harrison, and his Foreign Office entourage the moment he landed on Soviet soil. Having observed a plane with Egyptian markings at Leningrad Airport, George Brown wanted to know who had arrived in it. He was told it had been Hakim Amer, then Colonel Nasser's deputy. As Egypt had broken off diplomatic relations with Britain it was assumed that, his curiosity satisfied, George Brown would let the matter rest. He ignored protestations from his staff and telephoned the Leningrad hotel where Hakim Amer was staying. They met the next day at a Soviet dacha on the outskirts of Moscow where George Brown conducted his own unorthodox diplomacy to the surprise of the Russians as well as the Egyptians. He claimed it was his intervention which enabled diplomatic relations to be restored the following year.

Where Brown did make his mark in the tortuous trail towards a Middle East settlement was at the time of the Six-Day War in

June 1967. That was one occasion when he was able to claim 'I'm in charge' without any serious challenge from Wilson. It earned him a place in the United Nations records as the prime mover in the achievement of the famous UN Security Council Resolution 242 passed on 22 November 1967 and the subject of endless scrutiny for its deliberate ambiguity ever since. As an anti-Zionist politician who had married a woman of Jewish faith, George Brown was quick to focus on the real priority for Israel: recognition by the Arabs in return for ceding territory. He held thirty separate interviews with ministers in one day at the UN. Teams of secretaries filed in and out taking the record of the meetings in relays. His enthusiasm swept everyone along in agreement with the centrepiece of the resolution: 'Withdrawal of Israel armed forces from territories occupied in the recent conflict' (carefully omitting the definite article before 'territories') and 'respect for the acknowledgement of the sovereignty, territorial integrity and political independence of every State in the area'. With that formula as the basis for carrying the rest of the Security Council with him, Britain's Ambassador Lord Caradon finished the job. It was such a significant achievement that George Brown was almost forgiven for all his bad behaviour – but not quite.

He also earned great credit for the way his enthusiasm for Europe led to a negotiating tour of the six Community capitals with Wilson, resulting in the Government applying for membership in July 1967. His head and his heart made him fully committed. For Wilson it was a matter of cool calculation. It suited the Prime Minister at the time not to be seen sharing his Foreign Secretary's enthusiasm. That would have weakened his negotiating position with the Six and made it more difficult to overcome the strong opposition within his own Cabinet. In fact, Wilson had privately come to the conclusion before he won the 1964 election that Britain's future lay inevitably with the European Community.

The decision to make the tour of the six capitals was announced by Wilson, much to the surprise of George Brown, at a special session of ministers at Chequers. George Brown wanted to make the tour on his own but the Prime Minister shrewdly realized the danger of his ebullient Foreign Secretary going over the top. He judged that he had to be on hand to keep him under control and to provide the intellectual thrust on the monetary aspects of the talks. Wilson wanted it to be regarded as an exploratory tour while it was actually undertaken largely for party reasons.

Even though the major credit for the way the tour went belonged to Wilson, it was an occasion where George Brown marshalled the staff work of the Foreign Office as a good helmsman, ensuring that they took account of the shift of political currents in each capital. Briefs and speaking notes were revised all the time by the Foreign Office team to adjust from the arguments of one government to those of the next. One particular Foreign Office contribution won praise from Wilson when he went to the Elysée Palace for his meeting with President de Gaulle on 24 January 1967 – the skill of his interpreter, Sir Michael Palliser, who later became Head of the Diplomatic Service. The French President always regarded his interpreter, Prince Andronikov, as matchless, but he met his match in Sir Michael who was then on loan from the Foreign Office as the Prime Minister's Private Secretary.

The test comes when one interpreter has to intervene to correct the other's choice of words in translating the opposing statesman's remarks to his own leader. Wilson emerged jubilant that Sir Michael had won seven to two in having to correct Andronikov more often in his translations from English into French for de Gaulle. On his way out of the Elysée Palace George Brown was not quite so fluent in French. He brushed aside reporters with the first words that came to mind: '*Pas de comment.*' His efforts to get Britain into the Community were not universally appreciated. Labour MP Michael English, speaking for the anti-Marketeers, commented: 'George Brown should be given Cruft's First Prize in the class of spaniels.'

George Brown's relations with Harold Wilson were punctuated with angry outbursts, threats of resignation, and periods of sulks, particularly as his drinking bouts became more frequent. The bitter clash over the arms ban on South Africa in December 1967 marked a turning-point. Thereafter it was only a question of how long it would be before he finally quit as Foreign Secretary. Although his departure was a relief to most around him at the Foreign Office, that feeling was mixed with a sense of regret that he had had a raw deal in Cabinet over the South African issue –

an emphatic confirmation that a Foreign Secretary needs to have clout in the Cabinet to control foreign policy. Like many political crises it was triggered off by an apparently off-the-cuff remark, on this occasion by James Callaghan as newly appointed Home Secretary after his stint as Chancellor of the Exchequer. He hinted to a meeting of Labour MPs that the Government was considering easing the ban on the sale of arms to South Africa.

Harold Wilson was responsible for the issue coming to the boil since he had asked George Brown to find out whether the South African Government still wanted to buy naval weapons. It did – and since they were not considered the sort of weapons liable to be used against the blacks in the enforcement of apartheid, George Brown gave the sale his blessing. Although there were some reservations in the Overseas Policy Committee under the chairmanship of the Prime Minister, there was a general disposition to agree to the sale. However, once the Callaghan hint spread to the left wing of the Labour Party, Wilson was worried by the prospect of a major split. The question was the main item for the Cabinet meeting called for 14 December. George Brown and Defence Secretary Denis Healey were at NATO conferences in Brussels. In their absence they were both being blamed at Westminster for trying to railroad the Prime Minister. Denis Healey on his return before George Brown stood loyally behind him, denounced the smear campaign, and alerted him in Brussels.

Fog prevented Brown from flying back from Brussels, so his PPS had to get him – somewhat unsteadily – onto the overnight train. At the delayed Cabinet meeting, Brown fought his corner vigorously and seemed to have a majority on his side agreeing to ease the arms ban. The Prime Minister deferred a decision over the weekend. With intense speculation about pressure on sterling following the devaluation of the pound a month earlier, and controversy over public expenditure cuts, the arms issue became part of a wider question of loyalties. In the end the choice for the rest of the Cabinet meeting on the Monday morning of sticking with Wilson or standing by Brown was no real popularity contest. Apart from Denis Healey and a few others, George Brown's supporters drifted away. The Prime Minister was able to tell Parliament that the Government was firmly committed to the UN arms ban. He admitted afterwards he had had to fight rough. The scars stayed until George Brown finally resigned in March 1968.

After second terms at the Foreign Office first for Michael Stewart and then for Lord Home, the Wilson Government in 1974 produced a new helmsman, James Callaghan. He had the advantage not only of apprenticeship as Shadow Foreign Secretary but of six years in government in the senior posts of Chancellor and Home Secretary. That status gave him great weight in Cabinet, especially in the last year of the Government when much of Wilson's earlier dynamism had subsided. Like George Brown he came into politics without having been to university. At the Foreign Office Brown, a working-class Londoner, felt *déraciné*. He often had a chip on his shoulder when dealing with his Oxbridge mandarins. Not James Callaghan. He had respect for the experts but was not overawed by them. He liked to hear what they had to say and he was a good listener. For him it was a matter of judicious selection, sucking in the expertise and deciding what to concentrate on as the grist.

Callaghan's strength was his ability to get the best out of people. He studied people closely, worked out his tactics, and if need be bullied them into co-operating with him. He was aptly described by one of his staff as 'a hugging bear with claws'. He had a very disciplined approach to paperwork. Unlike Wilson whose appetite was inexhaustible, Callaghan drew the line at one document box per night. But he relied upon his mandarins to keep him informed and leaned heavily on the judgement of his Permanent Under-Secretary, Sir Michael Palliser.

Callaghan came to the Foreign Office with the reputation as a fixer who knew where the scope for leverage lay in a complex political situation. That was put to the test right from the start since he had to confront his European Community partners over the Labour election manifesto pledge to 'renegotiate' Britain's terms of membership. As current chairman of the Labour Party he had to keep looking over his shoulder at the large anti-Market lobby. He also had to watch his step with Cabinet colleagues such as Peter Shore, one of the strongest opponents of the Community who sometimes travelled with him as Secretary of Trade to meetings in Luxembourg and Brussels. His European manoeuvres were complicated by a row blowing up between the Americans and the Community over what President Nixon considered a lack of support for US policy in the Middle East. As an Atlanticist, Callaghan had to tread carefully. While he did not want to lose whatever benefits there still remained from the special relationship, he dare not give cause for Britain to be suspected of being a Trojan horse for the US inside the Community.

In the end 'Fixer Jim', working his charm on West Germany's Foreign Minister, Hans-Dietrich Genscher, secured some cosmetic changes to the 144-page Treaty of Accession plus the promise of a sweetener – a cut of around £125m in Britain's budget contribution which was finally hammered out by Harold Wilson at the Dublin summit in March 1975. Getting the principle of a budgetary corrective mechanism for Britain accepted by his partners was Callaghan's main achievement. That was sufficient to ensure that the referendum on continued membership of the Community gave the Government more than a two-to-one majority of the votes in June 1975.

A tougher test of his ability as a fixer came in a 'Flash' telegram to the Foreign Office on 15 July 1974 from the British High Commission in Cyprus saying: 'Makarios overthrown – Nicos Sampson installed as President.' It was symptomatic of the neglect of the Cyprus problem by successive British Governments that Callaghan's first reaction to the takeover by the EOKA gunman-journalist Sampson was 'Nicos who?' His knowledge of the island was no worse than that of other ministers. No British Foreign Secretary has visited Nicosia in the last thirty years. After the Zurich Agreements on the island's independence between the Greek and Turkish Foreign Ministers, Averoff and Zorlu, which were imposed on the island by the London Agreement on 19 February 1959, Britain virtually washed its hands of any constitutional obligations, despite being a Guarantor Power with Greece and Turkey.

Although bewildered by the political implications of the crisis, Callaghan lost no time in mounting an extraordinary rescue operation to get Archbishop Makarios out of the island. An RAF helicopter picked him up from his hiding-place in Paphos and flew him to the British base at Akrotiri. From there he was taken to

Malta where the British High Commissioner, Sir Robin Haydon, made him presentable for meeting ministers in London by donating one of his large shirts to the diminutive archbishop. Within a few hours of his arrival at RAF Lyneham in Wiltshire on 17 July Turkey's Prime Minister Bülent Ecevit had flown to London, bringing the political crisis right to the doormat in Downing Street.

Callaghan looked to the Americans as traditional brokers between Greeks and Turks to get Britain off the hook. That was a miscalculation. Twice in the past, in 1964 and 1967, they had staved off Turkish intervention in Cyprus. This time, with President Nixon totally engulfed in the Watergate scandal, the Americans had neither the time nor the will to intervene. Over a working dinner at No. 10 Downing Street which went on until almost 1 a.m., Ecevit appealed for joint 'police action' by Britain and Turkey to stop the Greek-backed coup in Cyprus becoming irreversible. Harold Wilson tried to play for time by suggesting a summit meeting with the Greeks. But the Greeks refused to come to London. With Wilson exhausted, Callaghan carried on, holding weak diplomatic cards and pinning his hopes on enlisting the help of American Secretary of State Henry Kissinger.

The response was half-hearted. Dr Kissinger's deputy, Joseph Cisco, was dispatched to London but he arrived for talks with Ecevit empty-handed. The Turkish Prime Minister adjourned the meeting, taking a look at volumes of poetry in the Charing Cross Road bookshops while Callaghan turned to Kissinger on the hotline to Washington for any new solution. None was offered. Ecevit returned to Ankara. Twenty-four hours later on 20 July, the Turks invaded Cyprus. The verdict of the House of Commons Select Committee on the handling of the crisis was blunt: 'Britain had the legal right, a moral obligation, and the military capacity to intervene in Cyprus.'

Callaghan made sure that people in the British sovereign bases were shielded from the military upheaval and that evacuation arrangements for British holidaymakers were given top priority. With a ceasefire accepted two days later, he set about trying to regain his status as a fixer by flying to Geneva on 25 July for peace talks with the Greek and Turkish Foreign Ministers. As before, Callaghan's negotiating hand was weak as he struggled to get agreement on stabilizing the ceasefire. At one stage he thought of flying to Ankara with a warning that he was prepared to put Royal Navy warships between Cyprus and Turkey. But Dr Kissinger was strongly opposed to that and Wilson did not want a row with the Americans. Callaghan's patience and stamina were severely tested in edging Greeks and Turks to accept a ceasefire agreement.

After a brief toast to his wife Audrey on her 61st birthday and their 36th wedding anniversary, Callaghan went for thirty-one hours without sleep or a shave. He put bottles of Scotch on the negotiating table at the UN's Palais des Nations, saying: 'We're here for the night.' He had to coax Greek Foreign Minister George Mavros out of quitting and returning to Athens. He had to be tough when Turkey's Foreign Minister Turan Gunes walked out of the room and stayed away for six hours. On the Turk's return with the announcement, 'We're ready to resume', Callaghan snapped 'I'm not' and went for a walk in the gardens among the peacocks.

The agreement on 31 July was virtually an acknowledgement of partition on the island. Despite strong denials by Callaghan, Article IV of the UN resolution requiring the withdrawal of all foreign troops was quietly ignored. The resumption of the Geneva conference on 8 August proved to be a charade marking time for the final endorsement of the Ankara Government's decision that Turkish troops were the only real protection for Turkish Cypriots in 34 per cent of the island. One last-minute threat leaked by Callaghan to diplomatic correspondents, that British troops were empowered to open fire on the Turks to prevent a breach of the ceasefire, failed to make Turan Gunes any more flexible at the negotiating table.

All it achieved was to make Dr Kissinger angry since neither he nor the Turks believed it could be taken seriously. Kissinger's aides were heard anguishing about allowing 'Boy Scouts loose at the negotiating table'. Gunes refused an appeal for a 36-hour period of reflection which Mavros sought for consultations in Athens. His abrupt walk-out at 3 a.m. on 14 August ended the conference and signalled further Turkish troop movements to straighten the Attila line and put a total of 37 per cent of Cyprus under their control. With the Americans not prepared to put any pressure on the Ankara Government, Callaghan had to accept that there was a limit to his role as a fixer.

His successor at the helm in the Foreign Office, Anthony Crosland, was totally different in temperament and character. A thinker rather than a doer, he did not like improvisation. He wanted time to analyse a situation from its fundamental elements. His intellectual training made him suspicious of any attempt to rush into a decision. At times he displayed a dislike of taking decisions at all even when there was no hurry. It was difficult for him to adjust to the transition from the Department of the Environment, where he could absorb himself in the broad sweep of policy, to the Foreign Office where sudden developments required small, but important, decisions on detail over a wide range of issues.

Despite his passion for football, which resulted in matters of state being interrupted so that he could watch BBC coverage on *Match of the Day*, Crosland was not a man of the people. Although he liked humankind, he preferred it in the abstract. He found himself ill at ease when hemmed in by warm bodies, especially warm bodies of foreigners. When he disappeared in the middle of a lunch at Luxembourg, one of his aides found him wandering in the garden 'to get away from those bores indoors'. Yet he enjoyed large meetings at the Foreign Office where he could go round the table asking people for their views. Crosland insisted on beginning with the discussion document before reading the recommendations so that he could introduce the subject as an intellectual exercise. He encouraged people by making flattering remarks about the quality of the papers and the research behind them. Although there was a certain shyness about him, he had the talent of being a stimulating chairman. He found time for the desk officers, listening to them as attentively as the under-secretaries. A nervous-looking junior diplomat wondering whether he dare say anything was sought out by Crosland. But he was fanatical about time. Debates had to be wound up after twenty-five minutes so that he could have the last five minutes to sum up. Even his sandwich lunch had to be brought in precisely at the minute he ordered it. When he was hosting a Central Treaty Organization lunch at the Banqueting House in London, he refused to keep the guests waiting just because Dr Kissinger had not arrived on time. After allowing him ten minutes' grace, Crosland announced: 'People here have work to do. We shall begin lunch without Dr Kissinger.'

His patience had a short fuse. During a visit to China in May 1976, less than a month after becoming Foreign Secretary, he looked forward to academic discussions when he was taken to Peking University. Instead, he had to listen for half an hour to a tirade against Vice-Premier Deng Xiaoping as a 'capitalist roader'. In a bored drawl he turned to his wife Susan on the platform and asked: 'What is a capitalist rodent?' Although she always tried to please her Chinese hosts at banquets by using chopsticks, her husband demonstrated his pride in England by sticking to the knife and fork the Chinese provided as alternatives.

As a minister not given to quick decision-making he surprised the Foreign Office by coming back from China with his mind made up to end the Cod War with Iceland – a brave decision for an MP whose constituents depended so much on fish for their livelihood. It was not easy. After eight months of confrontation, resulting in fourteen Royal Navy frigates rammed and forty-two trawler skippers laid off, emotions were running high on Humberside. But Crosland realized that if he as MP for Grimsby accepted an agreement, there could be no gainsaying it. After two days of negotiations at Oslo he took Iceland's Foreign Minister Einar Agustsson off to dinner at The Queen restaurant in the harbour and struck a deal on 1 June. Buoyed up by one decision he took another, an unprecedented one, a month later. He broke off diplomatic relations with Uganda – the first time Britain had done so against a Commonwealth country. Crosland decided he could stomach Amin's tyranny no longer.

Like Callaghan, he was mesmerized by Dr Henry Kissinger. By diplomatic sleight of hand Kissinger lined up the various parties for a Rhodesia conference on the basis of double talk. In an eleven-day shuttle across Africa he sold one set of ideas to the African nationalists and another to the whites. Delegates therefore arrived for the opening of the Geneva conference on 28 October 1976 under false optimism. At least Crosland was shrewd enough to avoid being trapped into running the conference himself after sizing up the risks with his African expert Dennis Grennan. He passed what the Foreign Office saw as the 'poisoned chalice' to Ivor Richard, former Labour minister who was made UN Ambassador. After seven weeks, when all delegations had seen through the Kissinger fast deal, the conference collapsed.

The sudden death of Anthony Crosland after less than eleven months as Foreign Secretary resulted in Dr David Owen at the age of thirty-eight becoming the youngest helmsman at the Foreign Office since the appointment of Anthony Eden in 1935. Succeeding a senior politician in these circumstances was difficult. Owen was not a member of Labour's National Executive Committee. He had little clout in Cabinet, particularly alongside Denis Healey, who would have been the automatic choice for the Foreign Office if circumstances had not tied him to the Treasury. Although Owen had been Minister for the Navy and had gained some experience as Minister of State at the Foreign Office, he was initially looked upon as someone out of his depth. Because the Government was fragile, dependent on Liberal support under the Lib-Lab pact, Owen gave the impression of being a brash young man in a hurry, insecure, not knowing how long he would be Foreign Secretary. Crosland's arrogance was moderated by an impish sense of humour and a certain raffish style. Owen's arrogance, though subsequently mellowed, was undiluted when he was appointed on 22 February 1977.

His style was abrasive, even to those whose loyalty was important to him at the Foreign Office. He would never think of going into the registry at the Private Office and saying 'Thank you', as Crosland did, to the girls working long hours typing documents. He was the sort of person who would give a secretary a book on human rights at Christmas instead of a box of chocolates. Senior advisers, such as 'Ham' Whyte, his chief spokesman held in high regard by correspondents, had to endure the humiliation of being dressed down by Owen in public. His assumption at the outset that he was surrounded by supercilious experts who regarded diplomacy as being on a much higher plane than politics made him distrustful of the Foreign Office. He even kept the Permanent Under-Secretary of State, Sir Michael Palliser, at a distance.

In recent years, however, the verdict on Owen's performance as

Foreign Secretary has been revised inside the Foreign Office. There are some diplomats who now admit that while Owen often treated the Service badly and did not get the best out of it, he was not served as well as he should have been. There were obstacles put in Owen's way because people in the Foreign Office would say something was not possible merely on the grounds that it was not in accordance with the way things were usually done. Owen refused to accept the eternal verities. He had an original, questioning mind which made him keep asking 'Why?' He was a stimulating lateral thinker unafraid of shaking up the traditionalists in the Foreign Office whose views run along straight lines.

Although he was pro-European, he felt that many in the Diplomatic Service dealing with European affairs were not prepared to fight hard enough for Britain's interests. He had a belligerency towards Brussels bureaucrats which people admired in Mrs Thatcher but not in him. Much of his irascibility was due to exhaustion. He worked his way through mounds of paper, reading every telegram carefully to make sure he never missed any nuance. Crosland would sometimes not appear in the Foreign Office until after lunch on a Monday and disappear at midday on Friday to his constituency. Owen was always at his desk before 9 a.m. and stayed on duty until eight o'clock every night. His attention to details and procedures – often derided inside the Foreign Office – was a key factor in securing the passage of the Bill on direct elections to the European Parliament through the House of Commons in defiance of Home Office draftsmen who tried to quote Erskine May against him.

Owen's political lifeline was being Callaghan's nominee. But he strained it to the limits by the way he appointed the Prime Minister's son-in-law, Peter Jay, to be Britain's Ambassador in Washington on 11 May 1977. It was done so crudely that it provoked accusations of nepotism by Callaghan and of skulduggery by Owen to ingratiate himself with his leader. Rarely has there been such a row in Westminster over an ambassadorial appointment. Nobody questioned Peter Jay's ability in the political arena. He had proved it as a highly professional journalist on *The Times* and on *Weekend World*. The incumbent Ambassador, Sir Peter Ramsbotham, had won high praise for boosting British exports when he was in Iran and for overcoming opposition in the US Congress to British Airways flying Concorde into New York. The way for Owen to make the switch without much fuss would have been to find an appropriate prestigious posting elsewhere for Sir Peter Ramsbotham and announce it. Then he could have made an announcement that his successor would be Peter Jay. Instead, Owen kept the announcement until the end of a briefing to diplomatic correspondents and then, almost as an afterthought, revealed that he was appointing Peter Jay Ambassador to Washington. It was left to the correspondents to discover that Sir Peter was being pensioned off as Governor of Bermuda.

The dirty-tricks department took over on the next day, 12 May, with a savage denigration of Sir Peter Ramsbotham as an 'old fuddy-duddy' out of touch with the new mood of America under President Carter. They ignored the fact that Ramsbotham had contacts envied by every other ambassador in Washington. He knew Secretary of State Cyrus Vance better than any other envoy. They played tennis together regularly. The wrath of Westminster was focused on the Prime Minister's spokesman Tom McCaffrey, who normally had a sharp sense of fairness in handling Press issues for the Government. Technically, he was correct in denying that 'any personal observations' about Sir Peter had been made during Press briefings. But in the corridor afterwards he gave a nod and a wink to John Dickinson of the London *Evening News* and Robert Carvel of the *Evening Standard*. It was enough for the astute Dickinson to write that Sir Peter had been ousted simply because he was thought to be old-fashioned and stuffy. Carvel followed suit. To be fair, McCaffrey did not use the word 'snob' but he was crucified when the two evening papers carried the same banner headline: 'Snob' Envoy Had To Go.

Owen had flown to Saudi Arabia immediately after the announcement and was very angry when he saw news agency reports of the versions in the newspapers. He telephoned the Foreign Office to dissociate himself from the smear campaign. What was not revealed at the time was that Callaghan's political adviser Tom McNally had not been consulted about the Jay appointment. Callaghan knew that if he had disclosed that he was thinking of agreeing to Owen's suggestion of appointing Jay to

Washington, McNally would have been determined to talk him out of it. McNally was so angry at the way it was handled after the announcement that he went with Tom McCaffrey to the Prime Minister to offer their resignations. Callaghan rejected them but warned that civil servants who had no chance to reply should never be subjected to such treatment again. He had winced at the jibe from the Liberal MP Sir Cyril Smith: 'It is time the Diplomatic Service was renamed the Court of St Jim.'

When the Conservative Party won the 1979 general election, Owen was succeeded by Lord Carrington, who knew where he was going and had the right track record to get there. Having served in the governments of Churchill, Macmillan, Home, and Heath, as well as having spent three years in Australia as High Commissioner, Lord Carrington took over at the helm in the Foreign Office on 5 May 1979 in a position of strength such as Owen never commanded. Mrs Thatcher looked to Lord Carrington as the expert on foreign affairs. He could talk back to his Prime Minister – a liberty Owen dared not take.

One reason for that was that Lord Carrington was no political threat to Mrs Thatcher. Whenever he was asked what he would do if a No. 9 bus were to go over Mrs Thatcher, he gave the whimsical answer: 'A No. 9 bus wouldn't dare.' She was well aware that Lord Carrington would never consider leaving the House of Lords to contest the leadership of the Conservative Party and seek the key to No. 10 Downing Street. When she held her first Cabinet meeting, the imminent arrival of her first visiting statesman, Germany's Chancellor Helmut Schmidt, was the top item on the foreign agenda. She rattled off a long list of questions which would have to be tackled at the talks. Then Lord Carrington interrupted her, as no one else could, with the observation: 'Won't Chancellor Schmidt have some points of his own to raise?'

Lord Carrington gave the impression of being the right man in the right place at the right time: a tailor-made Foreign Secretary for the Tories. It was, he admitted, the job he had always wanted, 'the summit of my political ambitions'. But even at the outset he was not wholly trusted by Mrs Thatcher. Although she admitted in the early days of her premiership that she knew very little about foreign affairs, she realized she had instincts like America's President Reagan. She was, one of her Cabinet colleagues observed out of earshot, 'the thinking person's Reagan'. Her instincts, she believed, were usually more accurate than the Foreign Office advice Lord Carrington relied on. He admitted he was no ideologue and knew little about economics. So, while she let him pick his own team of ministers for the Foreign Office – and it was a particularly strong team he chose with Sir Ian Gilmour, Douglas Hurd, Peter Blaker, Richard Luce, and Neil Marten – Mrs Thatcher insisted on adding one watchdog to keep him on the rails: Nicholas Ridley. Instead of brooding over the economics of foreign policy, however, Nicholas Ridley proved to be an innovative thinker, especially promoting the leaseback idea for the Falklands in the hope of settling the dispute with Argentina.

Lord Carrington's style at the helm of the Foreign Office was patrician. He only wanted to be shown what was 'really important'. So his PPS, Brian Fall, had to winnow the daily harvest of telegrams down to the bare minimum. Lord Carrington read submissions quickly, took very few notes, and relied on a good memory. Instead of studying long dossiers he preferred to sit in his armchair and talk through the issues with his experts. Making long speeches bored him. He made ten times the number of speeches as NATO Secretary-General after he left government than he did when he was Foreign Secretary.

From the outset he made Rhodesia his top priority, as will be seen in the next chapter. In between crises he had to be a sherpa preparing for Mrs Thatcher's summit battles over Britain's contribution to the European Community budget. Even when he managed to secure concessions from the French at a foreign ministers' meeting and returned expecting plaudits from the Prime Minister, she chastised him for not doing better. He found it exceedingly irksome to sit alongside her at summits while she harangued her EC partners for a better budget deal. Although he admitted that it needed someone of her iron will to hammer out the best terms, he often felt she went over the top. It meant there was very little camaraderie between them. His home at Bledlow was not far from Chequers but he rarely went to the Prime Minister's residence at weekends. He did not disguise the reason. He told his colleagues he saw enough of her through the week and needed a rest from her on Sundays.

Apart from the diplomatic furore over the TV documentary *Death of a Princess* in April 1980, which caused great offence to the Saudi Arabian ruling family and great embarrassment to Lord Carrington (an incident to be examined in Chapter VII), he enjoyed getting to grips with the problems of the Middle East. Because he played a leading role in the European Community's Venice Declaration in June 1980 pledging self-determination for the Palestinians, Lord Carrington became a target for the wrath of the Israelis. When he talked of Israel as 'an occupying power' and warned against any attempt to move the Prime Minister's office to the Arab quarter in East Jerusalem, he was bitterly denounced. Prime Minister Menachem Begin said it was none of Lord Carrington's business and told him to keep out of Israel's affairs.

It was ultimately Carrington's persistence in pursuing the Arab–Israeli problem which was his undoing as Foreign Secretary. He was so beguiled by trying to 'sort out the Israelis' that he lost sight of how urgent it was to keep a close focus on the Argentine threat to the Falklands in the last fateful days of March 1982. Instead of abandoning the EC summit in Brussels and staying in charge at the Foreign Office, Lord Carrington went ahead with a visit to Israel on Tuesday, 30 March. On his return the invasion of the Falklands ended his political career. Although he was unrepentant, saying 'My eye was not off the ball', he admitted at his resignation on 5 April: 'My judgement was wrong.'

No one could have been placed at the helm of the Foreign Office in more difficult circumstances than Francis Pym. The country on the brink of war with Argentina, the Foreign Office in disgrace, and the rest of the world totally bewildered at the way Britain appeared humiliated. The new Foreign Secretary inherited all the distrust of the Prime Minister for the Foreign Office but none of the trust that Carrington enjoyed as a person. Mrs Thatcher did not want to promote Pym to the job. She would have preferred William Whitelaw. She disliked Pym. He was a 'wet' who had defied her and got away with it. As her first Defence Secretary he had refused to accept swingeing expenditure cuts and won the battle over them. In the famous weeding out of the 'wets' known as 'Maggie's Monday Massacre' on 14 September 1981, Soames, Gilmour, and Thorneycroft were among the forty party stalwarts uprooted. But Francis Pym did not even cross his fingers. He knew he would survive. His standing in the Conservative Party was high and she realized that.

Lord Carrington was no political rival. Pym was. If the Falklands crisis had been botched, Mrs Thatcher would have been blamed. The price of failure would have been political hara-kiri. In the eyes of many in the party, the natural successor in those circumstances would be Pym. But in the anxious days of April 1982, the simplest way for Mrs Thatcher to fill the gap left by Lord Carrington was to move Francis Pym from Leader of the House and avoid any ministerial changes. Nonetheless Mrs Thatcher never took a single political step at that time without looking over her shoulder at what Francis Pym was doing.

Ironically, he proved to be the man of the moment – to the surprise of Mrs Thatcher herself. Not even his best friends would claim he was a great expert on foreign affairs, despite having been Shadow Foreign Secretary. His strength was that he was a very experienced parliamentarian from the vintage year of 1959. His first decision at the Foreign Office was a parliamentary one. There was a political crisis and the country required a lead from Parliament. There had to be a debate on the Falklands crisis and he would open it. Pym felt it was crucial, as Churchill had in the dark days of 1940, to hold the House of Commons together in order to have the nation united behind the Government. As a former Chief Whip he had the experience of knowing how to rally the waverers as well as the faithful. Never was that more important than when Francis Pym shored up the House of Commons behind the Government in a series of major speeches – eight in under two months.

His induction as Foreign Secretary was further complicated by his being plunged simultaneously into another crisis – the Battle of the Budget with Britain's European Community partners. In between rallying Parliament and the country behind the Government over the Falklands, Francis Pym had only ten days to become familiar with the huge dossier on Britain's claims for a better deal over her financial contributions. The other members had spent six months locked in debate with the British delegation haggling over the terms. They had heard every possible variant of the British case. After analysing all the options with the Foreign Office experts, Francis Pym reached the conclusion that Mrs Thatcher's demand for a three-year guarantee of a reduced contribution was a totally unrealistic negotiating position. When he told the Prime Minister she became very angry. Her attitude was imperious: 'I don't care what you say, just do as I tell you.' Still defiant, Francis Pym argued that if she put herself in the position of any of the other nine members they would all reject Britain's demands. He stuck to his strategy and eventually reached agreement on 24 May 1982 for a one-year package worth £476m in budgetary concessions. Trying to push his partners further would have jeopardized the chances of retaining their support against the Argentinian invasion of the Falklands.

One of the most important changes Pym made at the helm of the Foreign Office was to make MPs more aware of the problems of conducting foreign policy and, conversely, to make senior diplomats understand the parliamentary background against which a Foreign Secretary has to operate. Pym launched a system of seminars between backbench MPs and members of the Foreign Office. It was not a brainwashing operation to get support in the Commons. Pym did not hover around at the meetings. He left it to the PUS, Sir Antony Acland, to organize the discussion groups at the Foreign Office.

Although he was out of his depth in the Middle East and failed to make any impact on an ill-starred tour in April 1983, Pym was well ahead of other European statesmen in recognizing that it was time the West made overtures to exploit the prospects of breaking the East–West logjam. As soon as the Falklands war was over, he suggested a series of new moves to establish a sensible working relationship with the Soviet Union. He proposed visits to Eastern Europe, starting with Hungary. Then he urged talks with the Russians to break the ice and pave the way for successful disarmament negotiations. It produced no spark of enthusiasm from Mrs Thatcher. She had no interest in being a bridge-builder between East and West. Yet eighteen months later she did a somersault and suddenly became enthusiastic about Eastern Europe and the openings for change in the Soviet Union.

By then Francis Pym was gone, ousted by Mrs Thatcher the day after her victory in the general election of June 1983. As Thatcher's first Chancellor of the Exchequer, Sir Geoffrey Howe had been a steady, dependable manager of the country's economy. With that record and the training of a barrister at the Middle Temple, Sir Geoffrey was chosen as the member of her Cabinet best suited to conduct Britain's campaign with the European Community in the second round of the Battle of the Budget. During his six years as Foreign Secretary – the longest term since Sir Edward Grey's eleven years ended in 1916 – he proved he had the steadiest hands at the helm that the Foreign Office had known for a very long time.

His loyalty and reliability, his willingness to accept in silence the excesses of the Prime Minister and the humiliations she often heaped on him made Howe the butt of derision at Westminster. His soporific droning at the Dispatch Box invited ridicule as Mogadon Man. Denis Healey boasted of his prowess against Sir Geoffrey in the cut-and-thrust of debate in the House, saying an attack by Howe was like being 'savaged by a dead sheep'. But Sir Geoffrey made mincemeat of critics like that in his resignation speech. It was a question of timing. Sir Geoffrey came to the Foreign Office at a time when his patient diplomacy, his persistence with the nitty-gritty of complex negotiations, and his dedication to old-fashioned values matched the needs of the moment.

By any standards he was the hardest-working Foreign Secretary of the last three decades. For long periods he managed to keep going on only four or five hours' sleep a night. He often worked on the boxes of papers until after one in the morning and then would wake at 5.30 and work for an hour and a half before breakfast. He was usually discussing the day's problems with his PPS on the telephone before getting to his desk at eight o'clock. Every day was a long day. No one would call him a dynamic leader. He was slow, methodical, and not disposed to be rushed into decisions. At times his staff would wring their hands in despair. When they thought they had exhausted all the options and were at the stage of reaching a conclusion he would force them back to the beginning with the Socratic question: 'But what if we were just to do nothing?' It often had the effect of stopping the drift into doing something just for the sake of being seen to be taking action.

A calm Foreign Secretary meant no tantrums, no panicking. Yet the public persona of a man without emotions, a cool, calculating legal brain, was wide of the mark. Howe's eyes were moist when over 1,000 Poles defied General Jaruzelski's martial law to be with him at St Stanislaw Kostka Church in Warsaw on 12 April 1985 as he lit a candle at the grave of Father Jerzy Popieluszko, the young priest murdered by state security police. There was a quavering in his voice singing the hymn 'Fatherland and Freedom' along with the supporters of Solidarity saluting him with a 'V for Victory' sign. Sir Geoffrey could be carried away with the elation of a crowd, too. Although not suspected of being the Fred Astaire of the Foreign Office, he joined Mozambicans doing the Dong, a fertility dance, at Magude, a war-ravaged junction on the Limpopo railway. For those in the Foreign Office who never imagined they would see a Conservative minister give the clenched fist salute Sir Geoffrey left the villagers, who were fighting the RENAMO rebels, with a memorable gesture. His right arm held high, he shouted: 'The struggle continues. *A luta continua.* Long live the friendship of the peoples of Mozambique and Great Britain.'

Sir Geoffrey's deliberate use of ambiguous language gave rise to the term 'Hoveism'. His obfuscations irritated Mrs Thatcher to the point where she would stop in her tracks and say: 'Geoffrey, tell me straight: does that mean you are for or against the idea?' But his tendency to resort to bland expressions was ideally suited to one of his first tasks: taking on the Chinese after an embarrassing gaffe by Mrs Thatcher. Despite a forty-page brief for her first visit to Peking in September 1982, Mrs Thatcher made a cardinal error over Hong Kong by insisting: 'Treaties are treaties. If a country will not stand by one treaty, it will not stand by another.' It was that answer given at a Press conference in Hong Kong after her visit to China which angered the Chinese and set back talks in Peking for months. To the Chinese they were 'unequal treaties' signed under duress. Any attempt to insist on their enforcement was misguided since only 8 per cent of the colony was owned in perpetuity. The rest was under leasehold expiring in 1997 – and the Chinese controlled the water supply to the colony.

On her return Mrs Thatcher realized she had made a mistake and handed over the problem as the first of many hot potatoes to Sir Geoffrey. From then on until it was settled two years later, Sir Geoffrey spent at least one hour every day dealing with telegrams on the negotiations with China. Sir Percy Cradock as chief negotiator found his meetings with Wen Jong, the Vice-Minister for European Affairs, were left to mark time after Mrs Thatcher's 'insult'. When Sir Geoffrey decided on a fresh start after talks with Sir Percy and Sir Edward Youde, the Governor of Hong Kong, he set out to convince the Chinese that he was ready for genuine negotiations. He made his mark at the United Nations in New York with Wu Xueqian, the Chinese Foreign Minister. That paved the way for serious talks in Peking in December 1983. His first dividend was to get an extension of the deadline set by the Chinese.

The principle of One-Country-Two-Systems, allowing Hong Kong to stay capitalist for at least fifty years after the handover, was not a British idea. It came from the Chinese leader Deng Xiaoping. He refused to have any discussion of details. So Sir Geoffrey said the British negotiators were not interested in 'details'. Instead he chose the general description 'substance' and expanded the framework under that term. Deng had confined himself to six sentences on the principles of an agreement. That was enough for the dictionary of Hoveisms to be employed to flesh it all out. On his flight to Hong Kong in April 1984, Sir Geoffrey spent six hours on the RAF VC 10 enlarging one Chinese sentence into a lengthy appendix to what became the final agreement in the Joint Declaration by Britain and China. As Head of the Hong Kong desk, Tony Galsworthy, who became Sir Geoffrey's PPS afterwards, got to know his mind so well that most of the bland amendments in the final four months were inserted before the draft reached his desk. Right to the last minute, however, Sir Geoffrey had to intervene to ensure he got the most out of a bad bargaining hand. His final push with China's Mr Wu produced one unexpected concession. He got the Chinese to accept that Hong Kong's legislature should be constituted by elections. After all his patient manoeuvring to regain points following Mrs

Thatcher's gaffe, she upstaged him in the last round. Deng Xiao-ping insisted that she should sign the final agreement with him.

Another hot potato that the Prime Minister landed in his lap – the crisis over Grenada in October 1983 – ended with Sir Geoffrey taking the blame for dithering. For ten days there was confusion in the Caribbean following the murder of Grenada's Marxist leader Maurice Bishop and his replacement by an even more savage left-wing regime. Some neighbouring states wanted US inter-vention. Others did not. In Downing Street there was a natural assumption that Mrs Thatcher's special relationship with Presi-dent Reagan would enable the British Government to be informed in advance of any American military action. That was the under-pinning for Sir Geoffrey's statement to the Commons on 24 October that the Government was 'in the closest possible touch' with the US Government and he knew of no intention to invade. Less than twenty-four hours later, 1,500 US Marines landed in Grenada. Mrs Thatcher was furious. Reagan had promised: 'I'll get back to you.' He kept her in the dark. Her tirade over the phone to the White House was so fierce that a Reagan aide said the President took the phone away from his ear at one stage.

Initially, much of the criticism in the Commons was focused on the Prime Minister. Shadow Foreign Secretary Denis Healey accused her of 'fecklessness' and of being a poodle to Reagan. But six months later, Sir Geoffrey was the main target of attack in a scathing report by a Parliamentary Committee after on-the-spot investigations in the Caribbean led by a former Conservative Foreign Office minister, Peter Thomas. The Committee's verdict was blunt: 'The evidence given to us by the Foreign Secretary paints a picture of a British administration reacting passively to the events unfolding in the Caribbean and basing its reaction to those events entirely on the advice received from Washington, which in the event proved to be unreliable.'

The Committee acknowledged that the crisis blew up at an awkward time on the weekend of 22 and 23 October. Sir Geoffrey was in Athens for an EC meeting. His deputy, Baroness Young, was out of the country. But the Prime Minister was at Chequers – a point which the Committee did not think absolved the Foreign Secretary. It blamed the Government for not taking any initiative over that weekend to find out the views of Caribbean leaders. When Sir Geoffrey told the Committee that there was reluctance to use an open telephone line and the Foreign Office preferred 'normal diplomatic channels', the Committee was not impressed: 'This seems to us a somewhat lethargic approach.'

Sir Geoffrey's endless patience with softly-softly diplomacy was severely tested over South Africa. Mrs Thatcher had little time for the Commonwealth. She demonstrated that at the Nassau summit in 1985 with a contemptuous gesture of forefinger and thumb indicating that she had yielded only a 'tiny little bit' on sanctions. But she wanted to make it seem that her Government cared about exploring every possibility for a solution before the special Commonwealth summit in London in August. So Sir Geoffrey was dispatched to southern Africa in the guise of a 'last-chance peacemaker' on behalf of the European Community as its current chairman in the summer of 1986.

It was mission impossible, and he knew it from the start. At every stage he was rebuffed. South Africa's President P. W. Botha slapped him down as hard as the leaders of the Front Line states. Zambia's President Kaunda gave him a public dressing down. He told Sir Geoffrey he would have barred him from State House but for his 'love and respect' for the Queen. Undaunted, Sir Geoffrey plodded on. 'Just because it's difficult, it's no reason to give up.' He was often asked on the VC 10 why he put up with it and did not walk out. His answer was a justification of his style: 'Diplomacy is not about walk-outs. It's about talks through.' But it was all in vain. At the London summit Mrs Thatcher was left isolated, attacked by President Mugabe of Zimbabwe as 'an ally of apartheid'.

Sometimes Sir Geoffrey caught his critics by surprise and showed himself as a pacemaker, not a plodder. Such an occasion came during the Star Wars controversy over the extent to which the United States should pursue the Strategic Defence Initiative. Even the Prime Minister was taken aback by the way Sir Geoffrey opened up new approaches to the problem in a speech to the Royal United Services Institute in London on 15 March 1985. Mrs Thatcher believed she had closed down the transatlantic debate by her famous four-point agreement after her talks with President

Reagan at Camp David in December 1984. Sir Geoffrey's speech had been prepared for delivery in the autumn before Camp David, but the international calendar delayed it for six months.

There is still a debate over whether Mrs Thatcher realized how much her Camp David success was to be undermined by Sir Geoffrey in his seminal speech. The version of the Thatcher camp is that although she received an advance copy on her way to Moscow to attend the funeral of President Chernenko she was so tired on the return flight that she fell asleep with the text on her lap. It remained unread, according to No. 10 Downing Street. The Foreign Office version is that she was so content with the introductory passage affirming the need for nuclear deterrence that she nodded off happily on the flight. But there was no doubting her outrage when the speech was delivered and caused great anguish in Washington. The Camp David deal implied that Britain would support the SDI programme within the agreed limits on research and deployment. Yet here was a senior member of her Cabinet asking some more Socratic questions in typical Hoveism terms. It touched a nerve in Washington, prompting a bitter denunciation by Assistant Secretary of Defense Richard Perle. In an unprecedented rebuke delivered in London Perle said: 'It was a speech that proved again an old axiom of geometry that length is no substitute for depth.' He claimed that Sir Geoffrey 'succeeded in rewriting the recent history of the Soviet-American strategic relationship, rendering it unrecognizable to anyone who has charted its course'.

The cogently argued 4,000-word speech was a masterly thesis crafted by the Hon. Michael Pakenham, then head of the Foreign Office's Arms Control Department. The final polish was given by Sir Geoffrey's PPS Len Appleyard who came up with the headline phrase 'A New Maginot Line?' Sir Geoffrey posed all sorts of politically embarrassing questions which sent America's right wing into a rage. He raised the spectre of a new Maginot Line being outflanked by relatively simple and demonstrably cheaper counter-measures. 'What other defences in addition to space-based defences would need to be developed? We shall have to ask ourselves not only whether the West can afford active defences against nuclear missiles. We must also ask whether the enormous

funds devoted to such systems might be better employed. Are
more cost-effective and affordable ways of enhancing deterrence.
Might it be better to use the available funds to improve our capa-
bility to oppose a potential aggressor at a time of crisis with a
credible, sustainable and controllable mix of conventional and
nuclear forces?' Howe's speech reflected many of the legitimate
anxieties of Britain's NATO allies which they were too scared to
articulate for fear of offending their American protectors. It taught
Mrs Thatcher a lesson: never underestimate someone you usually
take for granted.

In the light of their bitter parting with his dismissal from the
Foreign Office in July 1989, it has become politically fashionable
to maintain that the Thatcher–Howe chemistry was wrong from
the outset. Not so. They were ideal foils for each other in the
Battle of the Budget Phase II from June 1983 to June 1984. The
Prime Minister played the Iron Lady, belabouring everyone who
opposed her with her handbag. She gave no quarter in demanding
a fair deal, knowing she had a trump card. With the Community
running short of funds any increase in *ressources propres* – the
Community's revenue – required unanimous approval. Unless the
package provided for an acceptable Budget rebate for Britain, she
would use her veto.

When the Italian Prime Minister Bettino Craxi blamed Mrs
Thatcher for paralysing the Community summit at Brussels in
March 1984, she turned to Sir Geoffrey to employ his patient
diplomacy on her partners. He worked on French Foreign Minister Roland Dumas, taking him through the fine print of amendments to the Community package during three long sessions at
Chevening, the eighteenth-century lakeside residence of the
Foreign Secretary in Kent. By the time they went to Fontainebleau
for the next summit under the presidency of the French, they had
a game plan for success. President François Mitterrand did not
relish being saddled with another deadlock so he agreed on the
first day, 24 June, to refer the issue of the £150m gap to foreign
ministers.

That enabled Sir Geoffrey to build on the structures prepared
in his private talks with Roland Dumas. The following day Mrs
Thatcher kept her nerve and held out for a better deal than was

offered at the Brussels summit. In the end she secured a mechanism for reducing Britain's budgetary burden by two-thirds and waived her opposition to an increase in Community funding by raising VAT contributions from 1 per cent to 1.4 per cent. The headline 'Maggie is home with a bargain' gave the triumph to the Prime Minister. But she acknowledged it was the outcome of her close partnership with Sir Geoffrey. Over the next four years that partnership was steadily soured by increasing differences over the strategy for Britain's role in a Europe accelerating towards economic and monetary union. It came to a head at the Community summit at Madrid in June 1989. Ganging up against Mrs Thatcher in her isolation from her European partners, Sir Geoffrey and Chancellor Nigel Lawson pressured her with threats of resignation into a positive statement committing Britain to make an early start on economic and monetary union from 1 July 1990 'as a matter of urgency'. Having pushed her so far, Sir Geoffrey should have braced himself for the pendulum swinging back against him.

Instead, he misread the warning signals from the Prime Minister. In an interview with the *Glasgow Herald*, she put on one of her glacial smiles and said: 'Geoffrey is a very good Foreign Secretary.' Then she added: 'I'm not going any further.' That menacing addendum should have put Sir Geoffrey on his guard. Yet he continued blithely assuming he was safe. Asked on Independent Television News if he accepted that he would never be Prime Minister, Sir Geoffrey said: 'I do not think anyone ever accepts that. We all come into politics believing we have a Field Marshal's baton in our knapsack.' That baton was snapped and cast into the Downing Street dustbin on 24 July when Mrs Thatcher gave him his marching orders out of the Foreign Office.

No one ever imagined that John Major would leap to the helm at the Foreign Office in one bound from being Chief Secretary at the Treasury. Mrs Thatcher's choice of successor to Sir Geoffrey stunned the Conservative Party – and the new Foreign Secretary himself. At the age of forty-six the MP for Huntingdon had been plucked from obscurity on the back benches five years earlier. Little was known of him except that he was the son of a trapeze artist. He arrived full of enthusiasm on his first day at the Foreign Office ten minutes early. 'I don't wear a watch,' he explained.

It was instant immersion for him in the Byzantine world of Middle East politics. He had to take over an appointment made for Sir Geoffrey and discuss the problems of the Gulf with Sheikh Zayed, President of the United Arab Emirates. 'The job is immensely interesting – but frankly daunting,' he gulped at the end of his fourteen-hour day.

Comparisons were made with Dr David Owen who was thrust into the Foreign Secretary's chair equally unexpectedly as a relatively unknown political figure. But Dr Owen had some international experience from having been Navy Minister and Deputy Foreign Secretary. John Major had to start from scratch, as one mandarin put it, 'with a bundle of briefs in one hand and an atlas in the other'. He had six days in which to prepare for heading the British delegation at the Cambodian Peace Conference in Paris on 30 July.

His main task in Paris was a delicate one. As the first Western minister to sit down with Chinese Foreign Minister Qian Qichen since the Tiananmen Square massacres the previous month in Peking, he had to deliver a strong warning over Hong Kong without provoking a backlash against the colony. It required skilful diplomatic handling to convey to Qian Qichen the anxiety in Hong Kong over Article 18 in the draft Basic law, the so-called 'turmoil clause'. John Major had to establish the need for the Chinese to restore confidence that after the handover of the colony to them in 1997, they would not create a state of emergency and order troops to shoot at students as had happened in Peking. After the forty-minute meeting there were signs that he had made his mark in what he described as 'very frank discussions'.

With Parliament in recess he was spared the grilling of Question Time. He eschewed the comforts of the official residence at No. 1 Carlton Gardens. He was not tempted to take his study programme of international affairs in the gracious 19,000-volume library at Chevening which was one of the attractions Sir Geoffrey Howe enjoyed showing to his guests. Instead, he hid himself away at his Great Stukeley home in Huntingdonshire. Telegrams and submissions were sent to him twice a day by road. Unclassified documents were dispatched by fax. He was so conscientious that he lost three-quarters of a stone in weight by the time he set off with the Prime Minister on 16 October for the Commonwealth Heads of Government meeting at Kuala Lumpur.

If John Major arrived imagining he could enjoy the Malaysian sunshine and let Mrs Thatcher take all the diplomatic flak over South Africa at the 49-nation conference, he was quickly disillusioned. The Prime Minister staked out her pragmatic position, calling for carrots not sticks to dangle in front of the South African Government and warning the others that they were starry-eyed over sanctions. Then she went off to the informal weekend upcountry at Langkawi, 300 miles north of Kuala Lumpur, leaving John Major to hammer out a document at a marathon session of foreign ministers. It turned into 'one hell of a fight' with Australia's Gareth Evans. Major had his back to the wall for nine hours trying to argue that sanctions were hurting South Africa's poor blacks more than the whites. He was so frustrated at one point that he rose to his feet and thrust a clenched fist at Evans.

In the end Major thought he had done 'a damn good job' protecting Britain's interests. He seemed quite proud to put his name to the final statement, 'Southern Africa – the Way Ahead', which the Commonwealth Secretary-General Sonny Ramphal hailed as 'one of the largest measures of unanimity ever achieved'. Then his troubles began, not with his Commonwealth colleagues but with the Prime Minister. He thought he would get a pat on the back for making her seem less isolated with only four reservations in the communiqué marked 'with the exception of Great Britain' instead of the six at the previous Commonwealth Conference in Vancouver. At first she seemed pleased enough with the document. She said so at Langkawi and was applauded by the other leaders. But when she studied it closely she was fuming. Mrs Thatcher did not want to be less isolated. She wanted her differences set out fully.

She summoned her faithful Private Secretary Charles Powell to work out an appropriate riposte. When word of this started to circulate in Kuala Lumpur, John Major was asked about reports that the Prime Minister was not satisfied with the 49-nation document. His usual genial expression gave way to a frown. 'What? She didn't say that to me,' he snapped. There was further humiliation for him in the abruptness of Mrs Thatcher's reaction. For

the first time at a Commonwealth Conference a separate communiqué was issued without the other delegations being informed
in advance. It was a slap in the face for all who had worked on the
Kuala Lumpur statement – including John Major. To rub in her
displeasure she entitled her five-page minority report: 'Southern
Africa – the Way Ahead: Britain's View'. It declared: 'Britain
believes the Commonwealth can help a new South Africa to
emerge in much more positive ways than those set out in the
Kuala Lumpur Statement.' The clear implication was that her new
Foreign Secretary had not fought hard enough to have Britain's
opposition to sanctions against South Africa fully explained. At its
most charitable it was a reflection on John Major's inexperience
in letting hmself be outmanoeuvred. In the chorus of dismay at
the British behaviour Canada's Prime Minister Brian Mulroney
charged both John Major and Mrs Thatcher with bad faith: 'When
you sign a document at five o'clock you don't repudiate it at six.'

It was no surprise that John Major did not wait until the end of
the conference. He gave the impression of being out of his depth
and ill-prepared for the infighting at such a large international
gathering. The reason given for his sudden departure on Monday,
24 October was that he wanted to be in the Commons for his first
Question Time as Foreign Secretary. It was also to be his last.
Nigel Lawson's resignation as Chancellor brought an end to John
Major's ninety-three days as Foreign Secretary – seven fewer than
Patrick Gordon Walker and the shortest time of anyone this century. When he walked across the road to No. 11 Downing Street
to become Chancellor, John Major opened the door for the one
person to take over the helm at the Foreign Office who seemed as
if his entire career had been shaped for that very purpose: Douglas
Hurd.

As the 55th Foreign Secretary since Charles James Fox began
the sequence in 1782, Douglas Hurd had the sort of curriculum
vitae which a headhunter for the job would have been delighted
to find. Captain of School at Eton (where he had a reputation for
caning boys because of 'insufficient effort'). Second Lieutenant in
the Royal Horse Artillery. Trinity College, Cambridge and President of the Union. Chairman of the University Conservative
Association. Member of the Diplomatic Service for fourteen years,

serving in Peking, New York, and Rome. Political Secretary to Conservative Party leader Edward Heath. Foreign Office Minister, Home Office Minister, Northern Ireland Secretary, and then Home Secretary. Fluent in French and Italian plus knowledge of Mandarin. Recreations: writing thrillers and reading French poetry on planes. Last of the politicians in office who could say: 'My father knew Lloyd George – and I met him in the Central Lobby at Westminster (aged nine).' One extra advantage, all too rare in ministers: a sense of humour.

When Douglas Hurd returned to the Foreign Office on 26 October 1989, there was no need for him to 'read himself in' on the files. He had what the Service calls 'the knowledge'. He had a family connection with the Falklands. His father was the first MP to visit the islands. He is remembered for bringing a special type of grass, known as Yorkshire Fog, for the islanders' sheep. Hurd's expertise on the Middle East made him in much demand as a junior Foreign Office minister. Whenever Mrs Thatcher had a stopover in the Gulf on her way back from the Far East, he would be flown out to be at her side advising her at her meetings with the sheikhs. That Middle East background went back to his days in New York as Private Secretary to Britain's UN Ambassador Sir Pierson Dixon. On the night of Israel's invasion of Suez in October 1956, Douglas Hurd was in white tie and tails in a box at the Metropolitan Opera alongside the Ambassador listening to Maria Callas singing *Norma*. In the next box was US Ambassador Henry Cabot Lodge. When news of the invasion reached them, Hurd was the go-between carrying notes back and forward about the crisis.

His familiarity with the Middle East and its problems steadied nerves in Whitehall in the uncertain days after Iraq's invasion of Kuwait in August 1990. This ability to keep a cool head in a crisis enhanced Hurd's position in Cabinet when John Major took over as Prime Minister from Mrs Thatcher. During the Thatcher era Sir Geoffrey Howe had to defer to her on all key international issues. While Major adjusted himself to the new burdens of the premiership he passed over the day-to-day business of the Overseas and Defence Committee to Douglas Hurd. His crisp style quickened the pace of decision-making on foreign policy. He usually set out five questions and called on his staff at the Foreign Office to provide assessments of the options in no more than two or three lines. He cut down on the paperwork and insisted that when he called for answers he wanted them all on one side of a sheet of paper.

When reams of paper had to be read in a major crisis, however, there was no one faster than Douglas Hurd. He amazed the mandarins who had taken fast-reading courses and still found they could not keep pace with him. In the tumultuous days of the Kremlin upheavals after the failure of the Communist hardliners' coup on 19 August 1991, Hurd not only read all the telegrams which flooded into the Foreign Office, transcripts of Gorbachev's speeches as he fought for his political survival, and summaries of Boris Yeltsin's defiant statements in the Russian Parliament. Hurd also found time to read Frederick Forsyth's new spy thriller *The Deceiver* and write a long review of it for the *Daily Telegraph* as a highly acclaimed thriller writer himself.

Hurd established a pragmatic pattern of direct diplomacy. In one month he saw the French Foreign Minister seventeen times – more than he saw his Cabinet colleagues. He would pick up the telephone and thrash out a problem instantly with US Secretary of State James Baker or the German Foreign Minister Hans-Dietrich Genscher. In his first year he travelled 130,000 miles by air. In September 1990, one month after Iraq invaded Kuwait, he flew 21,529 miles including journeys to Tokyo, Moscow, and New York and a six-day trip with eight stops in the Middle East. His seniority in the Conservative Party gave him the clout to stand up for his policies in Cabinet and against sniping from former ministers. That position of strength plus his knowledge of China – gained from being a diplomat there and having visited it subsequently with Edward Heath and then with Mrs Thatcher – enabled Douglas Hurd to withstand sustained attacks in January 1990 from hardline Tories over immigration from Hong Kong.

During his first six months, he was not at ease alongside Mrs Thatcher at Community summits. When he joined her she knew everybody and had all the background to every issue coming up for discussion. His grasp of economics and finance was shaky. Mrs Thatcher did not seem confident that he could carry off the role of second fiddle. On the final day of one summit Mrs Thatcher divided the workload on arguing for amendments to the draft conclusions. She took the difficult ones. Hurd was allocated the simpler elements left for argument in square brackets in the draft. But it requires a very alert mind to keep pace with the rapid interventions. When Hurd raised his hand to indicate an objection, other heads of government were amazed to see Mrs Thatcher grab the microphone from him. President Mitterrand was nonplussed to hear her loud stage-whisper to Hurd: 'Don't worry – they're used to me.' They were all aware of the substance of the British objection from a preliminary interjection by Hurd. But Mrs Thatcher felt that Hurd's polished old Etonian tones were not sufficient. She had to give them a handbagging herself.

Under the premiership of John Major it was much easier for Douglas Hurd to adopt a softer negotiating strategy. His first fence-mending signal after Mrs Thatcher's departure was significant. He pledged that the Major–Hurd approach would be to seek consensus – a word that was anathema to Mrs Thatcher – in the European Community. 'We're not going to sit there as wreckers,' he told the Commons Foreign Affairs Committee in December 1990. The evolution from his earlier days at the Foreign Office required new techniques, especially in lunchtime diplomacy. Working lunches used to be sociable occasions for leisurely political exchanges. In recent times they have become the forum for decision-making.

Ministers sit down for lunch from 1.30 p.m. until four o'clock doing business previously scheduled for formal sessions on the 14th floor of the Charlemagne building in Brussels. Only politicians are round the table. No officials are present. No note-takers. That meant that Hurd's PPS had to slip a notebook into his chief's pocket as he disappeared for lunch since that would be the sole record of the meeting. With eleven other ministers around him Hurd had to eat, drink, listen, speak and take notes all the time. Not surprisingly, there were frequently disputes among foreign ministry officials after such occasions as to precisely what had been decided, for example, on a new framework for discussions with the Palestinians.

One notable change with Hurd at the helm was the importance

given to the junior ministers at the Foreign Office. Apart from Lord Carrington, who chose his team carefully and required an eloquent No. 2 in Sir Ian Gilmour to answer for the Government in the Commons, most Foreign Secretaries in the past three decades have been loath to delegate authority. There is always a weekly meeting of the Foreign Secretary with his ministerial team but it has rarely led to responsibility being devolved on any issue liable to go to Cabinet. Dr Owen was a workaholic without much method in his work and no time for his Ministers of State Frank Judd and Ted Rowlands, although both of them were politicians with experience in Commonwealth affairs. Sir Geoffrey Howe never let much out of his grasp. Nonetheless, Timothy Renton made the most of his opportunities in disarmament negotiations and David Mellor jumped in with both feet whenever there was the slightest chance of grabbing a headline in the Occupied Territories of Israel and elsewhere.

As a junior minister who was given his head by Carrington in the early 1980s, Douglas Hurd established at the start of his regime as Foreign Secretary that his ministers should be a ginger group challenging the attitudes of the Foreign Office mandarins and exploring the prospects of changes in various deadlocked situations. For Young Turks like Francis Maude and William Waldegrave it was a chance to prove themselves – which they did on occasion with *élan*. Maude tussled in Hanoi with the Vietnamese authorities over the return of the boat people from Hong Kong, and any other issue he could get his teeth into. Waldegrave had a voracious appetite for material on the Middle East and became deeply engrossed in the Palestinian question. He would get the experts such as the Hon. David Gore-Booth, Roger Tomkys, and Alan Goulty round his desk to test his analysis of the latest developments against theirs. Even under Sir Geoffrey Howe, Waldegrave was the pacemaker in getting the Government to acknowledge that the Palestine Liberation Organization was making a fundamental shift in its position towards Israel in 1989 after the Algiers Declaration of the Palestine National Council. Having built up a close understanding with Bassam Abu Sharif, the adviser of the PLO Chairman Yasser Arafat, William Waldegrave proved an important Middle East linkman for Hurd. Whenever he left for Tunis with his tennis racket it was a signal that he was setting out for some backhand diplomacy on court with the US Ambassador acting as intermediary with the Palestinians.

Although much of that bridge-building was undermined by Arafat's disastrous alignment with Saddam Hussein after Iraq's invasion of Kuwait, the objectives pursued by Waldegrave in terms of self-determination for the Palestinians were not abandoned. That was the legacy for the experts on the Middle East to tackle after the liberation of Kuwait in February 1991. With so many rival interests setting conflicting conditions, it has proved very difficult to establish a framework for making progress. But diplomacy by conference can be extremely rewarding provided it is carefully organized and there is enough patience and stamina to see it through to the end – as Lord Carrington discovered after a diplomatic marathon in 1979.

VI

Conference Diplomacy

As the Royal Air Force VC 10 dipped down towards Lusaka International Airport on Monday, 30 July 1979, the Prime Minister opened her handbag and pulled out a large pair of dark sunglasses. It was eleven o'clock at night and pitch black down below. 'What on earth are those for?' asked Lord Carrington at her side. 'I'm scared they are going to throw acid in my face,' said Mrs Thatcher. After only eighty-eight days as Prime Minister she was nervous of the ordeal ahead. She knew nothing about Africa, the Dark Continent. There had been scare stories in London about the safety of the Queen going to Zambia to host the banquet on the opening night of the Commonwealth Heads of Government meeting. During her flight Mrs Thatcher read reports of mounting hostility to her on the eve of the 39-nation conference. The *Times of Zambia* accused her of 'blind and pusillanimous arrogance' towards the Rhodesia problem. The *Zambia Daily Mail* said that the Queen was unfortunate to have a Prime Minister in Britain 'who is so racially biased'.

Lord Carrington made light of her anxieties. The Zambian crowds at the airport would shout and dance. But they would not harm her, he tried to assure the Prime Minister. When the door of the VC 10 opened and she heard the loud ululating noise of the people on the tarmac, she turned to Lord Carrington: 'I don't believe you.' Still dubious, she put her sunglasses back in her handbag and gasped at seeing the throng of people: 'I think I'll be kidnapped.' Seconds later as she stepped off the plane she felt that could be her fate. Security arrangements collapsed as the crowd surged forward. Mrs Thatcher was engulfed. All around her people struggled in a heaving mass. Cameras and tape-recorders were sent crashing onto the tarmac. In the mêlée she was separated from her husband Denis. She looked as if she was frogmarched to a hangar for a Press conference. Lord Carrington's Press Secretary, Sir Nicholas Fenn, was swept away from the Foreign Secretary shouting 'Outrageous, absolutely outrageous.' Mrs Thatcher's Press Secretary, Henry James, was pushed aside and left twenty feet behind her. Her Cabinet Secretary Sir John Hunt could not get inside the building. He was standing, clutching the red box, straining to hear what she was saying outside the window.

Seven days later Mrs Thatcher was in the arms of President Kenneth Kaunda gliding across the dance floor at the Lusaka Press Club's annual ball to Zambia's top of the charts, 'Maggie is Beautiful'. Paying tribute to his 'dancing partner' afterwards, President Kaunda told her: 'You have brought a ray of hope to the world by your frankness.' Somewhat to her own surprise the Prime Minister admitted: 'There has been a fantastic convergence of will at this conference.' After delegates sang 'For She's a Jolly Good Lady', Jamaica's Prime Minister Michael Manley saluted her with the toast: 'She is obviously a woman of enormous ability, a woman with a great capacity for decision.'

That was the climax to the first phase of the moves to resolve the Rhodesia problem, fourteen years – and many failed attempts – after Ian Smith's UDI. It paved the way for what has come to be known as 'Carrington's Triumph', the agreement on Rhodesia's independence after fourteen weeks at the Lancaster House Conference in London. This was not the outcome of a sudden brain-wave at the Lusaka summit finding a way to end the deadlock which had eluded a succession of ministers since Harold Wilson. The armies fighting the bush war were at the point of exhaustion on both sides. The Foreign Office experts saw a new opportunity for negotiations on a new scenario for a settlement. That scenario deserves studying in detail as a textbook example of conference diplomacy which could be used as a model for demonstrating the importance of patient preparation of every stage. Like a child's house construction set, it required careful building, a block at a time.

The key to the success of conference diplomacy is having superb teamwork, and Lord Carrington acknowledged that he had the finest team a foreign secretary could have assembled at that time. His deputy, Sir Ian Gilmour, a very experienced politician, shared the chairmanship burden during the arduous three months. Lord Harlech, junior minister Richard Luce, and assistant under-secretary Derek Day had important liaison roles. The PUS Sir Michael Palliser kept a close watch on the co-ordination of the teamwork. For public presentation in front of the television cameras twice a day – and subtle guiding behind the scenes – Lord Carrington called his chief spokesman, Sir Nicholas Fenn, 'the star of the show'. The two figures who played Britain's hand across the table at private sessions with the African delegations were Sir Antony Duff, a quiet-spoken wartime submarine commander with the DSO and DSC who was an Africa expert as deputy to the PUS, and Sir Robin Renwick, then Head of Rhodesia Department who soared upwards to become Ambassador in South Africa and later in the United States. Their drafting skills were supplemented by Sir Charles Powell, who helped write the independence consti-tution and later became Mrs Thatcher's right-hand man, and Ronald Byatt, who was promoted to be the first British High Com-missioner in Zimbabwe. Lord Carrington often despaired, fre-quently lost his temper but never wavered in his admiration for them: 'I know that no institution but the Foreign Office could have produced such support and such skill.'

Forty-eight hours after his appointment as Foreign Secretary, Lord Carrington decided that the Rhodesia problem should be his first priority. It had become a drain on the energies of ministers, exposed Britain to denigration at the United Nations, threatened sanctions against Britain from its Commonwealth partners with the risk of breaking up the Commonwealth itself, and worst of all the war in Rhodesia was inflicting horrendous damage on a once-prosperous country. He summoned Sir Ian Gilmour, Sir Michael Palliser, and Sir Antony Duff to work out a strategy at a meeting on Sunday, 6 May. First, he sent Sir Antony Duff to Rhodesia to make an on-the-spot assessment. After talks with the recently installed Government of Bishop Muzorewa as the front man and Ian Smith, as Minister without Portfolio, pulling the strings from behind, Duff returned with the conviction that the time had come for a fresh attempt at a settlement. Next, Lord Harlech toured seven African states and came back with the report that none would recognize the Muzorewa Government. Richard Luce visited five other African countries and returned with the same assessment.

The main problem was to convince Mrs Thatcher of the need to make a fresh start. Even with all the persuasive powers possessed by Lord Carrington, it proved very difficult to win over the Prime Minister. His task was complicated by the Conservative election manifesto drawn up in February 1979. It stated: 'If the Six Principles, which all British Governments have supported for the last fifteen years, are fully satisfied following the Rhodesian elections the next Government will have the duty to return Rhodesia to a state of legality, move to lift sanctions, and do its utmost to ensure that the new independent state gains international recognition.' After the Rhodesian elections Mrs Thatcher – still in Opposition – sent out Lord Boyd who reported that the elections were 'fairly conducted and above reproach'. As a result Mrs Thatcher came to power convinced that Rhodesia was the only democracy in Africa and that Joshua Nkomo was 'a terrorist'.

Lord Carrington's strongest argument was the verdict from Lord Harlech on return from his travels that the so-called Internal Settlement in Rhodesia would never gain international recognition and that only an election with everyone allowed to participate would be considered valid. Mrs Thatcher seemed on the point of being won over when she lapsed back into hinting about a return to legality at a Press conference in Canberra on 1 July. She indicated that an attempt to extend the Government Order renewing sanctions against Rhodesia for a further twelve months might not get through Parliament in November. Australia's Prime Minister Malcolm Fraser was so worried about this backsliding that he sent his political adviser, Alan Griffiths, to London to urge Lord Carrington to get her off that line of thinking quickly or else there would be trouble at the Commonwealth summit in Lusaka.

Even when Lord Carrington redoubled his efforts to argue Mrs Thatcher into a more flexible state of mind about Rhodesia she fought against it until the moment when she boarded the VC 10. On the morning before she left she had a stormy meeting at No. 10 Downing Street on the final tactics. As Lord Carrington led in his team – Sir Ian Gilmour, Sir Michael Palliser, and Sir Antony Duff – they feared the worst. She flung back all the policy documents, dismissing them as 'a load of nonsense'. What was the point of calling for new elections in Rhodesia when 65 per cent of the electorate had just voted? Look what Alan (Lord Boyd) had said: the elections were fair. Why upset a perfectly reasonable arrangement with a black and white government? It took Lord Carrington over an hour to calm her down. He got her back on course by arguing that Rhodesia, like other British territories, was entitled to have a constitutional conference convened in London to work out an independence constitution. He reinforced that by pointing out that as she was convinced that Muzorewa had won fairly then she should have no doubt that he could win again in fresh elections.

The game plan worked out by Sir Antony Duff for the Lusaka conference was for Mrs Thatcher to sit back and listen without hinting that Britain was ready to offer a new constitutional conference open to all, including her so-called terrorists, Joshua Nkomo and Robert Mugabe. Sonny Ramphal, the Commonwealth Secretary-General, had been working in the background to calm the atmosphere on the other side. He persuaded Joshua Nkomo to suspend all cross-border fighting for the duration of the conference and drafted a unilateral ceasefire statement for him to issue. His other gambit was to get the Front Line leaders – Kaunda of Zambia, Nyerere of Tanzania, and Masire of Botswana – to put their case in moderate terms, not to harangue the British as happened in the days of Harold Wilson, and to avoid confrontation. They agreed to have a short opening debate on Rhodesia at the conference, not put Mrs Thatcher in the dock, and then adjourn on the Friday to allow time for quiet diplomacy during the weekend.

That plan was nearly upset on the opening day of the conference when Nigeria announced the nationalization of British Petroleum assets. Major-General Henry Adefope, Nigeria's External Affairs Commissioner, was caught on the hop. He had no advance warning of the Lagos announcement and was strutting around the opening conference reception in his bright blue robes when Lord Carrington pounced on him and gave him a blast in front of the television cameras. Once the eruption subsided the key players were able to get down to the real game.

As host, President Kaunda helped defuse the tension by holding a dinner for only the central characters – himself and Nyerere on one side, Mrs Thatcher and Lord Carrington on the other. The Prime Minister impressed her hosts. She listened patiently without butting in on their arguments. She surprised them by showing how well she had done her homework and how clearly she appreciated the tribal differences between Shona peoples and Ndebele. Late into the night Sir Antony Duff worked on her opening statement which highlighted her readiness to accept 'Britain's constitutional responsibility to bring Rhodesia to legal independence on a basis of justice and democracy fully comparable with the arrangements we have made for the independence of other countries'. It stressed that the British Government was 'wholly committed to genuine black majority rule' and that the present Rhodesian constitution was not satisfactory since it enabled the European minority to block all change. President Nyerere played his conciliatory role according to plan. In gentle tones he set out the consensus: 'I believe that no member of the Commonwealth is willing to acquiesce in the creation of another South Africa.' Mrs Thatcher kept her strident tones under control and promised: 'I shall listen with the greatest attention at this meeting.' She listed Britain's commitments to establish a truly democratic Rhodesia.

Next morning, while the rest of the delegates went down to Livingstone to see the Victoria Falls, Mrs Thatcher and Lord

Carrington began Phase II of the Lusaka game plan at a restricted session in President Kaunda's study at State House. Alongside them were President Kaunda, President Nyerere, Australia's Malcolm Fraser, Jamaica's Michael Manley, Nigeria's Major-General Adefope, and Sonny Ramphal. Overnight Sonny Ramphal had set the opening speeches of Kaunda, Nyerere, and Thatcher side by side and evolved 'elements of commonality'. When the discussions went ahead smoothly on that Saturday morning enough progress was made for the State House group to give a mandate to Sonny Ramphal and Sir Antony Duff to work out a synthesis as a basis for an agreed Lusaka Declaration. President Kaunda gave them his own room and left them to go through a draft line by line. By the end of the day they had completed it except for two divergencies on Commonwealth supervision.

The State House group reassembled on Sunday morning. They agreed the final text but Lord Carrington insisted on keeping it secret until the following morning so that the announcement could be made at the plenary session. Knowing he might be accused of sell-out by the right wing of the Conservative Party, he wanted time to get his version thoroughly digested in London first. President Kaunda also wanted time to explain what the agreement meant to Nkomo and Mugabe, who had been kept in the dark. But they had not reckoned on the ambitions of Australia's Malcolm Fraser. He was determined not to be upstaged by 'Maggie's triumph' reports in London. He gave an advance briefing on Sunday afternoon to Australian correspondents – and invited the *Daily Mail* and Independent Television News to sit unobtrusively at the back and listen to his version.

Leaks from that Australian briefing began to reach the British delegation at the Inter-Continental Hotel as they were giving a bland briefing to British correspondents. Spokesman Henry James was sticking to the rules. He was stating that good progress was being made but it was still too early to say if final agreement would be reached on a formula for a Rhodesia conference. When Fraser's pre-emptive disclosures were conveyed to Lord Carrington he was furious. Using his bad imitation of an Australian accent, he exploded: 'Melkom's blown it.'

He drafted a note for the Prime Minister. At that moment she was at the Cathedral of the Holy Cross listening to the Bishop of Lusaka thundering on about racism, totally out of tune with the new moves at the Commonwealth conference to put racism behind them and start afresh in Rhodesia. Mrs Thatcher's Private Secretary Ian Gow, who was the tragic victim of an IRA car bomb ten years later, slipped the message from Lord Carrington to her. It appeared to her that Lord Carrington had lost his nerve and was advising her to call the deal off. His message recommended that the State House statement should be released as a mere draft on which the British Government had not taken a final position. She passed the note to Sonny Ramphal sitting alongside and whispered, 'Sonny, we're in trouble.' With the Bishop still preaching Hellfire for racists, Sonny Ramphal wrote an answer on his Order of Service sheet, urging her to restrain Lord Carrington from throwing in his hand. 'Malcolm's behaviour cannot be allowed to frustrate this achievement. Stick with it and we will all help. Let's hold an emergency meeting and explain to the others what has happened. We can then get the statement out as an agreed text instead of waiting until tomorrow. Putting out a "draft" is a recipe for disaster.'

Mrs Thatcher decided it was worth holding on. She kept her nerve despite Lord Carrington's fretting. While she was waiting for President Kaunda to corral all the leaders, she made up her mind to pay the Australian back in full one day no matter how long it took. She waited ten years and then had the satisfaction of blocking Malcolm Fraser's bid to succeed Sonny as Commonwealth Secretary-General and enabling Chief Emeka Anyaoku of Nigeria to win the prize in 1989. When she was told that the special emergency session was to be held at Fraser's bungalow in Mulungushi Village, since they had all been invited there for a barbecue supper, Mrs Thatcher dug her heels in: 'I'm not going to his bloody party. I'll be damned if I'll be seen there.' But President Kaunda had a gentle touch and begged her to accompany him because her role was crucial to him in overcoming the crisis.

When she arrived, glowering, she was offered a seat alongside Kaunda. It was so cramped that Lord Carrington had to perch on the arm of her chair. Mrs Thatcher made it clear that a 'draft agreement' was not sufficient. A full, formal agreement had to be announced without delay. Fraser was nervous, hoping that his attempt to claim all the credit would not become a matter of debate. But his old Antipodean rival, New Zealand's Robert Muldoon, was not prepared to let Fraser get off without some public embarrassment. Responding to Kaunda's appeal to settle the whole matter there and then, Muldoon asked for some 'clarification' about how the agreement came about. 'This is all very well, President Kaunda, but I keep hearing all sorts of stories that one of our colleagues – I don't know who – has given this out to the media as his doing and I would like to know if there is any truth in this.' But as Fraser began to fear an inquisition, Zambia's Presbyterian President decided it was time for Christian charity and hushed it all up.

Mrs Thatcher's charity did not extend to supping with the devil Fraser. She walked out before the barbecue and held her own Press conference explaining how Britain would be in charge from then on at Lancaster House. She hailed it as a success for British diplomacy and was urged by photographers to hold up her copy of the final communiqué and wave it in the air. The voice of her spokesman Henry James cautioned her: 'Don't do it, Prime Minister.' She turned round rather startled and kept her hand down. 'But. why?' she asked afterwards as the Press conference broke up. 'Remember Chamberlain, remember Munich,' came the reply. 'Oh, my God. Yes,' she admitted with relief.

Lord Carrington's team had one month to organize the strangest constitutional conference ever staged at Lancaster House. The mandate as set out in the nine-point plan in the Lusaka conference communiqué presented no major problems for the British Government initially since it had been carefully phrased by Sir Antony Duff working in conjunction with Sonny Ramphal. It acknowledged that the constitution of the Internal Settlement was 'defective in certain important respects' and that a new constitution providing for genuine black majority rule was required. In accordance with the original game plan, the responsibility of the British Government for the entire proceedings through to independence was clearly defined.

From the outset Lord Carrington insisted on running the whole operation without any outside interference. He refused to be burdened, as Dr Owen had been, with the Americans as partners because their decision-making process was so slow and subject to so many Congressional qualifications. He would have nothing to do with the United Nations since that would put him at the mercy of the anti-colonialist lobby. He tried to rule out any intervention from the Commonwealth. Despite Sonny Ramphal's important role as a fixer at Lusaka, Lord Carrington regarded him as a dangerous meddler. In the end it was Sonny's intervention which saved the conference from one of its worst crises. Lord Carrington started the conference refusing to consult him or have anything to do with him unless protocol required it because he believed that Sonny Ramphal was in league with the Patriotic Front leaders, Joshua Nkomo and Robert Mugabe. But the Commonwealth could not be entirely bypassed because the Lusaka communiqué laid down that free and fair elections had to be 'properly supervised under British Government authority, and with Commonwealth observers'.

Invitations were issued for the opening ceremony at Lancaster House on 10 September with precisely calculated fairness. Lord Carrington's delegation numbered twenty-two. So did the Rhodesian Government delegation of Bishop Muzorewa. The African nationalists of the Patriotic Front also got twenty-two invitations – eleven for the Mugabe team and eleven for the Nkomo team. To make sure that Ian Smith as leader of the UDI rebellion was not threatened with a citizen's arrest, the Government provided legal immunity for him. Living allowances were paid by the Government to all delegates. When Robert Mugabe moved his delegation out of the Royal Garden Hotel in Kensington to apartments in Bayswater he claimed £950 a day. That claim was based on £125 a day for his suite, ten other delegates' rooms at £55 and eleven daily allowances at £25. But the Foreign Office put a limit of £550 a day on allowances for delegations taking private accommodation.

The Government clamped down on any squabbling over places at the conference table. The Foreign Office had learnt its lesson from the Kenya independence conference in 1960. Then the opening was delayed by a row over Mbiyu Koinange because of his activities during the Mau Mau rebellion. It was resolved by having Koinange in an ante-room as adviser outside the main conference room at Lancaster House. The Patriotic Front tried to make an issue out of the table plan. Dr Herbert Ushewokunze protested against the layout of Britain at the top with the Patriotic Front on one side and the Muzorewa delegation on the other. He called for a two-sided setting with the Muzorewa delegation alongside Lord Carrington's delegation since they were the 'puppets of the British'. But Lord Carrington stood firm: anyone not in his designated place for the opening address at four o'clock would forfeit his right to attend the conference. In fact, none wanted to miss an occasion they had dreamed of for years. For someone straight from the bush war, like guerrilla leader Lookout Mafela, going into Lancaster House, the mansion built in 1825 for the Grand Old Duke of York, the second son of King George III, was like entering 'an illustrated history book'. The African nationalists gazed in awe at the ceiling of the Great Gallery, 120 feet long, with its magnificent painting, Guercino's 'St Grisogonus borne to Heaven by Angels'.

As a protest both guerrilla leaders, Nkomo and Mugabe, boycotted the evening reception given by Lord Carrington on the opening day. A letter explaining their absence said: 'We felt we could not distinguish between the colour of the tea being given and the blood of the women and children which the puppet regime of Muzorewa and Smith are shedding at this moment.' But the refusal of African nationalists to shake hands with anyone having 'blood on his hands' did not last long. At the coffee break on the second day Mugabe's guerrilla commander, General Josiah Tongogara, broke away from a member of the British delegation saying: 'There's Mr Ian Smith. I must go and say "Hello". His mother used to give me sweets in Selukwe when I was a kid. That was back in 1952 and she was a lovely, kind lady.' That camaraderie soon evaporated as the high expectations of an early settlement disappeared. Most constitutional conferences in the 1960s managed to achieve agreement on independence in ten days. This one was recognized to be more complicated. But the British team were confident that they could settle it in three or four weeks. In the end it required all their reserves of ingenuity and stamina to stay the course for what turned out to be a fourteen-week marathon. Initially Lord Carrington's confidence in a successful outcome was shored up by the conviction that there was a good reason why almost everyone involved should want a settlement.

Lord Carrington believed Muzorewa was eager to work out an agreement since he thought that fresh elections would confirm him as Prime Minister. Ian Smith was losing heart over the war which was requiring heavy sacrifices from the beleaguered whites. Joshua Nkomo was tiring of the armed struggle and wanted the chance to be Father of the Nation, operating as leader inside, not outside, the country. President Kaunda wanted Nkomo's army out of Zambia. President Machel wanted Mugabe's forces out of Mozambique. South Africa was weary of supporting what was clearly becoming a lost cause. The only person not showing any signs of being in a hurry to come to terms was Robert Mugabe. His patience for waiting until the right terms were offered seemed limitless.

The game plan, which was devised by Sir Robin Renwick, was to build up the structure of a settlement block by block in such a way that no one would want to be blamed for knocking it down. The further the building went up the less likely people would be prepared to see squandered what had been achieved. He charted a course to settle first the new constitution, then the transitional arrangements to implement the constitution, and finally the terms of a ceasefire to ensure the necessary stability for elections. Had there not been such a disciplined approach Lord Carrington feared that the conference would slither into mere talks about talks on all the aspects of ending the war and making peace. In his opening speech Lord Carrington established his priority: 'It is essential to the prospects of success that we should first seek agreement on our destination – which is the independence constitution.' Joshua Nkomo tried to challenge Lord Carrington. He argued: 'This is our conference – not just yours. It is not enough to focus on constitution-making without seeking ways to ensure the irreversible transfer of power to the people of Zimbabwe. It is a collective decision on how we proceed.' Lord Carrington was blunt. He reminded the others of the Lusaka communiqué reaffirming Britain's constitutional responsibility: 'This is our show and I'm in charge.'

Many political analysts who were observing the events at Lancaster House came to the conclusion that the Carrington strategy was to wear down the Patriotic Front into making the maximum concessions and then sell that package as the best possible deal for Rhodesia's 230,000 whites. It was thought that the British team were manoeuvring all the time to split Nkomo from his more intellectual, more radical partner Mugabe in the hope of building a new partnership between Muzorewa and Nkomo. Alternatively, there were theorists who imagined that all the British negotiators were doing was trying to prove that a deal could not be done with the Patriotic Front and therefore the only way out of the deadlock was the 'Second Option', a deal with Muzorewa backed by Smith.

Both groups of pundits were wrong. The main focus of the British negotiators was on the whites. The game plan was to push the whites, who had all the levers of power in Rhodesia, into a position where they had to give them up. Basically, it was one big confidence trick. The tactics were to keep the number of plenary sessions to a minimum since they would merely be used as propaganda opportunities. That was where Mugabe with his sharp mind could score points. Clever debating sessions would not bring agreement any nearer. Lord Carrington was convinced that Ian Smith could not be driven into a corner and isolated at plenary meetings. By holding separate meetings and then reporting to the Patriotic Front what was the most that could be got out of the other delegation the British negotiators put themselves in a position to start serious bargaining.

Most of the serious talking took place away from the conference table at Lancaster House. Lord Carrington had little patience for long rambling discussions. He handed the hard bargaining over to Sir Antony Duff and Sir Robin Renwick who took delegates out in little groups for dinner and spent hours edging them into a more flexible frame of mind. Sometimes they went to Sir Antony Duff's club, the In and Out (Naval and Military), on other occasions to the Hyde Park Hotel. If it was the Patriotic Front people, they would take them to Italian restaurants in Soho. At other times there would be meetings late into the night after dinner. Sir Antony Duff would put a bottle of whisky on the table to keep the debate going until they reached the point of exhaustion and gave in. When they came to a crunch point it was often necessary to pass the baton back to Lord Carrington. Once when he had Mugabe and Nkomo in his room he began to eye a favourite table with some concern as Nkomo kept banging his flywhisk on it. 'Excuse me, Mr Nkomo, I'm rather fond of that piece of Chippendale,' he explained. 'I think I'd better remove it.'

The hardest part of the negotiations in the first phase came once the 34-page document on the constitutional framework drafted by Sir Charles Powell had been circulated. It meant that Muzorewa and the whites had to bite the bullet and accept that they had to begin all over again in the struggle for political power. Every one around Ian Smith had to be taken out separately for talks and argued with, not just once but in many cases three or four times. One by one they had to be isolated from Ian Smith. At the end only David Smith, the dour Finance Minister, remained to be convinced. Lord Carrington called him in alone to his room and urged him to swing his vote against his namesake. It took the Foreign Secretary over an hour. Then Muzorewa put the constitutional proposals to the vote and carried them with only one dissentient. Ian Smith flew home to appeal to the Rhodesian military but they had been squared by Sir Antony Duff behind his back and stayed loyal to Muzorewa.

Next to be convinced were Nkomo and Mugabe who strongly resented the proposal to have 20 seats out of the 100 in the new parliament reserved for whites. The African nationalists denounced it as racist. Their nine-page draft provided for an American-style executive president with supreme command of the armed forces and not a constitutional one as in the British plan which had authority vested in an elected prime minister. The objections to reserved seats for minorities were countered by Robin Renwick listing the other countries which made special provisions – an object lesson on the value of doing one's homework. They included India, New Zealand, Switzerland, and Tanzania. He enabled Lord Carrington to clinch his case by having a constitutional safeguard making it necessary for the whites to collect a further ten votes in order to meet the requirement of thirty votes to block changes. President Machel put pressure on Mugabe and the constitutional proposals were accepted after a fourteen-day deadlock.

The biggest clash over the constitution centred on land compensation. Nkomo and Mugabe told Lord Carrington at a private session that the land issue was vital and the conference could break down over it. With three-quarters of the land in the hands of only 6,000 people in the white population of 230,000, the Patriotic Front leaders were adamant that there had to be changes after the guerrilla forces returned home to claim their reward. But Lord Carrington insisted that the constitution contain guarantees of proper payment for land compulsorily acquired. Chapter V Section 3 of the Declaration of Rights in the constitution stipulated that compensation for loss of land 'will, within a reasonable time, be remittable to any country outside Zimbabwe, free from any deduction, tax or charge in respect of its remission'. Lord Carrington said that all independence constitutions drafted by British lawyers had such a provision written into them. Mugabe was emphatic: 'I don't care how many constitutions you've put this into. This time you'll have to do without it. I'm going into a situation where three-quarters of the land has been usurped. If the new Government is to survive some of this land has to be given back to the people.' He stood his ground on disowning any financial obligation: 'The principle is that we cannot be expected to compensate those who have dispossessed our people without paying for the land. The British were responsible for their people going there. It is up to them to compensate their kith and kin.' Mugabe and Nkomo left Lancaster House fuming.

The clash coincided with the arrival in London of Rhodesia's military supremo General Peter Walls and the Police Chief Peter Allun on 14 October. They were concerned that no concessions should be made on the security aspects for implementing the constitution. But it suited Lord Carrington's strategy to have them hovering as if their presence confirmed suspicions that he might turn to the 'second option' of a deal with the Muzorewa Government. Mugabe was determined not to be browbeaten. He would not budge. Nor would Lord Carrington. The deadlock required outside intervention – and to Lord Carrington's chagrin it had to come from two outsiders he wanted to isolate from the negotiations.

President Kaunda was anxious that the Lusaka Declaration for a Rhodesian settlement should not founder. Each day he telephoned two people for a report on the situation at Lancaster House: Sonny Ramphal and Zambia's observer at the conference, Mark Chona, known as Kaunda's Kissinger. When President Kaunda realized the seriousness of the crisis over the land he urged Sonny Ramphal and Mark Chona to move in quickly to resolve it. Both agreed that there was only one person to come to the rescue: America's President Jimmy Carter. Mark Chona laid the problem before the US liaison officer covering the conference, Gibb Lampher, at the American Embassy in London. Sonny Ramphal was very friendly with US Ambassador Kingman Brewster who had told him on the opening day of the Lancaster House meetings that if they ever came to a crunch he should drive straight to the Embassy. So Sonny Ramphal went directly from Mugabe to Kingman Brewster and told him: 'This is the crunch.'

He explained that Lord Carrington's problem was not really of his own making: the Conservative Party would be furious if he failed to get guarantees for the white farmers and their land. Mugabe could not deny his people land. But he could only buy it if he had money. Sonny Ramphal's solution was for President Carter to make a generous gesture and offer to underwrite a commitment for compensation in the new constitution. No one knew what that figure would be. Some estimates put it as high as £300m. It was decided not to mention any figures to Washington. Kingman Brewster agreed to put the proposition directly to Cyrus Vance, the US Secretary of State. The cause seemed a good one to Cyrus Vance. He undertook to win over the President. That he did, but then ran into a Congressional problem: how to get authorization for American taxpayers' money to be used to buy out white settlers in Rhodesia. But President Carter found a way to circumvent that. He suggested that the new Zimbabwe Government should create a Land Development Fund and the US Government could make a contribution to it. That solved the problem. Mugabe went back to Lancaster House and agreed to the constitution.

No one could have been more relieved than Lord Carrington –

although he did not raise a glass to the two intermediaries. He was thankful at not having to face the wrath of the right-wing Tories who had hounded him only the previous week at the party conference in Blackpool. On his way to the conference hall on 10 October he saw posters outside the building giving their verdict on his work at Lancaster House: 'Hang Carrington'. Leading the right wing in the debate, the former Foreign Office minister Julian Amery challenged Lord Carrington to end sanctions. There was no justification for continuing them and 'punishing the whole Rhodesian people'. Lord Carrington was attacked as 'the unacceptable face of Toryism' by Ian Wallace, a young Tory from Tynemouth. He urged Lord Carrington to stop sitting with 'those evil murdering bastards, the Patriotic Front'. But Lord Carrington's speech silenced his critics. He struck a high moral tone – an unusual posture for him and a clear indication of how worried he was. His mission at Lancaster House, he told the party, was directed at achieving a settlement in the best interests of all Rhodesians, black and white, and if successful would redound to the credit of the Conservative Government. The Tory faithful showed as ever how much they love a lord and sent him back to Lancaster House with an overwhelming vote of confidence.

He needed all the support he could get because he was soon faced with another major hurdle. Again, it required a great deal of concerted pressure on Muzorewa in order to overcome it. Lord Carrington realized that a well-balanced constitution was not enough. There had to be stability to ensure that it was implemented fairly in the transitional period between a ceasefire and the elections for the first government taking the country to independence. That was where trouble had hit other countries, so Lord Carrington had his team draft proposals to prevent it happening this time. He summoned a plenary session on 22 October and delivered a thirteen-point plan. The key provision was in Article 6 with the appointment of a British Governor who would have full executive and legislative authority. Joshua Nkomo could not believe it: 'Will he have white plumes and a horse?' he joked. 'If you send us a man with a cocked hat, we'll find a white charger for him,' he promised. But the serious aspect quickly sank in round the table: it meant that Bishop Muzorewa had to hand over his powers voluntarily and stand down.

It proved an extremely difficult exercise in persuasion even for an expert at massaging egos such as Lord Carrington. After a few days, however, it was made somewhat simpler by the Patriotic Front. They tabled radical counter-proposals which called for a four-man Governing Council – including Nkomo and Mugabe – to have executive authority during the transitional period. As Lord Carrington pointed out to Muzorewa: 'If you have to swallow medicine, mine is easier than Mugabe's.' A flash of inspiration by Sir Robin Renwick helped to make the medicine go down, and make the Patriotic Front let the crisis subside. The Foreign Office was asked to suggest a suitable candidate for Governor. The name that came up was Sir John Paul, an experienced administrator who had served in Commonwealth countries. But Sir Robin Renwick recalled his time in the Paris Embassy when Lord Soames was Ambassador and decided to put his name up to Lord Carrington. The suggestion was greeted with delight. 'Brilliant,' beamed Lord Carrington. He walked over to see his Cabinet colleague, then Lord President of the Council and Leader of the House of Lords, and put the proposition to him. Without a moment's hesitation Lord Soames agreed. No questions about when he should go or for how long. All he wanted to know was who would do the donkey-work day by day as his deputy. When he discovered it was to be Sir Antony Duff he felt more at ease with all that wealth of experience alongside him in facing what had all the makings of a nightmare assignment.

Apart from being at Alamein in the Second World War as a Coldstream Guards officer seconded on liaison duties to the French Foreign Legion (for which he was awarded the Croix de Guerre), Lord Soames had practically no knowledge of Africa. At the time of his appointment he had not met Mugabe, Nkomo, or Smith. But his status as son-in-law of Sir Winston Churchill, his experience as a senior Cabinet minister, a former ambassador, and a former vice-president of the European Commission gave him immense prestige as a charismatic figure presiding over the tempestuous period to independence. When he went out to Rhodesia on 11 December everything was still in the balance with the most critical issue of the entire Lancaster House negotiations, the cease-fire arrangements, still in dispute.

For Mrs Thatcher to give her consent for him to fly to Salisbury at such a time was a considerable political risk. If the situation had been plunged into violence before final agreement, the Prime Minister would have had to take the blame. It was also a measure of her trust in Lord Carrington. She demonstrated that several times during the various crises between the Lusaka conference and Independence Day in Zimbabwe. From the outset Mrs Thatcher made it clear that she would not be a court of appeal for disgruntled delegates at Lancaster House. Apart from occasional receptions, she kept aloof from the participants.

When President Kaunda flew to London on 8 November over the ceasefire crisis, Mrs Thatcher gave him a hearing at No. 10 Downing Street but she refused to negotiate behind Lord Carrington's back. President Kaunda brought a six-point plan for an interim period of four months – instead of the two months set as a maximum by Britain – with a Ceasefire Commission, an Election Council, and joint law-and-order arrangements giving the Patriotic Front equality with the Rhodesian forces. When Carrington became angry over some of the propositions Mrs Thatcher admonished him, saying: 'Fasten your seat belt, Peter.' But she did not appreciate her advice being capped by President Kaunda's Cabinet colleague Reuben Kamanga adding, 'And observe the No Smoking sign.'

Nothing caused more tension over the entire fourteen weeks of negotiations than the poring over maps on the arrangements for a ceasefire. Arguments raged night and day for three weeks on the number of assembly points for the forces engaged in the civil war and where they should be sited. Back and forward between the two sides went Sir Robin Renwick: in the morning with General Walls, and Kenneth Flower, Head of Rhodesian Security; in the afternoon with the Patriotic Front commanders, General Tongogara and General Dumiso Dabengwa. At first General Walls refused to have any guerrilla forces inside the country. He wanted them withdrawn across the borders to Zambia and Mozambique.

The British game plan for the ceasefire was to set a date for stopping the movement of forces into Rhodesia and have a complete cessation of hostilities by midnight seven days later. That gave the Patriotic Front only one week to move their forces into designated assembly points. Mugabe insisted that that was impossible and demanded six weeks because of the difficulties of communicating with scattered units in the bush. After a long wrangle Tongogara admitted that he could get orders through to everyone in three days and the deadline could be met. But although Nkomo was ready to agree to terms, Mugabe stalked out. After disappearing to Tanzania for four days, Mugabe returned to London and said he would take his case to the United Nations in New York.

Lord Carrington, frustrated by his deadlines being ignored, agreed to allocate an extra assembly point, making a total of sixteen for the Patriotic Front, provided the corralling of forces was completed in seven days. By this stage Mozambique's President Samora Machel ran out of patience with Mugabe's manoeuvrings. He believed Mugabe had done well in getting the terms for elections that could enable him to win and should settle for the deal on the table. President Machel was assured that the British Government would not cheat Mugabe out of power if he gained victory at the elections. He was convinced that he had to intervene and stop Mugabe taking a plane to New York. President Machel instructed his London envoy Fernando Honwana, who had been a very influential adviser throughout the negotiations at Lancaster House, to deliver an ultimatum to the Patriotic Front: accept the ceasefire arrangements or your barracks and bases will be shut down in Mozambique – and instead of a headquarters, Comrade Mugabe, you will have to be content with a villa in Maputo.

At noon on Friday 21 December, Robert Mugabe picked up the silver pen on the table at Lancaster House to sign the agreement which bound everyone to 'renounce the use of force for political objectives' and undertake to 'accept the outcome of the elections'. It was a proud moment for Lord Carrington. Mrs Thatcher made no attempt to steal the limelight as she did when she took over from Sir Geoffrey Howe after his laborious negotiations on Hong Kong and signed the Joint Declaration in Peking in 1984. She sat unostentatiously off-stage as Lord Carrington and Sir Ian Gilmour signed for the British Government, applauding what was being recorded as British conference diplomacy at its best. In his final speech as conference chairman, Lord Carrington stressed that there was a 'difficult period ahead', knowing that there would be moments of crisis for all signatories. He made it clear to everyone that the Governor in Salisbury was empowered to take all necessary action to ensure that the agreement they had all signed was properly upheld.

He felt it necessary to issue a final warning: 'No party or group could expect to take part in elections if it continued the war or systematically to break the ceasefire and to practise widespread intimidation.' But both he and Lord Soames realized that to ban Robert Mugabe's party from taking part – as they were urged to do several times by white Rhodesians – would destroy what they had so painstakingly achieved during the fourteen weeks at Lancaster House. They would sacrifice all prospect of international recognition for an independent Zimbabwe if the front-runner in the election campaign were to be disqualified.

The final phase of the game plan – for which Lord Carrington sent out his two key players, Sir Robin Renwick and Sir Nicholas Fenn, to work alongside Lord Soames and Sir Antony Duff – had two vital objectives. First of all, Lord Soames had to act as if he were quite prepared to disqualify candidates or even a party for unbridled intimidation or any other electoral malpractice. If that determination did not seem credible his authority would be lost from the outset of the campaign. Secondly, he had to prevent the whites from backing out of the agreement. With rumours of plots and preparations for coups swirling round Government House every day, Lord Soames had to keep his nerve and appear ready to clamp down on every defiance of his authority.

His toughness was demonstrated when he disqualified one of Mugabe's fiery lieutenants, Enos Nkala, and forbade his party from holding meetings in two areas. Three days before the elections began on 27 February, when intimidation seemed to be getting out of hand in the Victoria area, Lord Soames summoned Robert Mugabe to come alone to see him. The Patriotic Front leader feared he was about to have his entire list of candidates disqualified. He asked to bring his senior party aides with him. The message came back: 'The Governor wants to see you alone.'

For over an hour they sat alone, getting to know one another in a way that amazed people on both sides afterwards. The old Etonian graduate from the Royal Military College, Sandhurst, struck a secret deal with the Marxist prison graduate. Lord Soames told him: 'Get your forces under control and keep them from committing excesses between now and the time the polls close on 29 February. If you come out the winner at the election I will not deny you the victory. I shall call on you to form a Government and I shall help you to establish yourself as Zimbabwe's first Prime Minister.' He thrust his hand forward to shake Robert Mugabe's and told him: 'Let bygones be bygones.' Until then Robert Mugabe had conducted his campaign as the man of the people whom the British were determined to prevent at all costs from holding power. That meeting, in the eyes of those close to both participants, marked a significant chapter in the story of the handover of power without the bloodbath some eyewitnesses feared.

Problems on the other side were just as serious for Lord Soames. Difficulties arose with the Selous Scouts, the crack unit of white and black Government troops. A number of explosions were organized to look like the work of Nkomo's men intimidating Mugabe's supporters but no proof was ever produced to incriminate the Selous Scouts conclusively. One of the difficulties for Lord Soames on security questions was that he and General Walls could not get on. They hardly spoke to each other unless a matter of protocol required them to be in a discussion together. It was left to Sir Antony Duff and Sir Robin Renwick to tackle problems with General Walls. Often Renwick was assigned as mediator since he played tennis regularly with the General.

At one stage, when Muzorewa realized that the election was going to finish him politically, he thought the only way to stop a landslide was for him and Ian Smith to appeal to Lord Soames for a postponement. They wanted the election deferred on the grounds that there was too much harassment to permit a fair result. When this ploy came to the notice of Sir Antony Duff he sent Sir Robin Renwick to General Walls to stamp on the idea. The weakness of Smith's position was illustrated when General Walls and Ken Flower made it clear to the leaders of the former

Zimbabwe–Rhodesia Government that they could not support the move and the appeal was abandoned.

Another task for Sir Antony Duff was to get the South Africans to pull out their men and equipment after the Commonwealth Monitoring Force completed Operation Agilla, the supervision of the guerrilla forces being marshalled into assembly points. Under Major-General John Acland the small force of 850 men from Britain, Australia, Fiji, Kenya, and New Zealand rounded up 22,000 guerrillas with only two casualties incurred – two soldiers killed in a car crash. The South African exodus was not achieved as smoothly. They kept delaying their withdrawal and held on to military posts in the Beitbridge area for a long time. It took Sir Antony Duff two trips to Pretoria and meetings with both President P. W. Botha and Foreign Minister Pik Botha before authorization was given for the last phase of the withdrawal to be completed on 30 January.

As long as the South Africans were present, the hardliners among the white Rhodesians thought there was always the option of one last military stand against the tide of African nationalism. Even when the South Africans had gone, there were two scares that the whites would not abide by the verdict of the polling booths. Twenty-four hours after the voting ended, it became known that Robert Mugabe had won a landslide victory. Before the final results were announced – Mugabe 57 seats, Nkomo 20 and Muzorewa 3 – General Walls sent a message to Mrs Thatcher calling on her to declare the election invalid and appoint an interim Council of Ministers. The Prime Minister did not reply to his message. Instead, she instructed Sir Antony Duff to inform the General that the country must abide by the results of the elections.

That did not end the crisis. The whiff of a military coup in preparation became increasingly pungent at Combined Operations Headquarters. Emergency meetings were held throughout the weekend before the announcement of the results planned for Tuesday, 4 March. Ian Smith would have nothing to do with them: being a rebel once was enough for him. General Walls was not in the planning group. Its organizers included some brigadiers and a senior air force officer. They summoned Sir Antony Duff and Sir Robin Renwick for what became a tense and highly emotional meeting. They were in no doubt after the first ten minutes that the threat of a military takeover was genuine, not just vague talk at the Officers' Mess.

General Walls hovered round the anguished discussions, with the other officers urging him to lead them and the two emissaries from Government House calling on him not to plunge the country into more bloodshed. It was touch-and-go for a long time. General Walls seemed to lean to one side, then the other. Attempts to make Ian Smith change his mind were rebuffed. The meeting was adjourned. Anxious talks took place at Government House late into the night. Duff and Renwick returned to Combined Operations Headquarters on the Sunday for another round. They tried every argument they could think of, including the lesson of the Algerian coup in April 1961 which resulted in the coup leader, General Raoul Salan, being sentenced to life imprisonment. In the end it was the decision of General Walls to stay loyal which ended the crisis.

Immediately the results were announced, as planned, on Tuesday 4 March, Lord Soames invited Robert Mugabe to Government House and asked him to form a government. Their stiff formal relationship which existed throughout the election campaign was totally transformed. Robert Mugabe was so impressed with the outcome of Britain's conference diplomacy that he turned to Lord Soames as his mentor. The Governor's first question was: 'When do you want me to leave: tomorrow or next week?' The new Prime Minister seemed taken aback: 'No, No. You must stay for six months.' They struck a deal. Lord Soames agreed to remain for six weeks.

Sir Antony Duff was called in to join them in celebrating. He wanted to know why Robert Mugabe did not want to be rid of the British team right away. The answer from Mugabe showed his shrewdness. He admitted he was surprised by the sudden change: 'We never thought you would send for me and hand over power so quickly. There are two reasons why Lord Soames is important to us. First, my men have never had any experience in running a government department. We need help. Secondly, I am not going to pass up the chance of having advice from someone who has been a senior member of the British Cabinet going back to 1960.'

They agreed to meet and have long talks alone twice a week until Independence Day on 18 April when the Rev. Canaan Banana became President. Lord Carrington flew to Salisbury with the Prince of Wales for the last chapter of the labours at Lancaster House. He returned two years later with the Government's independence gift, a finely crafted symbol in silver of Zimbabwe's historic aspirations to nationhood. In making the presentation, Lord Carrington gave Robert Mugabe a word of encouragement: 'Keep it shining bright' – and handed him a tin of 'Silvo' polish.

No other minister since then has had to undertake such intensive conference diplomacy over a long period. The Hong Kong negotiations with China stretching for over a year until agreement in the Joint Declaration of 1984 were conducted by senior officials in Peking. Where ministers are regularly engaged in conference diplomacy is at European Community summits. These European Councils rarely last more than a day and a half but they require the same degree of careful preparation as was undertaken for the Lancaster House conference.

The principal figures whose negotiating tactics often determine the outcome are not inside the conference chamber. Each of the twelve nations at the summit has only two places at the negotiating table, one for the Head of Government, the other for the Foreign Secretary. But behind them in the delegation suite are the *éminences grises* – in Britain's case the Ambassador to the European Community in Brussels. From the Battle of the Budget begun by Mrs Thatcher in 1979 to the special summits on European Union started in 1991, Britain had three outstanding ambassadors as tactical advisers to the Prime Minister: Sir Michael Butler, Sir David Hannay, and Sir John Kerr. They sent a stream of 4,500 telegrams a year to Downing Street – plus as many faxes – assessing each new development in the Community affecting Britain. There is a strict rule on 'same-day reporting'. The account of a meeting must be sent to the Foreign Office immediately it ends. If it lasts until 3 a.m. the Embassy representative has to give a full report to London before going to bed – and that applies to the Ambassador as well. His assessment, his knowledge of the system and how it can best be used to serve Britain's interests are of crucial importance to the Prime Minister and the Foreign Secretary at summits.

Final preparations have to be left until almost the last minute because of the strange practice of allowing the Presidency, which rotates every six months in alphabetical order round the twelve members, to decide the agenda. The Presidency often waits until two or three weeks before the summit to give the broad outline of the issues which have to be addressed. Although the host President usually tours all the capitals and gets each government's views on current priorities, it is not until four or five days beforehand that he sends out a letter to the participants setting out the precise order of business. That informs them what is to be discussed at the opening session, what questions have to be tackled over dinner by heads of government, and which other issues have to be discussed by foreign ministers at their separate dinner.

Before then the British Ambassador has usually signposted the problems ahead and the arguments to be faced from other governments. Sir David Hannay made a practice of flying to London every Friday for a review at the Cabinet Office of the situation in the Community. He kept in close touch with the Community expert at the Foreign Office, Sir John Kerr, who succeeded him in Brussels in September 1990. That meant ten to fifteen telephone discussions a day between them. During the period when Sir Charles Powell was Mrs Thatcher's right-hand man, Sir David Hannay would have lunch with him three weeks before a summit to go over the main themes for the Prime Minister's attention. The European Commission would prepare papers on issues and circulate them to governments in readiness for discussion at the summit. But Mrs Thatcher had little time for Commission documents. For big issues such as the Structural Fund, the Single European Act, or the reform of the Common Agricultural Policy she preferred to have a teach-in at Downing Street with a small number of senior advisers who knew what she called 'all the nitty-gritty', such as Sir David Hannay and Sir John Kerr. At the summits she did not want hordes of advisers waiting in the delegation room. All she required was a small team who knew the problems inside out.

Conference diplomacy at Community summits requires swift

reaction to changing circumstances since there are twelve groups of mandarins all seeking to outmanoeuvre each other. There is always a lot of scurrying around at the last minute. Officials have to dig up facts and statistics to support a sudden switch in the presentation of a case. Once the meeting begins, the support staff start fretting, not knowing exactly how the discussion is going with the heads of government and foreign ministers locked inside the room. Foreign ministers are expected to take notes but the delegation has to wait for the running record of the debate supplied by the Council Secretariat known as the Antichi – the Ancients. Since that transcript – in French or English – is usually thirty minutes behind the course of the discussion inside the meeting, the ambassadors have to wait until an adjournment or a coffee break for a tactical review with ministers. This system can be very frustrating for the support staff when there is a protracted discussion late into the night in an attempt to resolve differences of view.

The prolonged uncertainty for everyone on the fringes of the summit gives devious mandarins the scope for gamesmanship with the circulation of 'leaks' or 'misleading guidance' in an attempt to influence the outcome of the verbal tug-o'-war inside the Council chamber. Sometimes it is put about by one delegation that it has the support of several others for a particular change of policy, in the hope that it will have a bandwagon effect and bring more supporters aboard. Press briefings are used (none more skilfully – or on occasion more blatantly – than by the British delegation, as will be analysed in Chapter XI) as part of the negotiating process. A tougher stance on a particular issue is projected in the style of an artillery barrage with the objective of softening the opposition. That operation was usually signalled from the British delegation by reports of 'hard pounding', a term that indicated it would be followed by some skirmishing at the negotiating table with Mrs Thatcher dealing out some 'handbagging' to those opposing her and mopping up the last pockets of resistance.

Other forms of conference diplomacy where there is no clearly defined objective for British interests tend to become damage-limitation exercises. The scenario presented to ministers is based on a simple hypothesis: if there is no glory in it for Britain, at least there should be no risk of Britain suffering a backlash from the failed expectations of others. That governed the tactics for the British delegation at refugee conferences in Geneva. There was no hope of getting international approval for Britain to go ahead with forcible repatriation of Vietnamese boat people from Hong Kong, even though the colony's camps were crammed with illegal entrants. Appeals for international action brought no response even when the flood of arrivals reached 1,000 a day and pushed the total in camps to over 40,000.

The Americans insisted on an open-door policy towards the Vietnamese escaping from the Communist system despite their own tough controls on Mexicans trying to enter the United States. All that British officials could do was to establish evidence of the real motives of the boat people through a screening process. Statistics showed that nine out of ten Vietnamese were not political refugees fleeing persecution but economic migrants seeking the chance of a better life in a capitalist society. One of the last moves made by Sir Geoffrey Howe at the Foreign Office was to arraign Vietnam's Foreign Minister Nguyen Co Thach for conniving at the export of his country's surplus population by not stopping the boat people from becoming a heavy burden on Hong Kong. As long as the US Government opposed mandatory repatriation until there was 'an improvement in Vietnam's economic, social, and political life', the Hanoi Government could get away with ignoring pressure and pleas from Britain. But it did not solve the British dilemma since the Chinese made it clear that they counted on Britain to have all refugees out of the colony by the time it was handed over in 1997.

Hong Kong's refugee problem, however intractable it seemed in the early 1990s, had at least some elements of predictability about it. There was the deadline of 1997 set for the political transformation of the colony. It allowed time to prepare for that eventuality and hold conferences to discuss the implications over a wide range of issues. Most exercises in conference diplomacy are set up with enough advance notice to enable them to be adequately prepared. But there are occasions when diplomatic incidents occur suddenly out of the blue. There is no point in thumbing through *Satow's Guide to Diplomatic Practice*. Such events are usually without precedent. There are no rules to follow, no guidelines. They require all the skills of diplomatic improvisation, sound judgement, steady nerves – and a measure of luck.

VII

Diplomatic Incidents

Major-General Haldu Hananiya checked his watch as he stepped
into his car at the Nigerian High Commission in Northumberland
Avenue on Thursday, 5 July 1984. It was 12.25 p.m. He had an
appointment, his first important one since he had arrived in London as High Commissioner on 31 May. He had to be punctual.
He was the guest of honour at a luncheon given by Malcolm
Rifkind, Minister of State at the Foreign Office.

Another Nigerian in London, Umaru Dikko, the former Transport Minister who was wanted in Lagos on charges of corruption
running into many millions of dollars, also checked his watch. It was
12.25 p.m. He had an appointment, too. He had promised to give
an interview to Elisabethe Ohene for the magazine *Talking Drums*.
He left his house in Porchester Terrace in Bayswater to walk there.

At 12.26 p.m. Major-General Hananiya was being driven past
Trafalgar Square to keep his appointment. At 12.26 p.m. Umaru
Dikko was seized by three men and bundled into a van. He never
kept his appointment. The General had seen to that. He had set up
the kidnapping. He had introduced a Nigerian Major, Mohammed
Yùsufu, as a diplomat to three Israelis at the High Commission

with the instructions: 'We are going to send Umaru Dikko home.'

What followed was an extraordinary diplomatic incident which came to be known as the Dikko Affair. It had all the ingredients of a paperback thriller, except that no fiction writer would have allowed a plot to be so badly handled. No one planning to kidnap Nigeria's most wanted man and smuggle him out of the country would normally choose the day on which the British Government was hosting a welcoming lunch for Nigeria's newly arrived High Commissioner. Relations with Britain had been uneasy since the overthrow of President Shehu Shagari and the installation of the military regime of Major-General Muhammad Buhari six months earlier. The Foreign Office had been eager to restore good relations. There was over £1bn of two-way trade at stake. The strong Nigerian connection was symbolized by the presence of 70,000 Nigerians in Britain. The kidnap drama forced a series of difficult decisions on the British Government which resulted in the expulsion of Nigerian diplomats and strained relations between the two countries for many months. Like most unpredictable events it had a momentum all its own. No training programme for diplomats has a course on how to deal with diplomatic incidents. They have to be played by ear.

The kidnappers who manacled and gagged Dikko transferred him to another van in Regent's Park. By the time they reached Stansted Airport Dikko was drugged and unconscious lying in a crate with an electrocardiogram monitor and two intravenous drips attached to his body. An Israeli doctor, Lev-Arie Shapiro, was alongside Dikko as his minder in the crate. A second, smaller crate of 4 feet by 4 feet had two other Israelis crouching inside: Alexander Barek, the ringleader, and Felix Abithol, his assistant. The crates – specially made by carpenters in Clapham for Yusufu who drew £500 from the Nigerian High Commission to pay for them – were to have been loaded onto a Nigerian Airways Boeing 707 cargo plane. But a Customs officer, Charles Morrow, became suspicious at seeing the crates addressed to the Ministry of External Affairs in Lagos being given a send-off by several diplomats from the Nigerian High Commission.

Not only was General Hananiya's timing wrong, he made the mistake of sending an attaché called Okan Edet, who was ignorant of diplomatic practice, to the airport. Edet did not use the term 'diplomatic bags' which ensures immunity from search under Article 27 of the Geneva Convention. He produced labels in red ink marked 'diplomatic baggage' which is not guaranteed total immunity from search under Article 36 of the Geneva Convention. Baggage can be searched if there are serious grounds for suspecting that it contains anything other than personal baggage belonging to an accredited diplomat or his family. That strengthened the suspicions already aroused. A call by Customs officers to check with the Foreign Office if there were any political reasons for a search not to be made paved the way for action.

Hananiya's biggest mistake was to underestimate the speed at which Commander Bill Hucklesby, the head of Scotland Yard's Anti-Terrorist Squad, would move to prevent the Nigerian Airways plane taking off with its extra cargo. Dikko's English secretary, Elizabeth Hayes, had watched him leave for the interview. Immediately she realized he had been abducted she telephoned Scotland Yard. Before Hananiya took his first bite of smoked salmon at the Rifkind luncheon, Commander Hucklesby had been alerted. He cancelled his lunch at the Gay Hussar in Soho and swung Scotland Yard's C-13 branch into action. He issued an 'All Ports Warning' to have any suspicious cargo held. Then he rushed with his anti-terrorist team to Dikko's house in Porchester Terrace. After talking to the secretary Elizabeth Hayes he was convinced that the kidnappers were heading for Stansted. His hunch was quickly proved correct when his team confirmed that a Nigerian Airways plane was waiting there. By the time the crates arrived at four o'clock Commander Hucklesby's team were at Stansted, ready to pounce. Hananiya was summoned to Stansted to see what was discovered when the crates were opened.

On the following day Sir Geoffrey Howe carpeted Hananiya at the Foreign Office. The High Commissioner denied any knowledge of the kidnap plot and refused to allow the police to question any member of the Nigerian High Commission. Two diplomats – the bungling Edet and Counsellor Peter Oyedele – were ordered out of the country. Hananiya said he was being recalled to Lagos for consultations. Sir Geoffrey said it would be 'inappropriate' if he returned. The Nigerians retaliated by stating that it would be equally inappropriate if Sir Hamilton Whyte, who had been Britain's High Commissioner for only six months and was in no way involved in the Dikko Affair, remained in Lagos. Subsequently at the Central Criminal Court Yusufu, who did not have diplomatic immunity, was sentenced to twelve years' imprisonment, the Israeli organizer got fourteen years in jail and his two accomplices ten years. But relations between the two countries remained tetchy for a long time, with Nigeria demanding the extradition of Dikko. The diplomatic incident also chilled relations between Britain and Israel. Even though there were denials of any direct involvement by Mossad, Israel's special operations intelligence organization, the 'fingerprints' on the organization of the Dikko kidnap were enough to convince British Intelligence of the Israeli connection.

Even more drastic consequences occurred after a British diplomat was kidnapped in Teheran in May 1987. The diplomatic incident escalated to the point where the Foreign Office withdrew its entire embassy staff of nineteen diplomats from Iran and the Iranians were left with one solitary diplomat in London. It began 3,500 miles from Teheran in Manchester on the afternoon of Saturday, 9 May, when police were summoned to the Arndale Centre to investigate a shoplifting incident. A 29-year-old man was accused of stealing a purse from C. & A. and a few pairs of socks from Burton's and Mothercare. As the total value of the goods was £7.75 there were some people at the Foreign Office who subsequently wished that the shoplifting accusations had been quietly dropped that afternoon. For the person accused of the theft was the Iranian Vice-Consul in Manchester, Ahmed Ghassemi. It was assumed in London that when he claimed diplomatic immunity that was the end of the incident.

Manchester police released Ghassemi but instructed him to report to 'A' Division headquarters in Bootle Street on Tuesday, 26 May. By then enquiries at the Foreign Office would have established that Ghassemi was who he said he was and that diplomatic relations with Khomeini's Islamic fundamentalist regime required handling with great care. However, when Ghassemi did not report to Bootle Street the police went looking for him. Ghassemi's car was spotted on the morning of Thursday, 28 May. The police gave chase. After a struggle Ghassemi was in police custody again, this time facing charges of reckless driving and assaulting a police officer.

Then the drama switched from the streets of Manchester to Avenue Ferdowsi in Teheran where Britain's No. 2 at the Embassy, Edward Chaplin, set out to drive home. With him in his Range Rover were his wife Nicola, their three-year-old daughter Stephanie and baby son Thomas. In the back seats were Annick Kershaw, wife of the Second Secretary, and her one-year-old daughter Gabrielle. Just after Chaplin overtook a large station wagon on Modaress Avenue it raced ahead of him and rammed the Range Rover into the side of the road. Chaplin, a fluent Farsi speaker, leapt out to complain about the damage. In seconds he was surrounded by six armed men from the station wagon. When they started attacking him, the 6 foot 6 inch diplomat fought back, while his wife and children watched terrified. The German Ambassador, Dr Armin Freitag, who was passing in his car, stopped and tried to rescue Chaplin. But he was hurled back. Chaplin was overpowered and driven off in the station wagon. A 'Flash' telegram from the Chargé d'Affaires Christopher MacRae reported the kidnapping to the Foreign Office. Back in England, Iran's Chargé d'Affaires Akhundzadeh Basti was summoned before Foreign Office Minister Timothy Renton for an angry session lasting ninety minutes. Instead of expressing regret for the assault on Edward Chaplin, Basti said that charges would be preferred against him. Ignoring protests over the attack, he went on to complain about the treatment of his Vice-Consul in Manchester. There, the police had planned to keep Ghassemi overnight in the cells before bringing him into court. But following consultations with the Foreign Office at six o'clock, they arranged a special hearing in No. 8 Magistrates' Court. After fifteen minutes in court, Ghassemi was released on bail.

In Teheran Edward Chaplin was kept in custody at the revolutionary guards' headquarters. Twenty-four hours after he had been seized, Chaplin was released. He was dumped out of a car a mile from his home and left to walk back to his wife. But he remained a virtual prisoner in his house with the threat of drug charges hanging over him. Sir Geoffrey Howe warned the Iranians not to bring any trumped-up charges against an innocent diplomat who had immunity. The charges against Ghassemi were dropped but Sir Geoffrey expelled him along with four other Iranians and closed the consulate in Manchester. When the Iranians backed down over Edward Chaplin and allowed him to leave Teheran, Sir Geoffrey imposed a diplomatic freeze to end the Chaplin Affair. Stopping short of a complete break, he expelled fifteen of the remaining sixteen Iranian diplomats and ruled that each side should be confined to one diplomatic representative.

For Edward Chaplin the ordeal was mercifully short. For Sir Geoffrey Jackson, the British Ambassador to Uruguay who was kidnapped by Tupamaros urban guerrillas, there was the agony of solitary confinement, most of it in underground dungeons, for almost nine months. After he was ambushed in his official Daimler on 8 January 1971 on his way to the embassy in Montevideo Sir Geoffrey was virtually a forgotten man, left to survive by his own indomitable spirit. The Foreign Office ruled out any deal to secure his freedom. While that was accepted as an inevitable consequence of the Government's policy not to pay ransom, many of his friends thought it was hard for his wife Evelyn to be left anxiously waiting without any attempt to contact his captors. There was strong discouragement in Whitehall of any publicity to highlight the plight of 'The Forgotten Man' on the grounds that it might stiffen the resolve of his captors to avoid being seen to give way to pressure from abroad. That policy turned out to be totally misguided. Sir Geoffrey Jackson's release on 9 September was the outcome of a decision by the Tupamaros and owed nothing to any Foreign Office intervention. Yet he emerged from captivity without a drop of malice towards anyone.

However traumatic such violent incidents are, they rarely leave their mark for a long time on diplomatic relations. Incidents liable to have lengthy, damaging repercussions are those involving matters of high policy. By far the most damaging are those between normally friendly nations. In recent years tensions have arisen more frequently to disturb the *entente cordiale* than any other partnership cherished by Britain. Angry exchanges over lorryloads of English lambs being attacked in France or immigration officers causing trouble for visitors from Britain with Commonwealth passports rippled the surface from time to time. But two major diplomatic incidents involving France left a legacy of ill-will and suspicion: the 'Soames Affair' and the 'Chalfont Affair'.

The first was the consequence of a lunch on 4 February 1969 at the Elysée Palace in Paris between President Charles de Gaulle and the new British Ambassador, Sir Christopher Soames. The Labour Government had set great store on the appointment of such a distinguished political figure to the British Embassy. After two vetoes from France had blocked Britain's entry into the European Community, the son-in-law of de Gaulle's wartime ally Churchill was considered the ideal person to make a fresh start. The thoughts of the General on what he described as 'Britain's movement towards continental Europe' in the course of over an hour were deemed by Soames to be political dynamite.

What de Gaulle was suggesting was a really radical new start. He had no liking for the Common Market, an institution he had had no part in creating. He wanted to scrap it and create in its place a looser organization, an enlarged European Economic Association. Expressing his traditional dislike of American domination, he held forth a vision of a truly independent Europe which would have no need for NATO. To begin with, he thought there should be secret talks between Britain and France to work out how this independent Europe would be established. His idea was for an Inner Council of France, Britain, Germany, and Italy to direct the European Economic Association. But he wanted the suggestion of a meeting to come from the British side and he would then concur.

These ideas were so important that Soames did not dash them off in a telegram that afternoon to the Foreign Office. He set them down with extreme care, added his own evaluation, and slept on it just to make sure he had the proper perspective before dispatching his telegram to London on Wednesday, 5 February. He was so anxious to be accurate that he took a rare step for an ambassador. He went back to the Elysée Palace on 6 February and handed a copy of his version to Bernard Tricot, the President's Secretary-General, for it to be verified. When the response came back on 8 February from Foreign Minister Michel Debré, he was assured it was accurate.

At the Foreign Office in London the Soames telegram landed

like a bombshell. It posed two problems: what to make of the General's ideas and how to handle the situation they created. A meeting was convened at once. It was attended by Foreign Secretary Michael Stewart, the Permanent Under-Secretary Sir Denis Greenhill, Deputy Under-Secretary Patrick Hancock, and the Head of the European Economic Integration Department John Robinson. Since it was Sir Denis Greenhill's first week as PUS he let the two experts Hancock and Robinson, known as the Office's 'Euro-fanatics', take over. Why Michael Stewart did not call over Soames for consultations in London on an issue of this importance baffled many observers. Some speculated that Soames was stopped from coming since he would have urged a cautious, but positive, approach with an attempt to explore the General's ideas.

The verdict of the Foreign Office experts was that this was a monstrous de Gaulle trap devised, as one diplomat put it, 'to enable him to have his British cake and eat it'. They believed that the General had contrived such a situation so that he could benefit from acceptance or rejection of his suggestions unless the British Government acted with great diplomatic dexterity. If the British went along with de Gaulle's ideas, it would greatly strengthen his hand in loosening the Community structure. If the British refused to fall in line, he could claim it demonstrated that they were not really interested in becoming part of continental Europe, preferring their 'special relationship' with America. Either way, they were trapped as anti-Market or anti-European. What was required was nimble diplomatic footwork and that was singularly lacking in Downing Street at that time.

There was no immediate attempt to seize back the initiative. That could have been done by a holding response to de Gaulle indicating interest in his thinking, enquiring if he had informed his five Common Market partners of it, and if so seeking clarification of his ideas. On Thursday, 6 February, both Michael Stewart and Foreign Office Minister Lord Chalfont were in Luxembourg with France's Jean de Lipkowski at a meeting of the Western European Union but no reference was made to de Gaulle's suggestions. Michael Stewart was not as interested in European matters as George Brown had been and his attention seemed distracted by the Nigeria–Biafra situation. His first step was to consult Prime Minister Harold Wilson who was due to visit the West German Chancellor, Kurt Kiesinger, in Bonn. Wilson was advised by his Private Secretary Michael Palliser, who had interpreted for him two years previously at his meeting with de Gaulle, that he could not have talks in Bonn without mentioning the General's suggestions. Palliser also stressed that Wilson could not speak to Kiesinger about these ideas without first advising the French President. Diplomatic protocol required him to give de Gaulle the opportunity to object. If he were to do so, then Wilson would be in a position to put de Gaulle on the spot by suggesting a joint Anglo-French approach to Kiesinger.

Stewart returned from No. 10 Downing Street to tell his Foreign Office team that Wilson was not convinced of the need to raise the matter in Bonn and that they must 'sort it out' with the Prime Minister on the way there. Wilson was always slow to reach decisions and did not want to do anything to jeopardize relations with de Gaulle. That resulted in the Prime Minister flying to Bonn on 11 February for two days of talks without sending any message to de Gaulle as he had still not made up his mind. On the plane Hancock and Robinson argued that it would greatly discredit the Government to be seen conspiring with de Gaulle about some vague new ideas for an independent Europe when Britain was still aiming at full membership of the Community. It was not the time to be concerned about de Gaulle's susceptibilities on not being consulted since he was not worried about Britain being put in an awkward position. Further discussions late into the night in Bonn ended with Wilson still vacillating. He went to bed telling the Foreign Office team to draft some speaking notes on the subject and he would decide whether to use them when he met Kiesinger.

That encounter went badly. The Foreign Office team's brief was much longer and stronger than Wilson expected. He tried to water it down as he delivered his account of Britain's approach to the Community. It sounded like waffling and became more confusing for Kiesinger in translation into German. Wilson endeavoured to retrieve the situation by getting Kiesinger to agree to a joint statement pledging themselves to 'work out together with other European Governments the means by which a new impetus can be given to the political unity of Europe'. His problems were compounded by the Foreign Office sending telegrams conveying the full speaking notes – not the watered-down version – to British embassies in the other Community countries to inform these governments of the Wilson–Kiesinger talks. Angry at the muddled meeting, Wilson flew back to London saying he would never have Patrick Hancock travel with him again.

Only after Wilson had spoken to Kiesinger was Soames instructed to seek a meeting with Michel Debré. He was kept waiting until the evening of 12 February. He then told Debré the British Government was ready for talks with the French but totally rejected de Gaulle's views on NATO. His disclosure that Britain had informed European governments of the proposals and Wilson's discussion of them with Kiesinger infuriated the French. The French were highly critical of the British version to their partners, using the word *directoire*. There was no official note-taker at the lunchtime meeting on 4 February, however, and de Gaulle was not in the habit of making a written record after his meetings. So the French relied, ironically, on the English version submitted by Soames to Tricot and that did not mention the word 'directorate'.

As a mark of the sudden chilling in relations with Britain, the French refused to attend a meeting of the Western European Union convened by Michael Stewart in London on 14 February. Three days later President de Gaulle ordered his London Ambassador, Geoffroy de Courcel, to boycott WEU council meetings until further notice. Significantly, the same day – Monday, 17 February – Reuters' Chief Diplomatic Correspondent, Mohsin Ali, a highly esteemed journalist with very good contacts, heard from sources in Paris that there was a row brewing over a lunchtime meeting between de Gaulle and Soames. Although the Foreign Office refused even to confirm that the meeting had taken place, the enquiry alerted them to prepare a contingency plan for leaking their version to the Italian newspaper *Il Messaggero* before any French leak. That project was dropped when senior officials convinced themselves that the storm would blow over. Mohsin Ali was convinced it would not and kept warning the Foreign Office that it was only a matter of time before the French spilled the beans.

Alarm bells began to ring in the Foreign Office on Friday, 21 February, when reports came in that the French version of the Soames Affair was running in the Paris newspapers *Figaro* and *France-Soir*. That was the signal for the Foreign Office to mount the counter-attack. One of the mandarins was exultant: 'We've got the bastards at last.' Sir Robin Haydon, the Foreign Secretary's chief spokesman, summoned selected correspondents for an off-the-record briefing. Long extracts from the 'Secret' telegram beginning 'General de Gaulle spoke to our Ambassador in Paris two weeks ago' were read out. It resulted in an international furore with headlines like 'De Gaulle's Secret Offer: Scrap Six'. The French tried to wriggle out of the dock by claiming it was a false version: 'The idea of a four-power directorate imposing its will on the small countries of Europe is so manifestly contrary to all that the French Government has always expressed on the necessity of independence of every people that it does not even merit a denial.'

For the first time since sending his famous telegram to the Foreign Office, Soames was called back to London for consultations. He arrived on Sunday, 23 February, before the Government faced challenges in the Commons over its clumsy handling of the affair. By then it was too late to search for excuses. Stewart's problems were increased when Soames was summoned on his return to Paris by Hervé Alphand, Secretary-General at the French Foreign Office. He was handed a strong protest at the way the Foreign Office had 'distorted' the President's observations. Stewart justified the Government's action on the grounds that the first public versions of the de Gaulle suggestions had been published in Paris: 'We, therefore, corrected these accounts.' He defended the disclosure to the other European governments, saying: 'It would not have been right to put ourselves in a position where we were in any sense to ask permission to inform our allies.'

It left Soames embittered, although his shrewd precaution of having his version of events verified at the Elysée absolved him from any personal responsibility for the crisis named after him. Wilson was annoyed at the setback to his hopes of better relations with de Gaulle, blaming everyone but himself and singling out the Foreign Office particularly for its perverse pleasure in scoring what he described as 'purely procedural victories'. His Press Secretary

Joe Haines gave his angry verdict afterwards in *The Politics of Power*. He said: 'At one stroke, the senior diplomats behind the move had destroyed any hope of Britain negotiating to enter Europe while General de Gaulle was still in power.' But the consequences of the Soames Affair were not as serious as they might have been. De Gaulle resigned on 28 April after losing a referendum and was succeeded by Georges Pompidou. That enabled Soames to make a fresh start and re-establish his credentials as a good European. It was not so easy for the British Government. Doubts about its real intentions lingered for a long time in the minds of French ministers.

Suspicions of Perfidious Albion were nurtured by the other notorious diplomatic incident of the Wilson era which soured the atmosphere between the two governments, the Chalfont Affair. It arose from what began as a mundane review of 'Britain's approach to Europe' given by Lord Chalfont as Foreign Office Minister of State to correspondents in his suite at Room 109 of the Beau Rivage Hotel in Lausanne on Thursday, 26 October 1967. It blew up into a storm across the front pages of the newspapers about the Government being ready to turn its back on Europe if France barred Britain from the Common Market. It brought calls for the Minister's dismissal, angry clashes in Parliament, and dismay among Britain's allies in Europe.

That such a controversy should have centred on Lord Chalfont was ironic. Before becoming a minister he was a highly respected professional journalist. Having been military correspondent of *The Times*, he added to his reputation by his self-assurance on tele-vision. It was assumed that he was well-equipped to 'handle the Press' when he arrived in Lausanne for a routine meeting of the European Free Trade Association together with Anthony Cros-land, President of the Board of Trade. The occasion was invested with a certain piquancy since it followed some abrasive comments by France's Foreign Minister Maurice Couve de Murville on the role of sterling and Britain's balance of payments problems which appeared to signal another French veto on Britain's application for membership of the Community. Those comments were capped by Wilson telling political correspondents at Westminster that France's intransigence could lead to EFTA being 'strengthened'.

When Anthony Crosland was asked on his arrival at Lausanne about what might happen if the French did veto Britain's application, he was shrewd enough to decline answering a hypothetical question – but not Lord Chalfont when he arrived at Room 109 at 6.15 p.m. He apologized for keeping correspondents waiting so close to their first edition deadlines – again an indication that he had not forgotten the pressures of his old profession – and talked at great length.

There had been considerable speculation about what sort of cards would be left for Britain if de Gaulle said 'No'. The percipient London correspondent of *Le Monde*, Alain Jacob, had written the day after Couve de Murville's hints in Luxembourg of another veto that there could be 'a new look' in London towards Europe. He posed the question: 'Has the Labour Government not already consented to heavy sacrifices to maintain sizeable forces in Germany in order to preclude being accused of undermining the Atlantic commitment in Europe?' In this tantalizing situation the correspondents in Room 109 were anxious to discover from Lord Chalfont whether the cards in Wilson's hands were really genuine or merely bluff.

He did not need any prompting. He listed four possible consequences of a French veto: abandonment of joint Anglo-French projects, withdrawal of Britain's 55,000-strong Rhine Army, the suspension of Britain's commitment to defend West Berlin, and the review of NATO obligations leading, if necessary, to a refusal to renew the treaty in two years' time after the statutory period of twenty years. These options were set out voluntarily by Lord Chalfont himself. It left experienced journalists bewildered that such a crude form of blackmail should be contemplated by a minister. Lord Chalfont was asked if this was merely his own personal assessment of the situation. He bridled. Why was he late? He had come straight from the PM, he retorted. Although this was technically a briefing which 'had not taken place' (the comments were not for quotation, and nothing was attributable to the Minister), there was no doubt that Chalfont wanted his views conveyed to the public – and not just the British public. When the *Daily Mirror* correspondent expressed his disbelief, Lord Chalfont told him if he did not believe it, not to write it.

The session broke up in considerable confusion just before the buffet supper at the hotel. Around the serve-yourself tables the correspondents twice resumed their debate with Lord Chalfont in an attempt to clarify various points. In a final attempt to 'get the story straight' he agreed to resume the briefing in Room 109 after supper at 11.45 p.m. He was specifically asked whether the French and the Germans had been made aware of what action the Government was considering if Britain's membership of the Market were blocked. He gave an unequivocal Yes. On two occasions he was given the opportunity to retract what he had said or modify some of the propositions he had made. Each time he insisted that he was not speaking without authority, which was taken by most people in the room to imply that he had the Prime Minister's approval.

By the time every opportunity to pick holes in the scenario set out by Lord Chalfont had been exhausted, it was too late to get a story into the last editions of the newspapers being printed for Friday, 27 October. All correspondents agreed to hold the story over until Saturday's paper, not to mention Lord Chalfont, and not to use Lausanne as the dateline. But there was no collusion as to an agreed 'story line' and when it broke there was pandemonium. Under the banner 'The Rumour that Shook Europe Last Night', the front page of the *Daily Mirror* revealed: 'A story reached the *Daily Mirror* from Europe last night that Prime Minister Harold Wilson is prepared to throw overboard all our European commitments if Britain is kept out of the Common Market.' After listing the four points of the threatened action, it added: 'On high authority the *Mirror* can say that the story is false.' The *Daily Express* carried it as the main story, stating that there was 'a serious split among Ministers' with George Brown at odds with Wilson over the threats.

The Chalfont Affair infuriated the French. Gaullist Party secretary André Fanton denounced it as a crude ploy: 'The British Government should know that neither threats nor manoeuvres of diversion or poisoning, nor vulgar and inferior blackmail are likely to facilitate Britain's entry into the Common Market.' Downing Street instructed the Foreign Office to issue fulsome denials: 'At no time has Lord Chalfont suggested that there was any change of policy, either actual or contemplated. Nor has he suggested that threats about such a change have been made to any country. Nor did he suggest that there was any difference between Ministers on any issue.' The Bonn Government tried to be helpful by denying that they had received any warnings from Britain, but that was taken as a diplomatic tactic in order not to appear being bullied by Britain into supporting its application to join the Common Market.

Prime Minister Wilson decided to lie low all weekend, staying at Chequers and refusing any comment. His spokesman, Henry James, was advised to fend off all suggestions of a reprimand for Chalfont and inform the queue of questioners on the telephone from the Press that the Prime Minister had no intention of seeing Chalfont. When it transpired that there had been a secret meeting between Wilson and Chalfont on the Sunday afternoon, the suspicion hardened that what had been said in Room 109 of the Beau Rivage Hotel was not just something off the top of Chalfont's head. Since Henry James was trusted as a spokesman who never lied to journalists, he insisted on making a statement to the Lobby in Westminster on Monday morning correcting what he had been told by the Prime Minister and confirming that Wilson had met Chalfont on Sunday.

The full fury of the Conservative Opposition was unleashed in the debate on the Address in Reply to the Queen's Speech in Parliament on Thursday, 2 November. In the Lords, the suggestion that it was all a misunderstanding was ruled out by Lord Carrington. Headlines that they had seen did not come about 'unless there was some substance of truth behind the story'. He warned of the dangers of flying kites – a manoeuvre on this occasion which he said had been 'conspicuously damaging and unsuccessful'. In the Commons, Edward Heath said the views were expressed in Lausanne by Lord Chalfont because he wanted them published to help his negotiating position. Instead they damaged it. They played into the hands of the critics who said Britain was not European at heart. His verdict was crushing: 'It was foolish because it is, in fact, an empty threat.' Sir Alec Douglas-Home enjoyed directing his scorn at Wilson himself: 'The damage is not that Socialist Ministers think aloud. It is that when they do, the thoughts they reveal are so awful. Lord Chalfont has offered to resign but the Prime Minister could not accept his resignation. It would be very odd if the pupil had been sacked by the master of the *double entendre*.'

As a strong pro-European, Foreign Secretary George Brown was clearly embarrassed. He took the line that it had been a 'think session' with Lord Chalfont speaking unattributably and off-the-record 'only to find his trust betrayed'. He said: 'Lord Chalfont will draw the lessons from this incident and so will many of us.' Chalfont took it nobly. In the Lords debate he said: 'I do not regard all this as a Press conspiracy or as an anti-Common Market plot. I bear no malice towards anybody involved in this unfortunate affair.' He insisted that Britain's place was in Europe and any alternatives were 'second-best'. The Prime Minister's perform-ance in the Commons was less gracious. He tried to explain it away by saying that Lord Chalfont had been asked a number of hypothetical questions. The Wilson version was: 'Most of the points made in subsequent Press comment came from the Press itself.' It was this clumsily contrived diplomatic incident that enabled de Gaulle to justify France's rejection of Britain's applica-tion for Market membership.

Drastic counter-measures affecting diplomatic and commercial relations with Saudi Arabia were threatened by the *Death of a Prin-cess* incident. It broke in a front-page exclusive in the *Daily Mail* on 10 April 1980 under the headline 'Storm over TV Princess'. It revealed that the Government faced retaliation from Saudi Arabia's King Khaled because of the screening of a dramatized documentary by ATV based on the public execution of the Saudi Princess Misha'al and her lover in 1977 for adultery. What really caused the greatest offence was the mixture of fact and fiction which used material based on gossip to indicate a debauched life-style by girls in the royal family. As the row flared up it put at stake British exports worth £1bn a year, jobs of thousands of Britons in Saudi Arabia, and a large volume of oil imports.

After a series of panic measures by the Foreign Office in an unsuccessful attempt to damp down the tensions, it was argued in Downing Street that this was the sort of diplomatic incident that could not have been avoided. In a free society no government could engage in censorship and forbid the showing of a programme on a commercial television network, the line of argument ran. But much of the heat could have been taken out of the row through sharper and quicker political reflexes by ministers at the Foreign Office. Britain's much respected Ambassador Sir James Craig had to be withdrawn from Saudi Arabia for over three months and the Saudi Embassy in London was left without an ambassador for six months – and neither need necessarily have happened if the incident had been more carefully handled.

Although there were doubts up to the last moment whether the TV film would be screened, it was known for many weeks in advance that film director Antony Thomas had been working on a television documentary about the Saudi execution for a long time. It could have been assumed that if the television programme was based on a reconstruction of such a controversial event then there was a risk of its creating serious problems for relations between Britain and Saudi Arabia. But no action was taken at the Foreign Office until Maundy Thursday, 3 April. Assistant Under-Secretary John Moberley telephoned Ambassador Craig who was on holiday in Paris that a big row was brewing and he was required to be in the Foreign Office on Good Friday for an emergency meeting. Sir Ian Gilmour, Lord Privy Seal and deputy to Lord Carrington, explained that the Saudis had summoned Chargé d'Affaires John Gray and expressed 'deep concern' over the prospect of the ATV documentary being shown. When it was suggested that Sir Ian might use the 'old boy network' to lean on Lord Windlesham, managing director of ATV and a former Lord Privy Seal, that was brusquely rejected on the ground that such an intervention might be leaked to the Press and cause a row over attempted censorship.

No one in the Foreign Office at that stage asked to see the television film in advance of its screening to assess the extent of the offence it would cause to the Saudis. No move was made to propose that the familiar formula of providing the right of reply in a studio debate after the TV film might give a sense of balance that could moderate objections by Moslems. After the meeting on Friday, Ambassador Craig was instructed to abandon his leave and fly back to Saudi Arabia with a message to King Khaled expressing regret that the matter should be causing such concern. When he saw Prince Saud al-Faisal, the sophisticated Foreign Minister, well aware of the ways of the West from his education at Harvard and the London School of Economics, Ambassador Craig stressed that it was impossible to interfere with freedom of expression on television in England. Nonetheless, the Saudi Minister made one further plea that the British Government should be made aware that the Saudi Government counted on something being done to avoid a damaging deterioration in relations.

When the story broke, Lord Carrington was in Lisbon for a Council of Europe meeting. On being asked about the disclosure in the *Daily Mail* he claimed he knew nothing about it. Yet copies of telegrams and submissions on an issue of this importance must have been circulated to his Private Office. Prince Saud al-Faisal's appeal, which was conveyed by Ambassador Craig, was a matter for Cabinet decision. Even if Lord Carrington had not been present, the normal procedure would have been to notify him of the outcome. The Foreign Office admitted on 10 April that as well as a letter from Sir Ian Gilmour to Prince Saud al-Faisal carried by Ambassador Craig on 5 April there was 'a separate message from Lord Carrington to Prince Saud sent by telegram'.

The Downing Street decision that nothing could be done to stop the TV film being shown did not excuse ministers for not seeking a separate TV discussion with experts from the Arab world putting their side of the case. Saudi concern was such that they persuaded a former influential figure from Downing Street to intercede at ATV. They enlisted the help of Sir Philip de Zulueta, Private Secretary to Macmillan and a brother-in-law of Lord Windlesham. He went on Tuesday, 8 April, with Mustafa bin Halim, the London representative of Crown Prince Fahd, and saw parts of the film showing princesses driving around in Cadillacs looking for lovers. The next morning, the day the programme was being shown, they returned to make one last appeal for the film to be withdrawn, or, if not, at least to have the sex scenes excised. Lord Windlesham listened to them for half an hour but rejected their pleas.

Prince Saud al-Faisal summoned Sir James Craig and told him he would have to be withdrawn from his post. It was not presented as a crude reprisal for the decision to do nothing about the TV documentary being screened. The Minister said that in the present circumstances the new Saudi Ambassador, Sheikh Nasser Almanqour, would not be taking up his appointment in London for the time being and therefore it would not be 'symmetrical' for the United Kingdom to have an ambassador in Jedda. Because of his popularity, Sir James was not given the usual forty-eight hours to get out but was told to take his time. As the Saudis wanted him back, they let it be known to the Foreign Office that it would not be wise to post him elsewhere for the time being.

A campaign was launched to heal the breach caused by the documentary which cost £200,000 to make and cost an estimated £200m in lost business to British companies. Admitting somewhat late in the day that the incident could have been handled better, Lord Carrington made some very placatory remarks at a meeting of the Middle East Association which were transmitted on television to Saudi Arabia. Without going so far as to make an apology, he expressed his regrets: 'It was a bad film and I wish it had never been shown.' He sent Minister of State Douglas Hurd on a peace mission to Riyadh in July. A month later Sir James Craig had to cut short his holiday in Scotland and fly back to Saudi Arabia for the final reconciliation in a visit by Lord Carrington. It was agreed to have 'new procedures' to avoid another damaging diplomatic incident – a long overdue joint committee to consult each other on achieving a better understanding of the way of life in each other's country.

Another diplomatic incident involving Saudi Arabia did not have a happy ending. It barred a distinguished British ambassador, Sir Horace Phillips, whom the Foreign Office praised for his 'record of long service in the Arab world', from serving in an Arab country for the rest of his career. For an Arabist who was fifty years old at the time with ten years still to serve it was a severe setback – and through no fault of his. It illustrated, however, how a few lines in a newspaper can arouse the sensitivities of Saudi Arabia's rulers – who take pride in their traditional title 'Keeper of the two Holy Places' – to the point of outrage.

Sir Horace was one of the Foreign Office's rare self-made envoys who forged his way to the top without any Oxbridge qualifications. His Civil Service career began at the age of seventeen as a clerk at the Inland Revenue. After a good military record with the British Army and the Indian Army, he joined the Diplomatic Service in 1947 and became Vice-Consul in Shiraz and Bushire in Iran. By 1968, after a number of postings in the Arab world, he was Ambassador to Indonesia. It was then decided to promote him to the plum post in the Middle East, Ambassador in Saudi Arabia. The Queen gave her approval on 29 January 1968. King Faisal personally gave *agrément* – the diplomatic form of accepting the nomination. With these formalities over, the Foreign Office arranged for Sir Horace's heavy baggage to be sent by sea to Jedda while he went on a brief holiday.

Then out of the blue the Saudi Arabian Ambassador in London, Sheikh Abdulrahman al-Helaissi, called at the Foreign Office to make an unprecedented announcement: King Faisal had withdrawn his *agrément*. The reason: Sir Horace had Jewish origins. That disclosure had been made public in the *Jewish Chronicle* – almost by chance. The newspaper had started a series of articles about British Jews who had risen to high office. A reader in Glasgow wrote to the Editor, William Frankel, pointing out that there was no mention of the Jewish Glaswegian who was Ambassador in Indonesia and was rumoured to be going to Saudi Arabia. The *Jewish Chronicle* followed up the reader's information and published a short report about the former member of the Jewish Boy Scout troop in Glasgow being appointed to Jedda.

It was especially galling for Sir Horace to be deprived of such a prestigious appointment when he had already served in the British Embassy in Saudi Arabia. In his four years there from 1953 to 1956 he had run the Embassy as chargé d'affaires on four occasions in the absence of the ambassador. He had met King Saud and spoken to him in Arabic. Sir Horace, whose Christian wife, Idina, had their son and daughter baptized as Christians, was known by many Saudis to be Jewish. Ironically, one of those Saudis who was aware of that was the ambassador who announced the annulment of the appointment.

The Editor of the *Jewish Chronicle* had no regrets about being instrumental in spoiling Sir Horace's career. 'Our job is to record news,' William Frankel insisted. The Foreign Office was angry at the incident and sorry about its consequences but powerless to challenge the decision which was the royal prerogative of the ruler of Saudi Arabia. It tried to explain that Sir Horace was no longer a practising Jew, claiming that he had abandoned the faith of his mother and father who were emigrants from Eastern Europe. In fact, he remained a member of the Garnethill synagogue in Glasgow. To compensate Sir Horace for the disappointment at being denied the post, the Foreign Office chose him to be the first envoy to restore relations with Tanzania even though it meant bypassing senior political figures on the short-list – Arthur Bottomley and Humphrey Berkeley. Sir Horace ended his career as Ambassador in a Moslem country, Turkey, and was invited back after retirement to run courses in Ankara on diplomacy.

Attitudes towards diplomats, their role in any diplomatic incident, and the personal immunity they are entitled to enjoy have changed in the past few decades. The penalties of being a representative of the British Government are that its enemies do not see the ambassador as a person but as a symbol of what they hate. If he speaks for a government, putting forth the policies of that government whether he is in agreement with them or not, an ambassador is at risk as a target for those who want to overturn those policies. In two tragic cases diplomatic incidents became fatal for the ambassadors: Christopher Ewart-Biggs, who was killed by a bomb which blew up his car only sixteen days after he took up his post in Dublin in 1976, and Sir Richard Sykes, who was shot dead in The Hague in 1979.

VIII

Crisis Diplomacy

> *Foreign Office officials are the butt of many jokes but, whatever their shortcomings, it has been my happy experience that whenever a real emergency does arise they will accept any challenge, however remote from their daily experience, assume great responsibilities, and work tirelessly and with skill.*
>
> Lord Callaghan,
> *Time and Chance*

At four o'clock in the morning of Thursday, 2 August 1990, Rob Young scrambled out of bed, dressed quickly, crept quietly downstairs so as not to disturb his family, and drove to the Foreign Office. As Head of Middle East Department he did not usually have such an early start. He knew he had something big to deal with – and not just for a day or two. An Arabist trained at the Middle East Centre for Arab Studies, Rob Young was well aware that this was more than a diplomatic incident. All night he had been taking telephone calls at home about the invasion of Kuwait by the forces of President Saddam Hussein of Iraq. As soon as he reached his department, he began gathering a team of experts around him. He was consulted by William Waldegrave, the Minister of State, about the line to be taken in a BBC interview at 7.30 a.m. on the *Today* programme. After listening to the interview, he went into conference with Roger Tomkys, the Deputy Under-Secretary, at eight o'clock. Until then it was not officially a crisis.

In Foreign Office terms a crisis exists only when the crisis management team is formally assembled to deal with it in the specially constructed blast-proof basement headquarters of the Emergency Unit. Only one person can authorize this secret section of the Foreign Office to be opened: the Permanent Under-Secretary. Sir Patrick Wright gave the signal and the Gulf Crisis was official.

Crises used to be regarded as an intrusion into the really important business of the Foreign Office and were relegated to the 'backroom boys' in the attic of the building under the sloping roofs of rooms 117–220. All that was provided was a few extra telephones, teleprinters, a television set, tea-making facilities, and an additional noticeboard to mark up urgently required telephone numbers. The team allocated to the crisis had to run up and down two flights of stairs and along three long corridors to consult ministers or the PUS. The attic enclave was where the Cyprus crisis of 1974 was handled, often in great confusion such as when James Callaghan was stranded at 5 a.m. without a car on the morning of the Turkish invasion and had to hail a milk delivery van to get him to Downing Street.

For Douglas Hurd, the crisis management centre in the Emergency Unit was operating with all the high-tech efficiency of sophisticated communications immediately the PUS gave the signal. The nucleus of the team around Rob Young comprised three diplomats from Middle East Department and two members of Defence Department which has the managerial responsibility for the Emergency Unit. Grant Lindsay, a veteran unflappable consular officer, had a staff of 25 available round the clock to take an average of 2,000 telephone calls a day from anxious relatives of the 4,000 Britons in Kuwait and a further 800 in Iraq. Direct telephone lines to other key departments in Whitehall, to British posts in the Middle East, the United Nations, and Washington ensured a continuous flow of information. Situation reports flooded into the crisis management centre at the rate of three million groups of words a day on telegrams. Closed-circuit television enabled twenty people to take part in inter-departmental briefings from the Ministry of Defence, the Cabinet Office, the Home Office, and Transport Department. Unit Manager Peter Whiten ensured comfortable facilities for rest periods – two bedrooms, one for men, the other for women, each with five beds and shower baths. Meals were supplied by the Metropolitan Police across the road in Whitehall three times a day – pre-cooked and ready to be heated in microwave ovens when required.

Logistically, the Foreign Office was well prepared. Politically, it was taken by complete surprise. Neither the politicians nor the mandarins with all their knowledge of the Arab world imagined that Saddam Hussein would actually take over the entire country of Kuwait and do it so quickly. What they heard out of Baghdad in the last week of July they dismissed as sabre-rattling. Even the gloomiest prediction in Whitehall had been merely that the Iraqis might occupy the disputed islands of Bubiyan and Warba and threaten to seize the contested oilfield of Rumeilah. The build-up began with accusations from Saddam Hussein on 17 July that the Gulf States' manoeuvres to cut oil prices were 'stabbing Iraq in the back with a poisoned dagger'. On 22 July President Mubarak of Egypt dismissed the dispute between Iraq and its neighbour as 'a cloud which will soon pass'. Iraq's seriousness was demonstrated on 24 July when Saddam Hussein sent 30,000 troops with tank support to the Kuwaiti border.

At this stage it was seen in London and Washington as a show of force to influence the OPEC meeting assembling in Geneva on 26 July with Iraq demanding a price rise from 18 to 25 dollars a barrel. Douglas Hurd put down a mild diplomatic marker: 'We would deplore any threat or use of force.' President Bush's spokesman, Marlin Fitzwater, chimed in with: 'All disputes should be handled through peaceful means.' There was no emphatic warning to make it clear to Saddam Hussein that the West would not tolerate any aggression against Kuwait. Saddam's demand for £1.3bn as compensation for oil taken by Kuwait from the disputed oilfield was answered with an offer of £700m from Kuwait. Neither that nor the offer at the OPEC meeting of a price rise to 21 dollars a barrel was enough to satisfy Saddam Hussein. The last chance of a settlement ended with Iraq walking out of talks with Kuwait in Jedda on 1 August.

American intelligence assessments from satellite pictures of Iraqi troops massing on the borders were not taken in Washington or London as a serious indication of Saddam Hussein's intentions.

They stayed silent even when there was evidence on 30 July that there were 100,000 Iraqi troops with 300 tanks massing just across the border from Kuwait. Equally calamitous, Saddam Hussein miscalculated the Western will to resist his aggrandizement. His reading of the messages out of Washington was that the Americans would not intervene. He failed to realize the international outrage his invasion would arouse. He believed the opposition would fade away in days.

In one respect his calculations were correct when he first moved his troops to the Kuwaiti border. Saddam Hussein behaved with a boldness born of the conviction that the Americans would be hesitant about invoking anger in the Arab world by any counteraction with a show of force. Knowing the divisions within the Arab League, Saddam Hussein calculated that the Americans would be reluctant to issue high-profile warnings which could provoke accusations of unwarranted US interference in Arab affairs. America's slow initial response until the actual invasion and the slow build-up of forces afterwards gave Saddam Hussein time to consider a number of options. In the end he chose the wrong one: to stay until he was forced out of Kuwait.

His challenge posed immediate problems and a number of rapidly evolving ones. Rob Young, straight back from leave on 27 July, had a full-scale exercise in crisis management to organize on 2 August and keep going for months. Two top priorities got immediate attention. Britain's UN Ambassador, Sir Crispin Tickell, marshalled all his efforts in the Security Council for a quick resolution. Having played a major role in securing agreement on the ceasefire resolution ending the eight-year Iran–Iraq war, Sir Crispin urged the need for sustaining that solidarity among the five Permanent Members in standing against Saddam Hussein's aggression.

In a matter of a few hours the Security Council passed Resolution 660 by fourteen votes to nil with only Yemen abstaining. It called for complete withdrawal of Iraqi forces from Kuwait unconditionally and the restoration of the legitimate government. The next priority was the call from the Kuwaitis that all assets dispersed internationally should be frozen. To organize the necessary action on a Friday morning before the City closed for the weekend, an inter-departmental meeting under the chairmanship of Roger Tomkys brought together representatives from the Treasury, the Export Credits Guarantee Department, the Bank of England, the Cabinet Office, and the Department of Trade and Industry. A Treasury order was issued to prevent the Iraqis getting their hands on any Kuwaiti assets.

With the Prime Minister out of the country in Aspen, Colorado, for talks with President Bush which had been arranged before the crisis, Douglas Hurd postponed his departure to Tuscany on a family holiday. He and William Waldegrave set out the guidelines for diplomatic action at a series of briefing meetings in the first twenty-four hours. The pattern of crisis management was established. Rob Young's fourteen-hour day began at 6 a.m., except when an emergency required him to take action at 4 a.m. His deputy, First Secretary Stewart Eldon, recently returned from the UK mission at the UN in New York, was on duty from 11 a.m. until midnight or later depending on developments. The day started with assessing the telegrams and any draft resolution sent overnight from the UK mission in New York. Comments had to be prepared for ministers answering questions on radio or television. Amendments to Security Council drafts and drafts for instructions to Middle East posts had to be worked out for ministers to approve.

Officials at the Emergency Unit had their first in-house meeting at 7.30 a.m. to discuss the day's agenda. Next came an inter-departmental briefing between the Foreign Office, Cabinet Office, and Ministry of Defence. They reviewed the early morning assessment of overnight developments compiled by Len Appleyard as Deputy Secretary to the Cabinet. The first main session of the day started at 8.30 a.m. with representatives from various departments in the Foreign Office – Middle East, Near East, Defence, United Nations, Economic Relations, Information, and News – plus the Cabinet Office and Ministry of Defence. At 9 a.m. Douglas Hurd or his deputy chaired a meeting of experts. These sessions were kept to thirty minutes. A smaller group, including Foreign Office and Defence ministers, under-secretaries, and Rob Young, met at the Cabinet Office at 11 a.m. Throughout the day groups of officials convened on special problems as they arose. A full-scale review of the day was held at 6 p.m. by the same officials who attended the first main session in the morning.

One of the first British objectives was to get all twelve European Community members firmly committed to a total trade embargo against Iraq. As the Political Director was not available, Roger Tomkys flew to Rome for a special EC meeting on Saturday, 4 August. The outcome was that the Community countries were the first to impose economic sanctions against Iraq. Their measures became the basis for Security Council Resolution 661 which was passed on Monday, 6 August, with Cuba and Yemen abstaining. There was a period of high-pressure diplomacy from the US and Britain on Turkey to cut off the pipelines from Iraq. Despite the importance of oil transit revenues and the fact that 60,000 Turkish jobs were at stake, President Turgut Özal gave his assent quickly.

Although Saddam Hussein insisted he had no intention of moving his forces on from Kuwait into Saudi Arabia, that possibility was the chief anxiety in the West for at least ten days after the invasion. It dominated discussions in Downing Street and the Bush–Thatcher talks at Aspen, Colorado. That was the reason why an announcement was rushed out the day after their talks that the US was sending out 4,000 men of the 82nd Airborne Division and F-15 fighters as a 'defensive measure' to Saudi Arabia. Britain became the first European country to send help to the Gulf with a squadron of Tornados and a squadron of Jaguar aircraft. Even as the planes were arriving, there was still concern that Saddam Hussein might strike to take advantage of the relatively thinly defended Saudi border. It was only when the troops took up position at the end of the week after the invasion that it was felt that the window of opportunity for the Iraqis had been closed.

Saddam Hussein's decision on 16 August to make foreigners in Kuwait hostages raised the most agonizing dilemma in human terms throughout the crisis for ministers and officials. The orders from Saddam Hussein were that the 4,000 British men, women, and children should report to the Regent Palace Hotel in Kuwait City. A telegram was sent at once to Ambassador Michael Weston in Kuwait asking for his assessment. The next the Emergency Unit heard was a broadcast on the BBC World Service with advice from the British Embassy which Ambassador Weston felt had to be given as a matter of urgency without waiting for approval from London. It stated that the Iraqis were warning of 'unspecified difficulties' if people did not assemble voluntarily. The British Embassy suggested those choosing to move should take no more than one suitcase each. The American Embassy was giving its nationals the same advice. But there was confusion when the US State Department made it clear that no Americans were going to be told what to do.

At the Foreign Office William Waldegrave was about to face a Press conference. Ideally, he would have liked to delay a response until he had sought clarification from the Iraqis through the British Embassy in Baghdad. But there was not time to get an answer back. In five minutes he had to decide whether to go along with Ambassador Weston's broadcast advice or countermand it and tell Britons to stay at home and ignore the Iraqi instructions. As Ambassador Weston had the advantage of knowing the situation on the spot, the Minister opted for saying that Britons should not offer resistance since there was a clear threat of trouble. In the end, when a number of Britons reported to the hotel, there were no Iraqis to deal with them and they went home. Waldegrave was subjected to severe criticism in the tabloid Press as 'Waldegrave the Wimp'. But the outcry would have been much greater if he had advised Britons to defy the Iraqis and some had been assaulted.

During this early period, there were many telephone calls to the Emergency Unit complaining that the Government was not doing enough to help people to get out of Kuwait. There was criticism that people were not being advised to make an escape across the desert. These views were still being expressed after a 49-year-old Ulsterman, Donald Croskery, had been shot dead by Iraqis while trying to get out by car to Saudi Arabia. Officially, it was impossible for the Foreign Office to advise people to make a dash for the safety of Saudi Arabia. Had that advice been given and other people shot dead, the Government would have faced angry questions in Parliament. The advice which ministers authorized was that any attempt to escape carried risks and it was up to individuals to decide whether to take those risks. Over 200 did so and were successful. Some of them were helped by convoys organized through the Embassy. Convoy leaders were made known to people through the wardens, the British residents who voluntarily keep in touch with other members of the British community. Diplomats from the British Embassy in Riyadh travelled to the Kuwaiti border to help people coming across.

When Britons were rounded up and kept in detention, and men were sent to installations in Iraq as human shields, the criticism of the Government increased. Calls came into the Foreign Office asking for rescue operations to be mounted by commandos from the Special Air Service. There were vociferous demands for the Government to negotiate with Saddam Hussein on hostages even though there was no question of negotiating with him on the withdrawal of his troops from Kuwait. The crisis management team had to repeat the position Mrs Thatcher had set out on 26 August: 'There will be no negotiation with a man who takes over by force someone else's country – except that he gets out completely. You are dealing with a dictator who is an absolute tyrant, who has had a callous charade on television with children.'

The Government's position came under attack as a cavalcade of elderly statesmen went to Baghdad to talk to Saddam Hussein and get their reward in hostages allowed home. Austria's President Kurt Waldheim, Germany's Willy Brandt, and former Prime Minister Edward Heath all helped to make it seem that Saddam Hussein had a case which deserved a hearing. The decision of Saddam Hussein to let all women and children go home did not make Douglas Hurd any more ready to listen. He condemned the tactics of the Iraqi President as 'a cat and mouse game – now a little mercy, now some more ruthlessness'. Even the announcement on 6 December that all foreigners in Iraq and Kuwait were being allowed to leave did not weaken the resolve in London and Washington to have the crisis settled either by Saddam Hussein getting out of Kuwait under the terms of the UN resolutions or by his being forced out.

Twenty-four hours after the deadline of 15 January had passed, with Saddam Hussein still holding on to Kuwait, Operation Desert Storm was launched under the terms of Security Council Resolution 678 which authorized the use of all necessary means to liberate the country. The nerve centre of crisis management shifted to the War Cabinet at No. 10 Downing Street. John Major, who had now replaced Margaret Thatcher as Prime Minister, had let Douglas Hurd chair the Overseas and Defence Committee of the Cabinet in its periodic reviews of the Gulf crisis before the fighting began. But once the course was set for war, John Major took charge. Diplomacy was not entirely set aside. It required considerable diplomatic skill on the part of the Americans and the British to persuade the Israeli Government not to intervene in retaliation for attacks by Iraq with Scud missiles. Immediately the fighting ended there were complex problems over the terms on which the state of war should be ended. It took until 3 April 1991 to get agreement on Security Council Resolution 687 setting out in over 3,700 words the 120-day timetable for establishing a formal cease-fire, with a UN observer force monitoring a buffer zone extending six miles into Iraq and three miles into Kuwait.

Throughout the crisis British diplomatic and military strategy was closely co-ordinated with the Americans who directed the international operations leading up to the conflict and played the predominant role in the liberation campaign. Apart from impatience over the hostage issue there was only one major question which aroused public debate in Britain and divided the parties: economic sanctions against Iraq. A body of left-wing opinion argued strongly against the resort to military force until there had been more time for economic sanctions to exert pressure on Saddam Hussein to withdraw his forces from Kuwait. They won support from many quarters where it was seen as a test case for sanctions.

One anxiety often cited was the prospect of heavy casualties in a prolonged war. London University's Centre for Defence Studies published a booklet called *The Gulf Crisis: Economic Implications* on 16 November 1990 with an extraordinary figure: 'Even if Saddam Hussein were defeated relatively quickly an estimated 60,000 allied troops might be killed.' In fact, in the operations from 16 January until the fighting ceased on 28 February, the total casualties sustained by the 482,000-strong forces from 30 nations were 166 dead and 207 wounded.

The quick end to the fighting and the avoidance of heavy casualties silenced the vast majority of the critics. The speed with which the Foreign Office responded to the crisis after the initial surprise put Britain well ahead of its European partners in diplomatic and military terms. Four weeks after the invasion Mrs Thatcher rebuked her Community partners for their 'slow and patchy' response. France was the only other major European contributor to the ground forces and their troops were not sent to the Gulf until 15 September. Manoeuvres inside the Community for separate talks with Iraq continued until Douglas Hurd blocked them on 18 December. Once the crisis was over, all the problems of finding a peaceful solution to the Arab–Israel dispute in the context of restoring stability to the Middle East returned to challenge the diplomats. But at least the Foreign Office emerged from the crisis with much more credit than it had been accustomed to receive and had a position of influence which previously had seemed to be declining fast.

That outcome was a sharp contrast to the way the Foreign Office shuffled out of the Falklands crisis in 1982, bruised and discredited. The resignation of Lord Carrington, his deputy Humphrey Atkins, and his junior minister Richard Luce immediately after the Argentine invasion began left the Foreign Office reeling, uncertain of itself, for over a year. The three ministers' departure resulted in the complete surrender of the Foreign Office to the Prime Minister for the duration of the crisis. All decisions on crisis management were taken at No. 10 Downing Street where the Prime Minister and her War Cabinet conducted the diplomatic and military campaigns. The Foreign Office was cast as scapegoat for the country being landed with a Falklands crisis.

It was not a new problem which suddenly surfaced when the Conservatives came to power in 1979. The dispute with Argentina over sovereignty of the Falkland Islands was an issue regularly reviewed by successive governments. Michael Stewart sent his Minister of State, Lord Chalfont, to the islands after the royal visit to Chile in 1968. As a result there was a pledge given on 11 December 1968 which became the benchmark for all subsequent ministerial statements: no transfer of sovereignty against the wishes of the people. Another Foreign Office minister, Ted Rowlands, talked to the islanders again in 1977 and reported back on the need for improving co-operation with Argentina. When Lord Carrington looked at his agenda on arriving at the Foreign

Office, one of the first moves he made was to dispatch his Minister of State, Nicholas Ridley, to the Falklands in July 1979. Ridley returned with an assessment of three options: sitting tight and refusing to talk with Argentina; offering talks with Argentina to work out a freeze on sovereignty for a limited period, then negotiations; talks on transferring sovereignty to Argentina with a leaseback arrangement enabling the UK to run the islands for ninety-nine years.

When Nicholas Ridley persuaded Lord Carrington that the only option with any chance of success was leaseback, he in turn put it to the Prime Minister. Her response was described as 'thermonuclear'. To Mrs Thatcher such a course was tantamount to selling the islanders down the river. Nicholas Ridley, however, was not to be shaken off the leaseback idea. Hawking it round the Tory hierarchy he got backing from William Whitelaw and Francis Pym. His persistence was sustained by strong support for leaseback in the Foreign Office. Although the Legislative Council in the Falklands opted for talks with Argentina on freezing sovereignty, Nicholas Ridley returned to Port Stanley in November 1980 in an attempt to make the islanders change their mind. When he reported no progress to the Commons in December he was bitterly attacked by the Tory right wing for undermining Britain's case in international law by even suggesting leaseback. With support from the left wing of the Labour Party, who opposed any dealings with a fascist regime, the backbench Tories forced the Government to suspend quiet diplomacy on the Falklands.

The arrival of General Galtieri on the Argentine political scene and his installation as President on 22 December 1981 changed the atmosphere and served notice that a crisis over the Falklands could not be avoided. How serious the crisis would become was not clear immediately. Some analysts seeking to amplify their case against the Foreign Office for not assessing the gravity of the crisis soon enough have blamed the Ambassador in Buenos Aires, Sir Anthony Williams, for playing down the danger signals. His record as a percipient observer of the Argentine scene gave the lie to such accusations. His first telegram on Galtieri's take-over warned that the President's closest friend was Admiral Anaya, Commander-in-Chief of the Navy, and both were the sort of hawks liable to be tempted into adventurist undertakings. He knew Galtieri well enough to make it clear to him that any resort to force to resolve the Malvinas (Falklands) question would be met by force. When Richard Luce, who took over responsibility for the Falklands from Nicholas Ridley in September 1981, resumed the dialogue with the Argentinians in New York in February 1982 Sir Anthony cautioned the Foreign Office not to be taken in by the superficial cordiality afterwards. He reported that no statement from Galtieri's men could be trusted. They were, in his view, merely biding their time for a showdown when their navy was ready.

Lord Carrington laid himself open to criticism subsequently by thinking that the New York talks had not gone 'too badly' and commenting that there was no reason to be too alarmist about the situation even as late as early March. But the same telegrams from Sir Anthony Williams in Buenos Aires also went to No. 10 Downing Street. Critics of the slowness of Lord Carrington's reaction to the build-up of the crisis could well have pondered why Mrs Thatcher, a voracious reader of telegrams receiving the same cautionary observations from Ambassador Williams, was not able to read the signals from Argentina herself. It was not until 3 March, only a month before the invasion, that the Prime Minister wrote on a telegram from Buenos Aires: 'We must make some contingency plans.'

At least the Foreign Office assessment of the tensions in the area advocated the retention of the survey ship HMS *Endurance* despite the decision of the Defence Secretary John Nott to withdraw it for the sake of saving £3m in the Defence Budget. Lord Carrington sent minutes on 22 January and 17 February to John Nott arguing that removing the *Endurance* would send the wrong signal to Argentina – that Britain was not even prepared to make a show of force. Mrs Thatcher did not support him. She sided with her Defence Secretary in answering a question in the Commons on 9 February. In the event the *Endurance* remained in the area when the crisis was reaching its climax.

It was during the first forty-eight hours of the week beginning Monday, 29 March, that Lord Carrington and his team lost their grip on the crisis. That weekend Mrs Thatcher caught up with the warnings in the telegrams and urged Lord Carrington to set in train the necessary measures to arrest the worsening situation. It was the main topic discussed on their flight to Brussels on 29 March for an EC summit in Brussels. Before leaving, Lord Carrington had sent a message to US Secretary of State Alexander Haig appealing for American pressure on Galtieri as possibly the one remaining factor capable of restraining Argentina's ships which were then on the high seas. A Royal Navy nuclear-powered submarine was on its way to the area and a second one was ordered to join it.

Even the increasing indications of Argentina's naval strength heading in the direction of the Falklands did not make Lord Carrington cancel his arrangements to fly to Israel on a routine visit at the end of the EC summit on Tuesday, 30 March. All he did was to re-route the RAF VC 10 to take him back to London first in order to make a statement in the House of Lords. On his return to the plane he dismissed the episode as 'some nonsense about scrap merchantmen'. He had made a statement warning about the consequences if British sovereignty continued to be violated by a party of thirty-nine workmen led by a scrap merchant dealer, Constantine Davidoff, on South Georgia. He was convinced by intelligence reports that the activities on South Georgia could not have any connection with the moves of the Argentine Navy.

The Argentine crisis took second place to Lord Carrington's preoccupation with the Arab–Israeli crisis over the arrest of the Arab mayors of Ramallah and Nablus. He wanted his Deputy Under-Secretary of State, Sir John Leahy, to help resolve the problem at a private meeting with the mayors. But he was snubbed by the Israelis who ruled out such a meeting. On top of that Lord Carrington was humiliated during a tour of Yad Vashem, the memorial to the victims of the Holocaust. When he stopped to look at a photograph of Neville Chamberlain returning from Munich, his guide from the Israeli Government commented: 'Appeasement 1938 – just like the appeasement of the PLO today.' After talks with Begin, Shamir and Peres he ended his visit with nothing to show for it.

In his absence Mrs Thatcher held a meeting in her room at the House of Commons to review the Falklands crisis for four hours with John Nott, Humphrey Atkins, Sir Michael Palliser as

PUS, and Sir Antony Acland as head of the Joint Intelligence Committee. On his return to London just before midnight on 1 April, it was too late for Lord Carrington to do anything to halt the Argentine Navy. Had he stayed in London on Tuesday instead of going to Israel it is just conceivable that something could have been achieved by calling an emergency meeting of the UN Security Council. According to American intelligence, Galtieri's final decision for the invasion of the Falklands to go ahead was not taken until Wednesday, 31 March.

At a joint Press conference with John Nott in the Foreign Office at 6 p.m. on Friday, Lord Carrington gave his observations on the invasion at dawn that day as if it were an event he never believed would have happened. He seemed surprised to be asked by journalists if he was considering resignation. After the fury unleashed in the extraordinary session of the Commons on the Saturday, when Nott had to take most of the flak since Lord Carrington belonged in the other House, the case for resignation became more compelling. It had the virtue of shielding the Prime Minister from further criticism and making it easier to unite the country. As a loyal party man he decided on that sacrifice despite appeals during the weekend from Mrs Thatcher, supported by Lord Home, Harold Macmillan, and William Whitelaw, for him to stay.

On his resignation on Monday, 5 April, Carrington realized that the Foreign Office would be blamed for what he acknowledged was 'a national humiliation'. He knew that the same signals he saw at the Foreign Office went to the Prime Minister. Yet it was, as usual, the messenger who was found guilty for nothing being done about his message. But before the management of the crisis passed to No. 10 Downing Street, the Foreign Office demonstrated that it was not as slow off the mark as its critics believed. Sir Anthony Parsons, the Ambassador at the UN, was roused before daybreak on Thursday morning with instructions to do his best to have the United Nations Security Council condemn Argentina the moment it invaded the Falklands. No one could have been quicker. He rounded up the necessary nine votes out of fifteen to have the Security Council summoned on 1 April on a matter of 'grave concern' before the invasion. He manoeuvred them into making a call for restraint. Next, he wrote a draft resolution, telling the Foreign Office minister Richard Luce what he was doing but not holding up the proceedings by getting it agreed line by line in London. He had to phrase it delicately so that he procured a demand for Argentina to withdraw its forces but avoided a parallel demand for Britain not to launch a task force.

Once the invasion had occurred, his main task was to avoid a veto by one of the five permanent members. He cleared that with the US, France and China, which with his own UK vote left only Russia. After prolonged discussion – since it was in the days of Gromyko – the Russians agreed to abstain. In the end one vote was needed – Jordan's. The Jordanian delegation sat on the fence, refusing to commit themselves without direct instructions from King Hussein in Amman. Sir Anthony could not wait. He telephoned Mrs Thatcher for help. She picked up the telephone and got through to King Hussein. He gave his vote at once. UN Security Council Resolution 502 was passed calling for the immediate withdrawal of Argentina from the Falklands precisely in the terms drafted by Sir Anthony before the invasion.

If the Government response to the Falklands crisis and the Gulf crisis is sometimes explained – at least partially – by the fact that ministers were taken by surprise at being suddenly confronted with them, that could not be used as an excuse for the way the Rhodesia crisis was handled in 1965. The rebellion of Ian Smith against the Crown by the Unilateral Declaration of Independence on 11 November 1965 was not an event which happened without any warning. It was an event waiting to be triggered off for months. The Rhodesia crisis had dominated the Commonwealth summit conference in London in June, even though Prime Minister Wilson tried to divert attention from it with a proposition for a Commonwealth mission of four prime ministers to solve the Vietnam problem. When Ian Smith left London after fruitless talks in Downing Street on 12 October any hopes of a settlement on anything but his own terms were no longer realistic. His parting comment, 'A vote in an African's hand is more dangerous than a rifle', ended any prospect of negotiating terms for majority rule.

Despite all the signals from Salisbury over several months, Wilson's handling of the crisis was extraordinarily naive for someone so alert to plots and counterplots within his own party. One of his best cards in keeping Smith guessing in the run-up to UDI was squandered when his Commonwealth Secretary, 'Honest' Arthur Bottomley, declared that the Government would never use force against a rebellion in Rhodesia. Wilson knew UDI was inevitable, but he had no clear-cut plan of action on the day to counter it. Instead, he summoned his security expert, Paymaster-General George Wigg, who had a special office inside No. 10 Downing Street next to the locked doors of the Cabinet Office.

Wilson sat puffing his pipe in wonderment at Wigg's 'battle plans'. His first idea was to have a combined army and police operation to storm Rhodesia House in the Strand – at the height of the morning rush hour with hundreds of commuters pouring onto the streets from Charing Cross Station. He planned to have abseilers clamber down the outside of the building, break into the office of the Commissioner, Brigadier Andrew Skeen, and charge him with treason at Bow Street Magistrates' Court. Wigg's next plan was put to Wilson as 'the master-stroke': kidnapping Ian Smith. He worked out a project for a raid on Salisbury by an SAS team. They were to infiltrate Milton Buildings and seize the rebel prime minister. Then the kidnappers would smuggle him over the border into Zambia and fly him back to London to be put on trial as a traitor. Wilson said he needed more time to consider what to do. Two months later, at the emergency Commonwealth summit conference in Lagos, Wilson was still floundering over how to handle the crisis. Ignoring the loopholes in the trade embargo through sanctions-busting by the Portuguese and the South Africans, he was rash enough to prophesy that the crisis would be over in 'weeks rather than months'. It lasted fourteen years.

Crises are usually much shorter than that and often extremely tense, as Mrs Lynda Chalker came to realize on Tuesday, 5 April 1988. It began as a quiet day at the Foreign Office, the first day after the Easter holiday. Parliament was in recess. Mrs Thatcher was setting out for an official visit to Turkey. Sir Geoffrey Howe had left London on Easter Monday for the Far East and was in Malaysia. As Minister of State and deputy to the Foreign Secretary, Mrs Chalker was in charge of the Office. One word shattered the calm: Hijack. The message flashed to London informed her that hijackers had taken control of flight KU 422, a Kuwait Airways Boeing 747 on its way from Bangkok to Kuwait.

It was timed precisely for the moment when radio links were weakest between the airspace monitored and controlled by Bombay and Muscat. The next information to reach London was that the plane with ninety-seven passengers and a crew of fifteen was in the hands of Arab extremists who demanded the release of seventeen militants imprisoned in Kuwait for terrorist activity. The first priority at the Foreign Office was to establish whether there were any British nationals aboard and if so how many. Ambassador Derek Tonkin in Bangkok was fortunate. Bangkok Airport authorities, unlike many others, still keep records of passengers' nationalities on each flight. He reported that there were twenty-two Britons aboard.

Mrs Chalker called in the PUS, Sir Patrick Wright, and the chief counter-terrorism expert, Ivor Roberts, Head of Security Co-ordination Department, to her room to assess their action programme. The PUS formally authorized the opening of the seven-room crisis management centre at six o'clock. It was the first time it had become operational. Mrs Chalker stayed in the bunker night and day except for a brief break for sleep between 2 a.m. and 6 a.m. From the RAF VC 10 Mrs Thatcher on her way to Turkey had instant communication with the crisis management centre. Sir Geoffrey Howe kept in touch from Kuala Lumpur by telephone and telegrams from the British High Commission. The Government's standard position on terrorism was reaffirmed: no concessions, no deals to get nationals released.

Two complications arose on the first day. The hijackers forced the pilot into Iranian airspace and secured permission for an emergency landing at Mashad, a holy city 500 miles east of Teheran close to the Soviet border. Following the row over the Chaplin kidnapping in May 1987, Britain's interests in Iran were handled by the Swedish Ambassador. But the Iranians refused to let him send anyone to the scene in Mashad. So the Foreign Office had no direct contact. The second problem was that the hijackers had an extra lever to press home their demands: the presence on the plane of three members of the Kuwaiti ruling family. The hijackers forced one of them, 34-year-old Fadil al-Sabah, to read from the

Koran over the plane's radio and to appeal for the release of the seventeen convicted prisoners in Kuwait. He and his two sisters, Anwar and Ibtissam Khaled al-Sabah, were stated to be 'in imminent danger' unless the demands were met.

Twenty-four hours after the plane had been hijacked, the gunmen suddenly freed 22 women, including 10 Britons. On the following day, Thursday 7 April, the hijackers released 32 more passengers, including the remaining 12 British men. But the drama did not end there for the Foreign Office crisis team. Iran agreed to refuel the plane. It took off for Beirut on Friday, 8 April, and had to circle the Lebanese capital for four hours with the airport refusing landing rights and the runways blocked. The Cyprus Government lifted its ban and allowed the plane to land at Larnaca Airport in the evening. As a new President only six weeks in office, George Vassiliou had a very inexperienced Cabinet to deal with an international crisis. He turned to the Foreign Office for advice. Mrs Chalker sent out David Ratford, an assistant under-secretary who knew the area well.

The crisis management team at the Foreign Office set out the three options: to storm the plane and overwhelm the gunmen; to refuse refuelling and sit tight; and to give the hijackers fuel and let an Arab country resolve what was basically an Arab problem. In contacts between Mrs Chalker and the Kuwaiti Government she was assured that they were firmly opposed to making any concessions and were against the plane being refuelled. Cyprus Interior Minister Christodoulos Veniamin remembered what had happened in 1986 when Pakistan's security forces stormed a Pan-Am jet at Karachi to dislodge the hijackers. The shoot-out left 21 dead and over 100 wounded. In Beirut the pro-Iranian Islamic Jihad movement threatened to kill Western hostages if the plane was stormed. Veniamin ruled that saving lives was the first priority and vetoed any commando raid on the plane. Mrs Chalker urged him to take the second option and deny the plane any fuel. It was argued that the only way to contain the crisis was to keep the plane in Cyprus and not pass on the problem to another government.

Intense diplomatic pressure was mounted on the Cyprus Foreign Minister, George Iacovou, not to yield to the hijackers' demands. Messages from London urged him to keep the plane on the ground at all costs. But Veniamin, watching the drama in Larnaca, was anxious not to have any more blood shed on Cyprus soil. His fears increased when the hijackers warned that they would start killing passengers if fuel was denied to them. They demonstrated their seriousness by dumping the body of a Kuwaiti on the tarmac on Monday, 11 April. The Cypriots refuelled the plane the next day. Twelve hostages were released. After the plane left for Algeria, Veniamin said he had been assured that the other passengers would be set free in Algeria. In fact, the threats of killing passengers continued for several days after the plane stopped at Algiers on Wednesday, 13 April. The hijackers asked for more fuel on Saturday, 16 April, to leave the country because they said they did not want a massacre in Algeria. The crisis ended four days later through Algerian mediation with all passengers safely evacuated.

Downing Street often cites the firmness of the Foreign Office crisis management team throughout the hijack drama as a model for dealing with terrorists. But there were many political observers who questioned whether the policy was the right one for dealing with the other type of hostage crisis involving men held captive for years in the Lebanon. From the day the Archbishop of Canterbury's special envoy Terry Waite was kidnapped in Beirut on 20 January 1987 until his release in November 1991 there was a constant search by the Foreign Office for ways of securing his release. The same concern was shown for ending the ordeals of journalist John McCarthy and ex-RAF pilot Jackie Mann. A succession of ambassadors in Beirut – John Gray, Allan Ramsay, and David Tatham – tried to track down every clue about them no matter how unlikely the report was. The Iranians, whose influence with the Hezbollah in the Lebanon was acknowledged to carry great weight, were repeatedly urged to intercede.

From the outset, however, the Government was adamant that. there would be no deals with terrorists and no ransom paid under any guise. The moment you indicate a readiness to negotiate on hostages, it was argued in Downing Street, is the time when you put at risk every other Briton in the Middle East who can be used as a pawn in further negotiations. In theory, it was the only honourable course. But as other nations, such as the French and the Germans, who put their names to EC declarations outlawing concessions to terrorists, made backdoor arrangements for their nationals to be freed, Britain's stubborn stand on principle came under increasing criticism. There were people with long experience of working in the Middle East who claimed that the Foreign Office could have been more active in making contact with Islamic fundamentalist leaders. They believed more use could have been made of well-known Arabists, not in government service, to travel as unofficial envoys and talk to some of the shadowy figures behind the kidnappers. During the Thatcher years it was difficult for anyone in an official position to deviate from her total opposition to any contacts with those regarded as even remotely connected with terrorism. But this inflexibility provoked criticism from many quarters that the traditional Foreign Office skills of bending the rules were not being discreetly employed. It perplexed many people that the Foreign Office, so renowned for its expertise in the Arab world from the time of the Sykes–Picot agreement of May 1916 which gave Britain a sphere of influence over Mesopotamia, could not have enlisted the help of its Arab friends at an early stage to end the ordeal of the hostages.

IX

Spies and Diplomacy

*The Russians knew that we knew exactly what
was happening and yet they kept on piling in
new agents. They reckoned that we would not
dare to face the public outcry of rooting them
out.*

Lord Home,
The Way the Wind Blows

*Even if relations between the governments of
East and West improve, Soviet intelligence operations will not be reduced. Intelligence work and
relations between states are totally independent
of one another and it is a great mistake to confuse
them. So the KGB and GRU will go on sending
their officers abroad in the guise of diplomats
and journalists and Western Governments will
go on expecting them.*

Ilya Dzhirkvelov, *Secret Servant*

Espionage is as old as diplomacy. Spies have been at work as long
as diplomats, long before Lenin's Polish comrade Felix Dzerzhinsky established his training school in Moscow's Lubianka Prison
for what eventually became known by the dreaded three initials
KGB (*Komitet Gosudarstvennoi Bezopasnosti*, or Committee of State
Security). In the eighteenth century, the employment of spies was
considered a basic requirement for any embassy to be able to
function properly. An ambassador was expected to provide
intelligence to his government on a wide range of matters. He

had to be well-informed not merely on the military strength of the country where he was serving but on the persons rising or declining in the favour of the monarch. He was also required to provide an assessment of what action the king's advisers might recommend in certain circumstances. Such intelligence-gathering could not normally be carried out without the resources of well-informed spies. They had to be richly recompensed but usually through an intermediary since an ambassador would want to be able to deny any direct involvement in case a spy tried to double-cross him.

Spies and diplomats operate in the same environment. There are those who would argue that a good ambassador functions as an efficient spy. That view is upheld by the eminent French diplomatist, François de Callières, whose famous book *De la manière de négocier avec les souverains* published in 1716 is still studied by aspiring diplomats. In describing the duties of a diplomat, he said: 'An Ambassador is called an honourable Spy because one of his principal occupations is to discover the secrets of the Court where he is situated and he acquits himself badly in his job if he does not know how to make the necessary payments to reward those who are appropriate to inform him of them.' Callières advised diplomats in England to keep in touch with Members of Parliament as good sources of information and recommended entertaining them well since they would talk more freely with good food and wine. He also thought it profitable to cultivate 'disgruntled courtiers' since men who were denied advancement were often tempted into indiscretions. It was important not to stay secluded in the embassy but to get out into the streets and become aware of the habits and customs of the people. Hasty judgements were to be avoided, however. That advice went unheeded, apparently, by the German Chancellor Konrad Adenauer on his only visit to Moscow. After his return he told his ministers that the Soviet economy was facing serious problems. When he was asked why, the Chancellor said it was because of the declining birth rate. How did he know that? He revealed that looking out of his car taking him through Moscow from one meeting to another he never once saw a woman wheeling a baby in a pushchair.

Observations in Moscow's Red Square are no longer a guide to what is happening in military terms. Western military attachés acting as 'honourable spies' at Soviet military parades in the 1950s and 1960s eagerly scrutinized the march-past to evaluate anything new in weapons and machines. Since the advent of the high-tech age in defence systems there is nothing of any interest to spies in the parades. Even in the escorted visits to military manoeuvres or installations in Communist countries, Western diplomats find there is little shown to them that is not already known. Technical advances have to be tracked down by other means. Communist military attachés have never baulked at behaving like burglars in Britain. In September 1988, three Czech attachés were expelled from their London Embassy after a break-in at the Farnborough Air Show. A ten-foot wall was scaled in order to photograph an American fighter pilot's helmet with an Eagle Eye device, a top-secret system enabling installations to be targeted with split-second accuracy. As frequently happened, the Czechs, who worked for StB (Statni Bezpecnost), the Czech Security Service, were operating on behalf of the KGB.

The intensity of Soviet espionage reached unprecedented levels in Britain when Moscow realized how much leeway they had to make up to match Western technology in many sectors, industrial as well as military. It led to the most extraordinary spy scandal being exposed by Lord Home on his return to the Foreign Office for his second term in 1970. How to handle it caused a row among Cabinet ministers which was hushed up at the time. Lord Home had strong suspicions that the Russians were abusing their diplomatic cover in an alarming way. To check on the extent of the Soviet spying he called in the Head of MI5, Sir Martin Furnival Jones. The security chief handed over a dossier which made riveting reading for the Foreign Secretary. In fifteen years the number of Soviet 'officials' working in Britain had quadrupled to 550. The heaviest concentration was at the Soviet Trade Delegation in Highgate, north London, which had added 60 'experts' to its staff in the previous two years, bringing its total strength to over 200. On top of that they had a rotating number of over 50 KGB 'commuters' from Moscow. The Russians had been obliged to withdraw 27 members of the Trade Delegation over the previous ten years.

Forty visa applications had been refused because the Russians tried to replace them with known KGB agents.

Lord Home was determined to have those he called Russia's 'nasties' cleared out of the country regardless of the rumpus it might cause. Under Article 9 of the Vienna Convention on Diplomatic Relations of 1961, a state may notify another state that a member of its mission is not acceptable without having to give a reason or make a public statement. After consultation with his PUS, Sir Denis Greenhill, Home decided to give a full explanation for taking action but to do it by quiet diplomacy. Although the veteran Soviet Foreign Minister Andrei Gromyko was a wily operator, normally well-informed across the entire spectrum of East–West relations, Lord Home believed it was just possible that the KGB had not disclosed the extent of their activities in Britain to the Minister.

He put the situation directly to Gromyko during an official visit to London on 28 October 1970. Whilst Gromyko had a good grasp of English, Lord Home took particular care to spell out the gravity of the problem, knowing that every word would be subsequently transcribed and studied since the Russians made tape-recordings of all discussions in their Embassy. He made it clear that he was prepared to allow the Russians six months to withdraw their KGB agents quietly. When his warning went unheeded he instructed Sir Denis Greenhill to take the matter up with Vice-Minister Kozyrev. Again, there was no response from the Russians.

Lord Home decided to give Gromyko more time but to set out a fresh warning in writing on 4 December 1970. In it he highlighted the concern at Soviet intelligence operations creating a serious obstacle to improved Anglo-Soviet relations. To give Gromyko an opportunity to dissociate himself from the abuses, he suggested that the competent Soviet authorities – he stopped short of identifying the KGB – could supply full information about the 'inadmissible activities' conducted from the Soviet Trade Delegation in Highgate. As an indication of what was in the MI5 dossier, Lord Home stated: 'They have included the running of agents, instruction in the use of clandestine techniques, the offer and payment of considerable sums of money to persons resident in this country either to suborn them or to secure their help in obtaining classified information (both official and commercial) or commodities subject to embargo or other restrictions.'

Not even that plain speaking produced any reaction. So Lord Home sent Sir Denis Greenhill to Moscow for talks with Gromyko and Kozyrev. This time they did react, accusing the 'British Special Services' of engaging in hostile and provocative activities against Soviet citizens and legitimate Soviet organizations in the United Kingdom. Kozyrev claimed that Anglo-Soviet relations were being damaged not only by these actions but by British authorities trapping Soviet citizens into defecting and seeking asylum in England. In spite of the Soviet bluster, Lord Home thought it worthwhile to give Gromyko one last chance to take action over the 'activities incompatible with the status of diplomats' and withdraw the offenders voluntarily.

A second letter from Lord Home to Gromyko on 4 August 1971 urged the Russians to think again and immediately end the abuses. He told Gromyko that if he were to list only those offenders whose activities had become known publicly in recent years it would be a long list. There were many more cases which were very serious and which, he insisted, were known to Gromyko. One in particular was gratuitously offensive. The Russians had applied at the British Embassy in Moscow for a visa for Boris Glushchenko as they were nominating him as a First Secretary at the Soviet Embassy in London. As they must have known his record would be checked, it was bewildering to MI5 that the Russians imagined that Glushchenko would slip through the espionage checknet.

Glushchenko had been in London from 1964 until 1968 under the guise of sales representative for Aviaexport at the Soviet Trade Delegation. He was such a clumsy KGB agent that he got himself into the British security files for trying to bribe the wrong person for details about military equipment. Lord Home expressed astonishment at the Russians' behaviour and answered Kozyrev's complaints to Sir Denis Greenhill by assuring Gromyko that any Soviet citizen who asked to stay in Britain and then decided to return to the Soviet Union would be free to do so. After waiting a month without a reply, Lord Home believed he had been patient long enough. Having given quiet diplomacy a year, he decided that the Russians would have to be publicly exposed with all offending officials being ordered to leave the country within fourteen days.

Before clearing the decision with his Cabinet colleagues, Lord Home asked Sir Martin Furnival Jones to give him a complete list of all the officials to be expelled. Back came an MI5 roll-call of offending KGB agents ten pages long. No one could have been more surprised than Lord Home and Sir Denis Greenhill. They stared at the list in disbelief. They knew that the espionage operations had been massive by any previous standards and the expulsions would go into the record books as the largest in one clear-out of spies. But they imagined that the list would have around 50 names on it. Instead there were 105 names: 90 officials currently living in Britain plus a further 15 who had gone back to Moscow temporarily. Until that dossier was drawn up, the occasional expulsions of Russian diplomats and denials of visas had been treated in Moscow as mere pinpricks. They had retaliated automatically by expelling a British diplomat from Moscow, realizing it inconvenienced the British to a greater extent since the UK Embassy was so much smaller than the Soviet mission in London. The blow Lord Home was about to deliver was to be the most devastating ever suffered publicly by Soviet Intelligence.

Armed with this dossier, Lord Home went across Downing Street to the Cabinet Room, taking Sir Denis Greenhill with him. Waiting for them were the Prime Minister, Edward Heath; the Home Secretary, Reginald Maudling; the Defence Secretary, Lord Carrington; and the Trade and Industry Secretary, John Davies. They were completely taken aback. Some expulsions had to take place, of course. They agreed with Lord Home that the Russians had to be taught a severe lesson. But there were murmurings about the dangers of going over the top by expelling as many as 105 Soviet officials at one time. The Prime Minister, somewhat reluctantly, indicated he was prepared to take Lord Home's word for it that this was no time for half measures and there had to be a total clear-out. But Reginald Maudling was incensed at the length of Lord Home's list. You must be joking, Alec, he said.

As Home Secretary, Reginald Maudling was convinced that the Government would make itself look ridiculous in Parliament with such a statement. It would be an admission of the total inadequacy of Britain's security services. To blackball so many Russians would make the Tories the laughing stock of the country, he fumed. Even if there was a case against 105 Russians he was opposed to expelling them instantly since it could mean that the Soviet ritual tit-for-tat could paralyse the British Embassy in Moscow. Lord Home stuck to his decision and told Maudling that if he did not like what he heard he should look at the evidence. He left Sir Denis Greenhill to go over the dossier with him. His hand was strengthened by the corroboration provided in disclosures made by the Soviet agent Oleg Lyalin who defected three weeks before the expulsion drama came to a head. Although the clash in the Cabinet continued, Edward Heath gave the nod for the go-ahead.

Lord Home instructed the PUS to summon the Minister at the Soviet Embassy, Ivan Ippolitov, on Friday, 24 September 1971, as Chargé d'Affaires in the absence of Ambassador Mikhail Smirnovsky. The ten-page list was handed over by Sir Denis Greenhill. Ippolitov read through the names in silence. After the standard Soviet comment – 'This is a very serious matter' – he bowed out. It left the Soviet Foreign Minister stunned, since the *aide-mémoire* handed over by the PUS put a ceiling on the Soviet presence in London, forbidding replacements for those expelled from the Soviet Embassy, the Trade Delegation, and other Soviet organizations. In Moscow, the Soviet Foreign Ministry summoned Britain's Ambassador, Sir John Killick, to inform him of the retaliation at 8 p.m. With unusual sang-froid for a newly arrived envoy, he sent back word: 'I am in the middle of my soup. I shall be there at 8.30 p.m.' The Russian revenge was less fierce than Reginald Maudling feared. They expelled eighteen of the Embassy staff of forty diplomats.

The chill that fell on Anglo-Soviet relations caused the cancellation of visits by Lord Home and by the Housing Minister, Julian Amery, to Moscow. It also stopped a visit to London of Soviet Foreign Trade Minister Nikolai Patolichev. But the fearsome predictions of Denis Healey as Shadow Foreign Secretary that the expulsions would make Britain's relations with Russia worse than at any time since the 1930s were not borne out by events. The Russians appeared chastened by the experience of being publicly denounced for spying. They realized that it had a knock-on effect on their espionage activities elsewhere, since the French and the

Italians also took the opportunity to get rid of a number of their obnoxious Soviet visitors masquerading as trade officials. In due course, as Lord Home forecast at the time, the Kremlin indicated that the diplomatic freeze was over by inviting him to Moscow in December 1973. A new chapter was opened with the Russians putting on a show of friendship. They thought it would please Lord Home to give him the chance to drive a train, even though he did not have a great reputation as a mechanical man. When the Gromykos came to London, the only daggers they saw were those on the stage for the murder of Rizzio in the production of *Vivat Regina*. The final reconciliation was inside the Cabinet when Reginald Maudling shook hands with Lord Home and told him: You were right.

The massive reduction in the KGB's strength in London and its awareness of being much more closely watched than the controllers in Dzerzhinsky Square had realized curbed the scale of spying in Britain for a long time. Yuri Voronin, the key figure running the network as London Resident under the guise of being one of the Embassy's eleven counsellors, was out of England at the time of the expulsion orders and never allowed back. He was severely handicapped in trying to reorganize a team of experienced operators to take the place of those expelled. MI5 supplied the Foreign Office with an additional list of Soviet intelligence agents who had operated in other English-speaking countries and who were to be banned from obtaining visas for Britain. The replacements kept their heads down to avoid angering their Moscow masters with more unwelcome publicity over expulsions. For over five years after Lord Home's big purge, there was no announcement of a Soviet diplomat being made *persona non grata*.

Professional standards in the KGB's London branch sharply declined. One of Voronin's successors, KGB General Arkadi Gouk, who was officially one of the six First Secretaries on Ambassador Viktor Popov's staff, bungled his espionage operations so badly that Moscow was relieved when he was expelled from Britain in May 1984. Although he moved smoothly round the embassy cocktail circuit in his Savile Row suit, Gouk was so slow-witted that he let opportunities slip for recruiting a spy. His hamfistedness was humiliatingly exposed when Michael Bettaney, a renegade MI5 officer, was sentenced at the Old Bailey to twenty-three years' imprisonment. Bettaney went to Gouk's apartment on Easter Sunday 1983 at 43 Holland Park and pushed an envelope through the letterbox. The documents gave details of how MI5 had tracked down three KGB agents who had been expelled the previous month. Bettaney offered himself as a recruit with the promise of more secret information.

In advance, apparently, Bettaney had done some research before choosing Gouk as the best person to contact, but clearly not enough, however. Gouk came to the conclusion that the envelope from Bettaney was a trap by MI5 to compromise him so that he could be expelled. When Bettaney repeated the delivery of secret material to Gouk's apartment in June and July the spymaster was convinced that his first suspicions were confirmed. The sentence on Bettaney, who was arrested as he was about to go to Vienna to seek a better response from the KGB there than Gouk had given, ended Gouk's fumbling four years as London Resident.

One important offer which the KGB did not spurn provided them with significant inside information from GCHQ, the Government Communications Headquarters at Cheltenham in Gloucestershire. It came in January 1968 from a corporal in RAF Signals Intelligence at Gatow in Berlin, Geoffrey Prime. Six months later when he left the RAF, Prime joined GCHQ and became the Russians' most valuable mole. Year after year for over ten years he passed on a cornucopia of secrets to Moscow. He gave the Russians highly detailed information on how the system worked at GCHQ. He revealed the names of key members of the staff at Cheltenham and in posts overseas. By informing the Russians of the extent of the penetrations made into Soviet intelligence material, he was able to alert his masters as to what parts of their system had been compromised.

Even more alarming to Britain's partners in the Central Intelligence Agency was the way Prime was able to supply the Russians with top-secret details on the operations of the latest American intelligence-gathering satellites. The Americans were furious at the failure of the British security vetting system in allowing Prime to continue his betrayal for so long. They began to question whether the risks of having an intelligence partnership with Britain were not beginning to outweigh the advantages. What worried the Americans was that the highly damaging drain of information was only stemmed when police arrested Prime in 1982 for sexually molesting young girls. It took a long time before their confidence was restored.

The advice of Callières about the usefulness of cultivating Members of Parliament was not lost on the KGB. But they were shrewd enough to realize that much less suspicion was created if initial approaches were made by Czech diplomats rather than by Russians. Labour MPs were their most favoured targets and were often invited to the Czech Embassy in Kensington Palace Gardens in the 1960s by Ambassador Zdenek Trhlik and his successor Miloslav Ruzek. One of the best catches by the Czech StB agents was Will Owen, Labour MP for Morpeth from 1954 until 1970. As a member of the Commons Committee on Defence Estimates, Owen was a source of valuable information to the Russians, via the Czechs, on Britain's Rhine Army activities. After being acquitted at the Old Bailey in May 1970, Owen made a confession to MI5 on condition that he was granted immunity from further prosecution. The Czechs also focused their attention on John Stonehouse who was appointed Minister of Posts and Telecommunications by Harold Wilson in 1968. He was cultivated after visiting Czechoslovakia as a backbencher, accepting invitations to the Embassy, but he always denied co-operating with them.

When Britons fall into the hands of Soviet security, as they do on rare occasions, the problem of spies and diplomacy becomes a complex question clogged with moral and political dilemmas. That particular challenge was thrust at the Foreign Office on 22 July 1965 when Gerald Brooke, a 28-year-old Russian-speaking lecturer from Holborn College, London, appeared in a Moscow court accused of anti-Soviet activities. It was a day the KGB had awaited eagerly since 22 March 1961 when Morris and Lona Cohen, otherwise known as Peter and Helen Kroger, were sentenced to twenty years' imprisonment for their part in the Portland spy case over submarine secrets sent to Russia. The appearance of Brooke in the dock provided the diplomatic lever the KGB wanted to press for the release of the Krogers.

Whatever else he was – naive, careless, muddled, and misguided

– Gerald Brooke was not a trained spy. The Krogers were veteran espionage agents trained in America with the Rosenbergs who were executed in 1953. Brooke, who should have known better since he had been a student at Moscow University in 1959, went to Russia with anti-Soviet propaganda from the émigré organization NTS – *Naradno Trudovoy Soyuz* (Popular Labour Alliance). When he was about to hand over the smuggled documents in the apartment of a Soviet doctor, Yuri Konstantinov, security officers burst into the room. As they arrested Brooke they praised Konstantinov as 'a patriot of the fatherland'.

In court Brooke was the victim of a show trial. It was held in a small theatre attached to a workers' club, lit by arc lights for television and film cameras to record the proceedings. The judge and the lawyers sat on the stage against a backdrop of red curtains. Some 600 spectators watched in the stalls. Outside there was a buffet for them with beer and smoked salmon sandwiches. Brooke was provided with a lawyer, Nikolai Borovik, who spoke of him as 'a good man who took the wrong path'. Borovik claimed that Brooke had been brainwashed by NTS and, 'snared by candies and biscuits', had been unaware of what he had smuggled into the country in his special underwear. After a scripted adjournment for 3 hours 25 minutes the court sentenced Brooke to five years' preventive detention. He had to spend the first year in prison at Vladimir, 100 miles from Moscow. Then he was transferred to the corrective labour camp at Potma in the Mordovian region 280 miles southeast of Moscow. There in the political prisoners' block of Camp V he had to carve white knight chess pieces – a daily quota of 250 – while the ordinary criminals in the other wing carved bishops and pawns.

The first Government intervention on behalf of Brooke was sixteen months after the trial when George Brown went to Moscow as Foreign Secretary in November 1966. It was not one of George Brown's best efforts at winning friends and influencing people. When the Foreign Minister, Andrei Gromyko, showed no great interest in his humanitarian appeal, George Brown launched himself into a tirade about Soviet labour camps. He became highly emotional and thumped the table to the embarrassment of everyone in the room, including the British delegation. His appeal left the Russians unmoved. The matter was put aside until the Soviet Prime Minister Alexai Kosygin came to London for talks with Harold Wilson on 8 February 1967. Then Wilson tried a plea for clemency but there was no response. The Government turned to open criticism in November 1967 when William Rodgers, Parliamentary Under-Secretary at the Foreign Office, condemned the detention of Brooke as 'disgraceful, indefensible and uncivilized'.

That was followed a month later by the first hint of Russian blackmail. It came in an article in the newspaper *Izvestia* on 28 December 1967 with a warning that Brooke's sentence could be trebled to fifteen years' preventive detention. It denounced Brooke as a 'fully fledged spy' who should have been given fifteen years' imprisonment. People complaining about his treatment were advised to be careful or else Brooke would find himself 'getting his full deserts as a spy'. The article pointed out that under Soviet law Brooke could be re-arrested and put on trial again. The Foreign Office called in the Soviet Ambassador Mikhail Smirnovsky and asked for an explanation of the Government-inspired references to a new trial. He was reminded that Anglo-Soviet relations could not flourish in an atmosphere of threats.

The question came up again in January 1968 when Wilson went to Moscow. Although most of the official talks in the Kremlin were spent on Wilson's manoeuvres for a Vietnam peace settlement, he raised the issue of Brooke with Leonid Brezhnev and Alexei Kosygin over lunch. Afterwards it was stated that he argued vehemently for Brooke's release. But from the version given out by the Soviet side it was clear that the Krogers' release had become the dominant factor in their presentation. Until then the Russians had denied that there was any direct link between the two issues, although they never failed to emphasize that the release of the Krogers would automatically lead to a review of the Brooke case. This time, however, the blackmail was set out, unmistakably and crudely.

Two months later, when Michael Stewart returned to the Foreign Office in March 1968, Sir Denis Greenhill as PUS suggested that it was time to reassess the Brooke case as a humanitarian problem. It was not a view shared by MI5. Sir Martin Furnival Jones as Head of MI5 was firmly opposed to any negotiations. His opinion was that since the Krogers were professional spies any deal to swap them for a petty smuggler of pamphlets would only serve to boost morale among Soviet agents. The MI5 argument to the Foreign Office was that Britons going to Russia should know the risks of violating Soviet laws and put up with the punishment if they were caught. Michael Stewart was impressed by the tough line taken by MI5 comments. Although a man sensitive to the moral content of foreign policy, he took a lot of convincing over several months that there was a case for getting Brooke out even at the cost of letting the Krogers go free.

The Greenhill argument was based on three main factors. First there was concern for Brooke's health. Reports from former inmates at Potma labour camp stated that Brooke had stomach trouble, which was being aggravated by the poor food. He had been taken to hospital for treatment of intestinal inflammation. After that his morale was not good. Secondly, there was the threat of a new show trial and the imposition of a further ten-year sentence which might break his spirit. Thirdly, there was the belief that as the Krogers had served over half their sentence and had been isolated from the outside world they were a spent force not capable of being reassigned as spies.

It was felt that other Soviet agents might not be very impressed by the fact that it took such a long time for the KGB to get their people back. It was also argued that despite ministerial assurances in the past that there would be no swap for Brooke there were precedents for exchanging people in detention. In April 1964 the Soviet spy Konon Trofgimovich Molody, otherwise known as Gordon Lonsdale, who was sentenced to twenty-five years' imprisonment in 1961 along with the Krogers, had been freed under an exchange deal. In return Britain secured the release of the British businessman Greville Wynne who was jailed for eight years after being arrested as an Intelligence courier to Oleg Penkovsky, the British agent shot after a show trial in May 1963. Three German students – Walter Naumann, Jurgen Schaffhauser, and Peter Sonntag – were released from the same camp at Potma as Brooke in February 1969 in exchange for the Soviet spy Heinz Felfe.

After the German swap Michael Stewart was convinced that he should authorize negotiations on Brooke. Following consultations with Home Secretary James Callaghan about the Krogers, Michael Stewart got Cabinet approval and gave the go-ahead to Sir Denis Greenhill. One new factor injected a sense of urgency into coming to terms. The KGB let it be known through Ambassador Smirnovsky that Brooke had been 'misbehaving' at the labour camp, allegedly stirring up trouble among the other inmates. This development, it was hinted, might lead to the 'troublesome prisoner' being given a further trial – and a further sentence. It was an elaboration of the earlier blackmail and, even though completely fabricated, Foreign Office experts believed that it could not be ignored.

On 14 June 1969, a front-page story in the *Daily Mail* disclosed that negotiations were taking place for Brooke to be freed in return for the release of the Krogers and that he could be back home in a few weeks. It caused much embarrassment in Downing Street since there had been an agreement with the Russians to keep the negotiations secret and to synchronize the release announcement later. Last-minute attempts were made by the Foreign Office to persuade the Editor of the *Daily Mail* not to publish the story. First, it was argued that the Russians might take it as a deliberate leak designed to improve the terms of the arrangements and call off the negotiations. That was countered by stating that as the Russians were getting two spies back they would not walk out of the deal. Then, a final appeal for the story to be withheld was made on the grounds that although Brooke's wife Barbara was aware of the negotiations his mother was not and it might be too much of a shock for her to read about them in a newspaper. The Editor's answer was that if he agreed not to publish something because it might give a reader a shock he would be left with blank columns every day.

After eleven weeks of negotiations conducted by Sir Denis Greenhill and Sir Thomas Brimelow, the Russian-speaking Deputy Under-Secretary of State, with Ambassador Smirnovsky, the agreement on the swap was officially announced on 24 July. It provided for the immediate release of Brooke followed three months later by that of the Krogers. As a bonus two other Britons, Anthony Lorraine and Michael Parsons, serving drug-trafficking sentences at Potma, were also freed. To head off any criticism at

Westminster for giving in to the Russians, Michael Stewart told the Commons that it was an agreement reached for humanitarian reasons. Although Stewart felt he was right to authorize the swap, he admitted afterwards: 'I am glad I did not often have to make decisions of this kind.'

If anyone ever doubted the importance of the interaction between espionage and diplomacy, impressive proof was provided when the superspy Oleg Gordievsky came in from the cold in 1985. For eleven years Gordievsky worked as a double agent supplying top-secret political and military information to MI6 while acting as a senior officer of the KGB. After being recruited by a British diplomat in Copenhagen in 1974, Gordievsky reached a peak of political influence unmatched by anyone in the East or the West as the person trusted to brief both superpower leaders, Gorbachev and Reagan. Before Mikhail Gorbachev's first meeting with Margaret Thatcher at Chequers in December 1984, he relied on Gordievsky's political reports – appropriately moulded by British Intelligence – as the best-informed briefing material. Shortly after Gordievsky's escape to England, his assessments of Gorbachev's political priorities formed an important part of the White House briefing material for President Reagan's first summit talks with Gorbachev at Geneva in November 1985. The American President was evidently so impressed by Gordievsky's personal notes on the man he was about to meet that he read them right down to the last word, which was rare for him in dealing with briefing papers.

Gordievsky's judgement of the way Gorbachev's mind worked was highly valued by the Americans as they prepared for subsequent summits. His knowledge of how intelligence appreciations were made in both East and West gave him a significant role in the evolution of a new understanding in Washington and London of the political transformation in Moscow. He was able to predict reactions in the Kremlin to hawkish rhetoric in Washington, which may explain why President Reagan switched away from his emphasis on Russia as 'the evil Empire'. Equally important, he was in a position to analyse the pressures of the military on Gorbachev to enable the West to adjust their strategy in disarmament negotiations. One of the most studied documents was a long analytical article by him under the title 'Soviet Perceptions of Nuclear Warfare'.

Gordievsky's three years with the KGB in England leading to his appointment as London Resident gave him a strange double life. Under the cover of the Embassy counsellor handling religious affairs, he met leading churchmen, including the former Archbishop of Canterbury, Dr Robert Runcie. For a time he would mingle at Soviet Embassy receptions in Kensington Palace Gardens picking up strands of ideas just like his fellow counsellors Lev Parshin and Alexei Nikiforov. He would compile reports to convince the Moscow chiefs that they were being kept closely informed of what people in high places were thinking. Then he would switch to his true allegiance and sift through the reports on activities of the agents in the Embassy and the Trade Delegation. This enabled him to forewarn British security of the clandestine manoeuvres being undertaken by Soviet officials.

Information from Gordievsky led to the largest number of Soviet officials being expelled since the Home clear-out of 105 in 1971. A total of 25 Soviet officials were given three weeks to leave the country in a Foreign Office announcement on 12 September 1985. That announcement coincided with the disclosure that Gordievsky had ended his amazing double life and had chosen asylum in Britain, although in fact his escape had taken place two months earlier. It triggered off an angry tit-for-tat series of expulsions by the Russians ending with 31 forced out on each side.

Since Gorbachev had only been in power at the Kremlin for six months, there were hopes that the restructuring of Soviet society promised by his programme of *perestroika* would extend to the KGB and curb the Russian obsession with espionage. Changes were made at the top. In October 1988 Gorbachev got rid of Viktor Chebrikov, the hardline Chairman of the KGB who joined forces with Yegor Ligachev in an attempt to put the brakes on *perestroika*. In his place he put Vladimir Kryuchkov, who had been the head of the Foreign Intelligence Directorate of the KGB. Kryuchkov gave the impression of being ready to co-operate with the West, especially in the struggle against terrorism. To improve the KGB's image he made it seem that the openness of Gorbachev's policy of *glasnost* had reached Dzerzhinsky Square. He appeared in a public relations film called *The KGB Today* and even opened the doors of the Lubianka to journalists. But in his first interview he made it clear that the days of the spy were far from over. 'Spying yields information that enables international problems to be solved by political, not military means,' Kryuchkov was quoted as saying in the *Sunday Times*.

That policy led to a bitter row between Britain and the Soviet Union in May 1989 after fourteen Russian officials were expelled for trying to bribe scientists and business executives in a large-scale campaign of industrial espionage. Far from winding down their spying, the KGB agents had been stepping up their activities with the aim of penetrating areas with access to high technology. MI5 investigations were accelerated after disclosures from a Czech defector from StB, Vlastimil Lubvik. Sir Geoffrey Howe gave the Russians several warnings and the chance to withdraw the offenders voluntarily. Even when the Russians refused to take action, Sir Geoffrey summoned Ambassador Leonid Zamyatin and handed him a list of eight diplomats and three journalists being given fourteen days to leave the country, but made no public announcement. He wanted to keep the diplomatic temperature down in the hope of minimizing the damage to Anglo-Soviet relations. Only six weeks earlier Mrs Thatcher and President Gorbachev had toasted their improved relationship at a Downing Street banquet.

The KGB were not disposed to co-operate in avoiding a public clash. Twenty-four hours after Zamyatin had been given the list of Soviet offenders, Britain's Moscow Ambassador Sir Rodric Braithwaite was summoned to the Soviet Foreign Ministry and presented with a parallel list for expulsion, rank for rank, including three British journalists. The spy crisis escalated two days later with a sudden announcement from the Soviet Foreign Ministry giving the British seven days to scale down their staffing in Moscow. They insisted on the ceiling being reduced from 375 to 205 and that figure had to include not just British diplomats, businessmen, and journalists but the Soviet citizens working for them. This decree was defended as matching the ceiling of 205 put on Soviet officials and journalists in London. There is no restriction, however, on the number of Britons working in Soviet enterprises in England.

Although the Russians backed off the seven-day ultimatum, it took a long time to defuse the tensions over the staffing numbers. Mrs Thatcher, normally ready to make allowances for the difficulties Gorbachev faced over his policies of openness under *perestroika*, was much chastened by the setback. 'It reveals that perhaps the Soviet Union has changed rather less than a number of people hope. I am disappointed. We gave them a chance. They have not taken it and have revealed their true nature,' she admitted. It confirmed suspicions in Downing Street that the KGB's open-door policy under Kryuchkov was just a public relations exercise.

Despite Kryuchkov's determination to clean up the image of the KGB inside the country, scale down its high-profile activity on the streets, and ensure that its operations were in accordance with 'Soviet legality', there was no change in its role abroad. His emphasis on the close co-ordination of spying and diplomacy remained undiminished. The handshake between President Bush and President Gorbachev at the Malta summit in December 1989 ending the Cold War was not a signal for the KGB to stop recruiting agents. Breaking down the Iron Curtain and demolishing the Berlin Wall transformed Eastern Europe in one significant respect for the KGB. It forced Kryuchkov to accelerate the recruitment of spies because the KGB was now left to operate on its own without any help from its former satellites. The political upheavals across Eastern Europe sent not just the Red Army packing: they ended the valuable intelligence-gathering which was done by the KGB's junior partners. A large proportion of foreign intelligence operations in the sixteen NATO countries was undertaken for the KGB by the Czechs and East Germans.

Even when it was left on its own, the KGB showed it was still capable of getting its faithful servants out of dangerous situations. One of the most spectacular examples was the KGB's abduction of Erich Honecker, Communist East Germany's leader for eighteen years, on 14 March 1991 from Federal German territory to the Soviet Union. Germany's Supreme Court pronounced that the Soviet Union had no legal right to intervene to prevent the arrest of Honecker. He was accused of personally ordering border guards to shoot to kill, a policy resulting in the deaths of over 200 East Germans trying to escape. But having sealed Honecker off in a Red Army hospital in the eastern zone for treatment of a serious kidney condition, the Russians said he was too ill to be served with an arrest warrant. That was a temporary manoeuvre to give the KGB time to outwit the German security system and get Honecker out of the country.

Despite the furious protests from the Government of Chancellor Helmut Kohl, there were signs of relief in Bonn that the KGB coup had removed a potential source of deep embarrassment. Germany's partners in Western intelligence, the CIA and MI5, could have been very worried if Honecker had not been silenced but had been left in Germany to speak in court about the political corruption under his leadership from 1971 until 1989. It could have been extremely awkward if Honecker had disclosed how the East German intelligence agency, HVA, had co-operated with the KGB to get compromising information from the Bonn administration. Revelations about how the controls on exporting technology from the West were circumvented between the two Germanies until unification would have aroused bitter controversy. These aspects of the abduction gave rise to suspicion that there were good reasons why the Germans and the Americans had not taken sterner measures to ensure that the KGB did not succeed in removing Honecker to Moscow.

The overthrow of the old Communist regimes in Eastern Europe removed the protective shield they provided for the Soviet Union against the penetration of Western intelligence. KGB officers at Soviet Embassies in Warsaw Pact countries were cut off from all the agencies which helped to monitor the movements of foreigners. All the political and industrial intelligence supplied to the KGB by the Bulgarians, East Germans, and Czechs dried up. Keeping track of the new technology in the West, which the Soviet Union fears as an increasing threat, was made much more difficult for the KGB without the back-up they used to have in the East European agencies. The Soviet Union felt much more exposed to what the KGB calls 'ideological subversion' without the tripwire of the Communist satellite system. The free flow of ideas throughout Eastern Europe was regarded by the hardline elements of the KGB as an extra danger since they were able to spread more easily across the Soviet borders.

For Western intelligence the changes in Eastern Europe transformed their operations. The unification of Germany and the break with the Communist system by its neighbours substantially reduced the amount of activity which had to be monitored by Western agents in East European capitals. There was an extra dividend in many capitals with the acquisition of dossiers from the discredited security services. Although much of the documentation incriminating the KGB was destroyed before it could fall into Western hands, there was a large amount of material made available which enhanced the files of the CIA and MI6. The dossiers of the Bulgarian Security Service revealed that the poison used in the umbrella ferrule to murder the dissident writer Georgi Markov in London in 1978 was supplied by the KGB. Gorbachev's *glasnost* not only transformed the atmosphere inside the Soviet Union, enabling people to talk freely to one another and say what they thought in public for the first time since 1917. Travellers from the West also enjoyed a new freedom to talk to people and acquire information. Diplomats, businessmen and journalists were able to mingle with ordinary citizens who were no longer scared to speak their minds.

One dramatic event changed the East–West power struggle in terms of espionage and diplomacy: the coup that failed in Moscow on 19 August 1991. The KGB bungled the operations designed to topple Gorbachev and turn back the clock on reform. Vladimir Kryuchkov, the KGB chairman who was one of the leaders of the junta, failed to silence Boris Yeltsin and Eduard Shevardnadze at the outset. The people defied the Communist old guard and took to the streets to proclaim their faith in freedom. The collapse of the coup opened the floodgates for reform. With Kryuchkov and the other plotters in the Emergency Committee arrested and charged with treason, the entire leadership of the KGB was purged. It was symbolic of the transformation that the first statue to be hauled down was not one of Lenin but that of Felix Dzerzhinsky outside the Lubianka in Moscow.

The backlash against the dictatorship of the Communist Party was bitter. People demanded an open society so that ordinary citizens could feel free of the spying eyes of the State Security. The files at the KGB headquarters were seized. Once the euphoria subsided, however, the xenophobia which was as marked in Tsarist times as in the heyday of Stalinism began to surface again. For foreigners there remained a certain barrier to trust which made it difficult to predict what is really going on in the Russian mind. Intelligence gathering was as challenging as it has always been. There seemed to be more straws visible in the wind once the heavy hand of the Communist system was lifted. But what to make of them was often as baffling as ever. It emphasized the eternal dilemma for the diplomat and the spy: when to be bold enough to believe you have the necessary foresight to get it right before it becomes self-evident in hindsight.

X

Foresight and Hindsight

*Some of the most intractable international issues
in which we have been involved in the last two
decades could, in our view, have been handled
better if their implications had been more fully
explored in advance.*

Plowden Report, 1964

*When you are 'planning' for a world of over
100 nations over most of whom you have little
influence, your powers of foresight are very
limited.*

Lord Gore-Booth,
With Truth and Great Respect

Hindsight is not an attractive thing.

John Major, March 1991

No one at the Foreign Office on 1 January 1989 predicted that
the Berlin Wall would come down later that year on 9 October.
Nor did anyone else in Washington or Moscow or even in Bonn.
Inside the Foreign Office there are those who would respond to the
initial observation with a question: Who forecast that the Korean
airliner KAL 007 would be shot down by a Soviet jet fighter on
its way from Anchorage, Alaska, to Seoul on 1 September 1983
with the loss of all 269 aboard? But posing that question does
nothing to allay the suspicion that there is a weakness in the system
as far as planning for future eventualities is concerned. There

are usually certain contingencies which can be anticipated when a situation, whose timing cannot be foreseen, actually does arise. Preparations can be made which ensure that the conduct of policy is much more efficient than if it had been left to improvisation at the time. East–West relations went through some of their most tense moments during the KAL 007 crisis of 1989. If the problems of mutual suspicion aroused by an airliner straying into Soviet airspace had been analysed thoroughly in advance, some of the angry recriminations of 'extreme adventurism' would have been avoided.

Formal policy planning was not taken seriously at the Foreign Office until relatively recently. Some planning functions were always accepted as a useful academic exercise, but they were tucked away for years under the umbrella of the Western Organizations and Co-ordination Department. In fact, when the Fulton Committee on the Home Civil Service recommended in 1968 that all government departments should have planning units the Foreign Office preened itself for having had one for the previous eleven years. But for the first few years after 1957 all the planning for the entire range of responsibilities of the Foreign Office across the globe was in the hands of one first secretary. There was no real enthusiasm for planning except for analysing the problems for NATO in the Cold War. There was no organized direction of its activities and little time for supervising the work done. It was only when the Plowden Committee in 1964 focused attention on the need for a proper planning staff that any priority was given to it by the Foreign Office. An upgraded department was established under a counsellor, a diplomat destined to become PUS, Michael Palliser. With advance notification of the Plowden recommendations from the Whitehall early-warning system, the Foreign Office had him rushed into the job in January 1964, a month before the criticisms of the Plowden Report were published.

What concerned the Plowden Committee then, and is still a matter of concern to many critics of the Foreign Office, is the need to have enough people in the senior echelons of the Foreign Office with time to think ahead beyond the day-to-day flow of telegrams on current issues. One basic comment made by Lord Plowden over twenty-five years ago is even more valid today: 'Most of those engaged in policy work, especially at home, seem to be overburdened.' He made a plea for the provision of experts 'who are free enough from current work to be able to germinate and develop ideas without being so remote from current work that their thinking becomes too academic'. That plea was answered by creating a staff of only three diplomats for the Planning Department under Michael Palliser, and one of these was assigned as a speechwriter for the Foreign Secretary. By 1973, when the department was further upgraded to have an assistant under-secretary temporarily as its head, the staff was enlarged to four. It was only in recent years that the Foreign Office recognized that the department required a minimum of six diplomats.

The objectives of the planning staff in terms of what to plan for – events or trends – remained confused. When another high flyer, the Hon. David Gore-Booth, was put in charge in January 1987 the title of the department was changed from Planning Staff to Policy Planning Staff. The uncertainty of his role was emphasized by an anonymous well-wisher who left a rhyme on his desk on his first day:

> A planner is a cautious man
> He wears not gun nor pistol
> He walks as carefully as he can
> His balls are made of crystal

Even with crystal balls, the planner's vision is limited. Lord Plowden acknowledged that situations could arise which no amount of expertise could predict. But he made the point for a succession of planners to ponder: 'Many issues can be foreseen at least in outline and it is better to prepare for these in advance than to improvise when they have arisen.' His thesis was that no one could operate with the precision of military contingency plans in an international arena where so many political influences were deployed. Yet it should be possible, he argued, to have studies made of the probable consequences which could flow from a particular event. Lord Plowden emphasized the need for planners to identify the options in advance, 'to foresee the choices with which Britain is likely to be faced at some stage in the future and to consider how we can use the intervening time to place ourselves in the best position to make a final choice when we have to'.

This is one of the responsibilities devolved upon the PUS as a sort of chairman of the board in the Foreign Office. He holds a meeting every month which brings together the deputy under-secretaries as a board of directors to look ahead with the Head of Policy Planning Staff Department. As PUS, Sir Michael Palliser put emphasis on having a strong economic input into these meet-ings so that the planners should not lose sight of the economic implications of the political consequences they examine on the horizon. Sometimes these meetings get down to specifics and lead to a further round-table session as happened in 1989 with up to ten people analysing all the aspects of economic aid to the Soviet Union. But the tendency is for the specifics to be clouded over by discussion of longer-range issues such as mass migratory pressures on the Mediterranean or the emergence of new national move-ments around the world.

It has always been a debatable question as to how deep a plan-ner's field of vision should be and how close to the real world of today and tomorrow he should focus. Lord Plowden warned against the folly of the ivory tower perspective: 'The planning staff should not spend too high a proportion of their time scanning the horizons of the distant future.' If there were any remnants of the ivory tower mentality still surviving in the Policy Planning Staff Department, they were buried in the sands of the Gulf War in 1991. Under the direction of Robert Cooper as Head of the Department the planners had to make instant responses to the rapidly changing scenario created by the unpredictable Iraqi leader. After attending the morning meeting in the crisis manage-ment centre, Cooper would have a list of imponderables to assess – the 'What ifs?' By the following morning his planning team would be required to have discussion papers ready on the way the situation might develop in certain circumstances – if there were a partial withdrawal of Iraqi troops from Kuwait, if there were a threat of chemical warfare, if sanctions were to be effective how long they would have to be maintained – plus assessments of a wide range of 'worst-case scenarios'. Sometimes the Foreign Secretary would ask for an analysis of certain options from the planning staff by six o'clock that day. In the first three months of 1991 the planning team produced twenty-four papers – more than are usually written in a year.

Despite this unprecedented amount of close-focus work, there was one extraordinary omission. No policy planning paper was commissioned in anticipation of the Kurdish crisis which followed the end of hostilities. It was only when the horrendous reports appeared in the newspapers and on television of the tragic exodus of Kurdish refugees towards the borders of Turkey and Iran that priority was given to planning emergency relief. Yet President Saddam Hussein's appalling record at the end of the eight-year Iraq–Iran war was still fresh in the memories of many observers of the Middle East. Less than forty-eight hours after Iran's President Khamenei agreed to abide by the ceasefire terms of UN Security Council Resolution 598 on 18 July 1988, Saddam Hussein ordered his forces into battle against the Kurds. His attacks with jet fighters and chemical weapons killed 3,000 Kurds. Over 60,000 Kurdish refugees fled to seek asylum in Turkey and a further 20,000 went into Iran.

Neither the US nor Britain moved quickly to protest at that time because of political anxieties about Iraq walking out of the peace talks in Geneva. Subsequently, there were pledges never to stand by and let Saddam Hussein resort to gassing Kurds again. Why ministers did not remember Saddam Hussein's record and order a paper on contingency arrangements for protecting the Kurds was a baffling oversight. Much valuable time would have been saved – and, more importantly, many lives spared – if the options on ways to prevent the Kurds being victimized again had been properly analysed so that decisions could have been taken immediately after the ceasefire.

An attempt by Prime Minister John Major to ease the plight of the refugees by advocating the establishment of a safe haven for the Kurds inside Iraq close to the Turkish border was well-intentioned, but it ran into trouble at the outset because it was politically half-baked. It was launched by him at the EC summit in Luxembourg on 8 April 1991 and became known as the 'Major Plan'. This caused some dismay among the Turks since President Turgut Özal on a television interview in Ankara twenty-four hours earlier had proposed a buffer zone inside Iraq to protect the Kurds under United Nations control. It prompted the wry observation: 'Others get the kudos – we get the Kurds.' The way the 'Major Plan' was presented caused problems in Washington and at the UN in New York. While Britain's EC partners immediately approved it – partly because it appeared to be upstaging the Americans – the US was distinctly cool.

In his rush to get the project first on the table at Luxembourg the Prime Minister had not taken time to clear it with President Bush. It had been embroidered into a four-point plan on the flight to Luxembourg and given to the Press as soon as it was tabled. It reached the US from the news agency reports. The Americans were chary about John Major's initial use of the term 'enclave', a word which John Weston, the Political Director at the Foreign Office, would have discouraged the Prime Minister from using if there had been the opportunity for last-minute consultation on the way to the meeting in Luxembourg. It aroused concern in Washington that the Americans might be trapped into supporting the establishment of a zone which could be the first step towards the creation of a separate Kurdish state. They were apprehensive at the prospect of another 'safe haven' like the Gaza Strip which was set up as a temporary protective zone in 1949 and remained an encampment of despair for 700,000 Palestinians two generations later. UN Secretary-General Perez de Cuellar had reservations over how Iraq would accept the intrusion of forces even on a humanitarian basis. These were the sort of points which a policy planning paper would have alerted ministers to tread carefully around because of the pitfalls of arousing Kurdish political aspirations and facing procedural problems at the UN.

It required some fast diplomatic sidestepping by Foreign Secretary Douglas Hurd, on his return from visiting China, to shift the emphasis away from the controversial term chosen by the Prime Minister and substitute 'area' for 'enclave'. He used the platform of the Lord Mayor's Banquet at the Mansion House in London to stress that there was no intention of imposing a government from the outside or of promoting a separate Kurdistan. To his credit John Major quickly changed tack on terminology but kept up the pressure for collective action to help the Kurds survive. Sir

David Hannay, Ambassador at the UN, smoothed over some of the hesitations at breaching the principle of non-interference in a member state's domestic affairs.

President Bush was more difficult to shift because of the pressures on him to bring the US servicemen home from the Gulf without further involvement. At Maxwell Air Force Base in Alabama, six days after the launch of the plan at Luxembourg, President Bush declared: 'I do not want one single soldier or airman shoved into a civil war in Iraq that's been going on for ages.' Undaunted, John Major persisted with his plan and was rewarded three days later when President Bush came round to acknowledge the need for more than air drops of food and clothing. The announcement by President Bush on 16 April 1991 that American, British, and French troops would establish six encampments inside Iraq as protected areas for feeding the Kurds fell short of the Major proposal for 'safe havens'. But it was close enough for Downing Street to claim credit for taking the diplomatic initiative. Belatedly, it helped to make up for the lack of foresight at the Foreign Office in preparing for an obvious problem that was bound to emerge at the end of the war.

Once the heat of a crisis subsides, the planners revert to their longer-term objectives of analysing the issues that are just over the horizon but may present serious problems before very long. Lord Plowden's recommendation that policy planning papers should answer 'specific well-defined questions and should lead to well-defined conclusions' is accepted as the ideal target even though it is often not attainable. One of the successful ventures was an analytical paper about German unification two years before it happened. While not forecasting the timing of the Berlin Wall coming down, it did focus the attention of mandarins and ministers on a problem which would otherwise have been left in the pending tray as an issue so far away as not to merit preparing for its consequences at that stage.

Another role for the planners is to identify the international trends which will require a different sort of expertise for international negotiations. A policy planning paper on environmental problems came to the conclusion that gradually over the next ten years these issues would be the dominant matter for international negotiations, taking over the priority traditionally given to arms control and disarmament conferences. As a consequence, instead of training more diplomats in handling the intricate problems of verifying arms reductions, the Foreign Office concentrated on building up a cadre of diplomatic expertise on environmental issues. After the World Drugs Summit hosted by the Government in London, there was a fresh impetus for gearing the Diplomatic Service to play a larger role in this area.

Planning staffs have developed an international brotherhood in order to feed each other ideas on various projects which are being studied in many capitals. Planners in the twelve European Community countries meet four times a year to share the results of their analyses of future trends. Projections in defence planning are discussed by the planners in the sixteen member countries of NATO twice a year. Individual exchanges take place regularly with British planners meeting their American, French, and German equivalents. On occasion the Head of the Department will go to discuss planning issues with experts in Japan, China, and Russia. There have even been clandestine arrangements to enable a planning project which failed to win support in one country to be floated by planners in another country.

An extra resource for the formulation of policy is available from what is termed the 'Brains Trust'. Provided their opinions are not required in a hurry, the Research and Analysis Department can be relied upon to come up with an erudite assessment. Accommodated separately in the Old Admiralty Building, they keep themselves at a distance from the hustle and bustle of daily decision-making in the Foreign Office. Their function, which was originally 'the collation of Political Intelligence from various regions of the world', is now officially described as furnishing 'advice based on specialist experience'. It is the part of the Office where the air of academe is strongest. The Director of Research, Anthony St John Figgis, has a large staff at work under nine assistant directors. They have specialists steeped in Soviet affairs, China, Africa, Eastern Europe, the Middle East, and the Far East. The donnish atmosphere is enhanced by extensive files on the history of all the principal issues of relevance to policy-making and an extraordinary index of over one million individuals whose activities or influence could be of some significance in evaluating a situation.

Determining the priorities inside the Foreign Office can be a test of wills. Some ministers give a free rein to the Planning Committee which brings together all the deputy under-secretaries once a month under the chairmanship of the PUS to set the directions for the planning staff. That could result in someone being given a month to produce a paper on a theme such as 'Islam as a Foreign Policy'. Another paper may be commissioned on the probable shape of the European Community in ten years' time with an assessment of its capacity to deal with its enlargement by three more or six more members. But strong-minded ministers can push their own priorities and convene seminars which sometimes overtake the papers under commission. Douglas Hurd had no time for lengthy treatises. He preferred to have ideas condensed onto one sheet of paper and then gather experts, planners, and academic authorities to sit round a table to discuss the trends implicit in current situations. He believed in the stimulus of debating great issues such as the impact on the West of a radical shift of the balance of power inside the Soviet Union. His emphasis was on having policy planning papers set out a course of action, not just a series of options. He wanted to have clear indicators of the direction to be taken.

Sir Geoffrey Howe had the greatest stamina of any minister for reading policy papers. On a long flight home from Hong Kong he would spend hours discussing where his experts should be focusing their attention. His PPS Stephen Wall would be asked to jot down pages of suggestions for the policy planners. He would continually question not just what the Foreign Office was not doing that it ought to be doing but, just as important, what the Foreign Office was doing that it should not be doing. In his methodical way, like a barrister steadily building up a case, Sir Geoffrey kept probing for possibilities of a change of direction in policy. One of these explorations led to the most significant transformation of relations with the Communist world for decades, 'Howe's Ostpolitik' as it was called.

From the moment when President Brezhnev sent Soviet troops into Afghanistan and installed the puppet regime of Babrak Karmal in Kabul in December 1979, Mrs Thatcher decided that the Russians were beyond the pale. She ruled out any visits. Lord Carrington was warned: 'I don't want you having anything to do with those bloody Russians.' Even after Brezhnev died in 1982 and Francis Pym as Foreign Secretary suggested in the wake of the Falklands victory that it was time to consider opening doors to the Soviet Union and Eastern Europe, Mrs Thatcher refused to see any reason for warming East–West relations. But on her return to Downing Street after the general election in June 1983 she was persuaded that it was time for a change.

In the honeymoon period of the new administration the Prime Minister was prepared to listen to ideas from her new Foreign Secretary, Sir Geoffrey Howe. Looking at the doddering old men in the Kremlin – Brezhnev's successor Yuri Andropov not expected to last very long and the next in line, Konstantin Chernenko, equally fragile – Sir Geoffrey persuaded Mrs Thatcher that it would be worth reviewing relations with the Soviet Union and Eastern Europe. A new approach to pave the way for fresh opportunities of dialogue with the next regime could be a very profitable initiative, it was suggested. But instead of coming back to the Foreign Office and commissioning a paper from the planning staff, Sir Geoffrey turned to two of his brightest experts. First he had a long session with Nigel Broomfield, who had served in Moscow and had risen to be Head of the Eastern European and Soviet Department. Next he summoned in John Birch, who had served in Hungary and Romania before being appointed the first Head of the separate Eastern European Department in October 1983. The two papers they produced for a fresh chapter in relations with the Soviet Union and Eastern European countries were the basis for a dramatic change of policy.

The Broomfield Report, which was delivered to Sir Geoffrey Howe in July 1983, charted the course for a gradual evolution from confrontation to better East–West understanding through increased contacts. It was a lengthy analysis of how to pursue the best interests of Britain in the realms of politics, defence, trade, and culture. The Birch Report in 1984 proposed that there should be a new concept of dealing with Eastern Europeans as separate units, not as a monolithic bloc. To test the theories, Mrs Thatcher made her first visit to Hungary in February 1984. She came away satisfied that there was a case for talking to Communist governments and edging them towards more respect for human rights while at the same time encouraging opposition groups. Her visit set a pattern for further ministerial contacts under the new 'policy of differentiation' which cast the Hungarians, the Czechs, and the Poles in a more progressive category than the East Germans, Bulgarians, and Romanians.

Mrs Thatcher's next visit through the Iron Curtain was a turning-point for Anglo-Soviet relations. She was persuaded to go to Moscow ten days after her return from Budapest. The occasion was the funeral of President Andropov. It was her first chance to assess the Soviet situation on her own in a forty-minute meeting alone with the new Soviet leader Chernenko – fifteen minutes more than was given to Vice-President Bush, who was standing in for President Reagan. Armed with the Broomfield Report, she looked at Andropov's 72-year-old successor, Chernenko, shuffling along, a very sick man with emphysema, and realized that important changes could not be long delayed in the Soviet Union. How to make the most of the new opportunities they could create for the West was one of the first questions she asked on her return. Mrs Thatcher was won over to the idea that it was time to break down the tension and mistrust caused by Russia's build-up of ss20 missiles and the West's response with the deployment of Cruise and Pershing missiles. She accepted that if arms control negotiations were to achieve any result there had to be confidence generated on both sides so that the negotiators could be given the mandate to get to an arms agreement.

The Broomfield Report urged that preparations for a new relationship could be made by seeking out one of 'Tomorrow's Men'. As one of the few Foreign Office experts bold enough to make a forecast, Nigel Broomfield reckoned that the choice lay between the youngest man among the eleven full members of the Politburo, Mikhail Gorbachev, and the Moscow party boss, Viktor Grishin. He picked the winner. Re-reading the Broomfield Report, Mrs Thatcher decided that no time should be lost in getting Gorbachev to come to London. She wanted to be the first European head of government to make her mark with the man destined to be the next General Secretary of the Communist Party of the Soviet Union – and be a step ahead of the US President as well.

How to get an invitation to Gorbachev in the Kremlin that he could not refuse or could not be passed to some other, and duller, member of the Politburo was the next task for Nigel Broomfield. It was not in accordance with protocol for anyone in the Foreign Office to write to the Soviet Politburo and say: please send us your No. 3. But he hit on a clever ploy of making it a parliamentary invitation. He drafted a letter for Sir Anthony Kershaw, Chairman of the Foreign Affairs Committee of the House of Commons, to send as an invitation to Mikhail Gorbachev as Head of the Foreign Relations Committee of the Supreme Soviet. Sir Anthony raised no objection. He signed the letter and it was sent to Moscow via the diplomatic bag.

Gorbachev realized what was at stake in making his first important appearance on a political stage in the West. As the first top Soviet leader to visit Britain for seventeen years, he wanted to make sure that it gave him the sort of platform that would establish his credentials as an international figure. He demanded an assurance in advance that there would be a long session of talks with Mrs Thatcher and a full statement on them at the end. It took a lot of to-ing and fro-ing by the British Ambassador, Sir Iain Sutherland, to settle the arrangements for the visit exactly to Gorbachev's requirements. At the time it was made to seem a casual, largely impromptu programme. In fact, everything was planned with an eye to maximum media coverage. The Prime Minister was always reluctant to accept terms from anyone – except, of course, President Reagan – for a visit to Britain, but she decided that this was a very special occasion which could bring substantial political dividends for her as well as Gorbachev. She bowed to his demands and invited him and his wife Raisa for lunch at Chequers followed by three hours of talks alone in the Hawtry Room.

That invitation and his acceptance were kept secret until shortly before Gorbachev arrived with his parliamentary delegation in December. Consultations with Washington about the visit were ruled out in Downing Street. Mrs Thatcher did not want to be upstaged by the White House. The Americans could have taken the edge off the visit by inviting Gorbachev to Washington or by trying to set the agenda with a long list of human rights questions. This was her show and she was determined not to have any meddling from outside. She took the preparations very seriously. All the briefs prepared at the Foreign Office for the discussions at Chequers were carefully read and reread.

The change of policy advocated by the Broomfield Report was completely vindicated by the outcome of the meeting and its consequences. Although Mrs Thatcher and Mikhail Gorbachev differed on many fundamental points, they accepted the value of each other's political acumen to the process of working out a more stable relationship between East and West. The new chapter was registered with Mrs Thatcher's seal of approval for Gorbachev as 'a man she could do business with'. Chernenko's death three months later and the succession of Gorbachev to supreme power in the Soviet Union gave Mrs Thatcher a position of influence between Moscow and Washington that no other Western leader could claim. It also put the Foreign Office on a pedestal for policy planning and forecasting – a place in which it can bask only rarely.

Arguments against encouraging short-range forecasting are largely based on the assumption that the geographical department is best placed with experts on the region to estimate what is most likely to happen immediately in any situation. But the advantage of the policy planners is in being able to stand aside from the swirling confusion of events and judge the probabilities from more detached standards. In the run-up to the invasion of Kuwait in August 1990 there should have been an opportunity for the planners to say: even if the Gulf experts think there is only a 30 per cent chance of it happening, there is a case for forecasting how it could affect everyone in the area and those dependent on Kuwait for oil. Although it is argued that nothing could have been done to stop the forces of Saddam Hussein, there would have been some benefit from forecasting what subsequent action would be most effective in dealing with certain eventualities. Under the present system of focusing the attention of the planners from one to ten years ahead, there is a danger that the experts in departments will be left without an intelligent forecast of events over the next three to nine months.

The fact that these inadequacies are highlighted by several critics is evidence that hindsight is as much neglected as foresight in the Foreign Office. Attempting to learn lessons from the way situations have been handled in the past involves the admission that mistakes have been made. That is a practice that ministers are trained to avoid since it is a basic rule of politics that MPs should never admit mistakes unless it is certain that they will be discovered. But there is a growing body of self-styled 'dissidents' in the Diplomatic Service who believe that it is their duty to keep asking awkward questions about why events have been handled badly. They resent being asked to select the facts and massage them in order to demonstrate afterwards that ministers, faced with circumstances which suddenly arose without warning, reacted in a way that was justified by the knowledge they had at the time.

One serious misjudgement which the Foreign Office failed to explain away was the closure of the mission in Afghanistan under chargé d'affaires Ian Mackley in February 1989. The reason given was that it would not be safe for the mission to stay in Kabul when the Soviet troops withdrew. That sounded unconvincing at the time, especially since the Foreign Office had no qualms about keeping the embassy open in Lebanon under far more perilous conditions with the ambassador in Beirut protected by an armed bodyguard of five men. The political assessment prompting the withdrawal was based on a rare experiment in prediction: that President Najibullah could not sustain himself in power after his Soviet military prop was removed and that the capital would be engulfed in civil war.

The Foreign Office went along with the US State Department in believing that the evacuation of Western embassies would be an important factor in destabilizing the regime of Najibullah's People's Democratic Party of Afghanistan. That was another miscalculation. It was confidently expected that after a short while the staff would return to the palatial embassy set in thirty acres which Lord Curzon once described as 'worth the presence of at least two divisions'. The intelligence verdict was that the mujahidin forces would occupy the capital and re-establish law and order quickly.

Two years later with Najibullah, however unpopular, still in power, and the mujahidin still squabbling among themselves and no nearer victory, the Foreign Office's Diplomatic Service List described the situation at the embassy as 'Staff temporarily withdrawn from post'. France and Italy quietly swallowed their pride and re-opened their embassies in Kabul. Mistakes never openly admitted by ministers take longer to rectify at the Foreign Office.

Diplomatic post-mortem examinations of policy are rare inside the Foreign Office. Occasionally papers are written to report on the way an event or a long period of negotiations were handled. That happened after the Lancaster House negotiations on Rhodesia, the negotiations on Hong Kong, and the Kuwait invasion crisis. It is unusual for the policy-making process to be reviewed after a major event. Normally that is left to be assessed in the course of investigations by parliamentary committees. After the Falklands war there was a review conducted inside the Foreign Office despite the fact that the Franks Committee was established to cover all the ground. The Foreign Office review was never made public for the very understandable reason that one of its principal conclusions was highly sensitive politically. The review affirmed that the mandarins believed their policy – the leaseback proposal of giving sovereignty to Argentina but having the islands run by the British – was right as the only feasible proposition, but the fault lay with the politicians who were responsible for its being badly presented in the House of Commons.

One important exception to the normal ostrich posture in the Foreign Office over learning lessons from mistakes occurred in 1979 a few weeks after the Shah of Iran abandoned his throne and flew to Egypt on 16 January. After writing a long report on his return from five years in Teheran, the Ambassador Sir Anthony Parsons was still perplexed at having lived through a genuine revolution almost of the magnitude of the 1789 revolution in France. Going round the corridors of the Foreign Office talking to other diplomats, he kept asking: 'Where did we go wrong? How did we fail to read the signs in time?' Because the search for answers was of interest to so many people, the PUS Sir Michael Palliser suggested a teach-in at the Foreign Office open to everyone.

An announcement was put on the notice-boards at the Foreign

Office of meetings being held by Sir Anthony Parsons under the auspices of the Diplomatic Staff Association. As an exercise in hindsight they drew about 100 people on three occasions at lunch-time to listen to Sir Anthony thinking aloud on the various factors leading up to the Khomeini revolution and dealing with questions about it. To have a senior ambassador stand up in front of everyone – including typists – and admit he made a big mistake required a large measure of courage. For many in his audience the meetings were a textbook example of how it can be worthwhile to learn the lessons of diplomacy by hindsight.

No one can be categoric about when it is advisable for a diplomat to send the Foreign Office warning of an imminent revolution. But one indicative event looked at in hindsight was on 9 January 1978 when Iranian troops opened fire on crowds for the first time for fifteen years. What made that particularly important was that the crowds attacked were in Qum, the spiritual home of Ayatollah Khomeini. Yet nine months later – and only three months before Ayatollah Khomeini took over – with tanks at the airport and the Shah admitting privately he was wondering whether he could survive, the Embassy was not warning that the end was near. 'I was still confident the armed forces would do their duty and I thought the Pahlavis had a fair chance of surviving,' Sir Anthony wrote in 1984 in his book *The Pride and the Fall*.

Many factors have to be weighed when an ambassador assesses the risks intrinsic in any situation. He has the safety of British nationals to consider. In Sir Anthony's case he had to take account of how a breakdown of law and order would affect the 20,000 Britons living in Iran. The protection of the British Council offices has also to be borne in mind. In Iran the Council had three centres outside Teheran at Shiraz, Ahwaz, and Mashad. One significant indicator in retrospect was the fact that when Mrs Thatcher went as Leader of the Opposition to Iran in April 1978 her planned visit to Isfahan was cancelled because of law-and-order problems. An ambassador has always to take account of the impact of events upon British trade and business interests. In 1978 Britain was enjoying a boom in exports to Iran. Any wavering in Britain's support for the Shah, it could have been argued, would have had a serious effect on the arms industry. With firm American support behind him the Shah would have felt it was a vote of no confidence if the British had not stayed four-square with him as well. Any hedging of bets could have undermined confidence throughout the Gulf in view of the importance of Iran's strategic position.

Allowing for all these factors, it was still legitimate to ask why so much store was set on the capacity of the armed forces and the strength of the sinister SAVAK secret police to ensure that the Peacock Throne was not overthrown. In his own defence Sir Anthony could argue that all the sources of discontent had been identified. Telegrams to the Foreign Office covered the student unrest, the factory strikes, the deep-seated opposition of the mullahs, and the anger of the bazaar traders at losing business in the modernization programme. But he admitted that there was a failure to realize how all these elements could be combined into one general uprising. In retrospect there should have been a greater awareness of how the mosque provides a roof for all the opponents of a regime to link themselves together. What many observers failed to appreciate early enough was how the mullahs used their influence to foment disobedience through demonstrations by students and by stoppages at factories by workers. Assumptions that the army could ensure that any protest would not get out of hand were flawed in many respects. They could not silence the mullahs. They could not force strikers to go back to work.

One of the principal lessons to be learned from the events in Iran was the danger of concentrating too much of the energies of an embassy on export promotion. There were times when the ambassador in Teheran was expected to see six company directors from Britain a day. In the intense competition of the economic boom all the diplomats in the embassy were regarded as commercial attachés almost to the extent of being blamed if a contract was not secured for a British company. That pressure of day-to-day commercial work did not leave enough time for the embassy staff to be circulating among the people who have the breadth of contacts to enable a comprehensive assessment to be made.

The teach-in highlighted the need for missions to have someone on the staff who is steeped in the affairs of the country and its politics. One of the classic examples was John Hyde, the Vice-Consul in Istanbul, whose encyclopaedic knowledge of Turkey and its people was of immense value to ambassadors, businessmen, and journalists. He spoke Turkish like a Turk and had a capacity to make friends with people in all sectors of Turkish life. His judgement of what were the causes of a sudden political develop- ment was usually far more reliable than most other sources of information in Turkey. Few young diplomats nowadays are allowed the time to develop such a knowledge of their area and the people who have influence in it. Those who are given the opportunity are often very impressive specialists such as Ralph Morton. As a Third Secretary in East Berlin from 1987 to 1991, he had a vast array of contacts with the dissidents in the city, which was invaluable to the Foreign Secretary when he wanted to have talks with a cross-section of the opposition. Another of the same breed, Patrick McGuinness, as Second Secretary in Sana'a from 1988 to 1990, acquired a deep understanding of the country and the thinking of its politicians which made him a highly regarded observer of the Yemeni scene.

Perhaps the most important lesson to be learned from past misreading of the signals is that it is time to abandon the assump- tion that only diplomatic intelligence counts in assessing a situ- ation. One senior ambassador made this criticism of the traditional arrogance of many of his colleagues: 'We are too convinced that only our information is really worth having and that outsiders don't know the score. We don't bring travelling academics, journalists, and businessmen into our area of discussion – and not just for the occasional seminar but for confidential talks, showing them our so-called secret stuff and asking them: "What do you think?"' People in these categories are able to have discussions with a wide range of individuals in circumstances that are ruled out for diplomats. It enables them to judge public figures away from their public personae. They often get access to information which it would be embarrassing for diplomats to be seen seeking.

This is not an argument for using journalists as the extra eyes and ears of an embassy. No correspondent is prepared to be an agent for his government – unless he works for a Soviet newspaper. The information a journalist acquires is for his newspaper, tele- vision, or radio programme. But in crisis situations assessments can sometimes be best put in perspective by diplomats and journalists taking soundings of each other. So far, however, correspondents find themselves kept at a distance at most diplomatic missions. Ambassadors – with exceptions occasionally in posts such as Moscow, Brussels, Paris, Pretoria, and Riyadh – rarely trust an outsider. Certainly not an outsider from the Press.

XI

The Press and Presentation of Policy

In 1930 most regular members of the Service had as little to do with the Press as possible. They were usually regarded with deep suspicion. There was a Press Section under a certain Mr Koppel; but it spent most of its time simply fobbing people off.

Lord Gladwyn, *Memoirs*

I think our spokesmen talk too much, and too much is attributed to them. I am instructing the Department to adopt a rather astringent attitude and on occasion to say flatly they have no statement to make. We want to have the output reduced and News Department confined as far as possible to statements which it is really in our interests to have published. We must get out of the habit of feeling obliged to provide information or answer questions simply because newspaper correspondents press us to do so.

Selwyn Lloyd to Harold Macmillan,
FO records,
1 November 1959

If a completely open society is ever established in Britain, the last bastion to surrender will be the Foreign Office. Ever since the beginnings of the Foreign Office in 1782 in Mr Fox's House, there has been an obsession with secrecy in the conduct of foreign policy. Most of the senior mandarins behave as if they belonged to a secret society. Papers and files are kept away from prying eyes in locked cupboards. Keys for opening red boxes or Lamson telegram tubes are given only to the highly trusted. Desks are cleared of every scrap of paper each evening before the rooms are vacated. All copies of telegrams no longer required are put through a shredder. Every word communicated to an outsider is very carefully weighed before it is conveyed in writing. Anyone not a member of the Diplomatic Service is made to feel that he or she does not belong to the elite and is an outsider. None more so than the Press.

The suspicions of the Press which Lord Gladwyn encountered in his early days were very clearly demonstrated in the procedures laid down for acquiring information before Percy Koppel's time. Correspondents were allowed through the gates in Downing Street provided they were properly dressed, and in those days a black bowler hat was *de rigueur* so that journalists could pass themselves off as gentlemen. The visitor from Fleet Street would be escorted to the Commissionaire's desk where he would present his visiting card and enquire if there was any news. His request would be conveyed to an attendant who would walk down to the PUS's room on the ground floor. More often than not, on his return the intrepid correspondent would be told: 'The Permanent Under-Secretary of State thanks you for your enquiry. He wishes to inform you that there is no news today but he invites you to call again tomorrow.' There are a number of diplomats who regret that such a system was abandoned.

Surprisingly for such a secretive organization, the Foreign Office was the first department in Whitehall to introduce a public relations system to deal with the Press. During the First World War Sir Edward Grey became concerned about morale and believed that diplomatic reporting could play an important role. To that end the Foreign Office created the News and Political Intelligence Department. For Fleet Street, however, the emphasis in the department was not so much on news as on propaganda – an impression which still emerges from time to time today from Downing Street. After the First World War the Foreign Office established a separate unit in 1921 to handle Press enquiries with two career diplomats as spokesmen. Its example spread extensively throughout Whitehall so that the latest list of government Press officers has over 1,000 names. By comparison with other departments, such as Employment which has 80 Press officers and the Ministry of Defence which has 36, the Foreign Office News Department is trim with only 9. Across the street at No. 10, where Press enquiries on foreign affairs are also handled, the Prime Minister's Press Secretary has a staff of 5, including one diplomat who is liaison officer for international correspondents based in London. In 1969 the Duncan Report highlighted the importance of the Foreign Office News Department, particularly in 'reaching the overseas public' through foreign correspondents in London. It recommended that News Department 'should be provided with adequate accommodation, equipment, staff and entertainment funds which in our view is not the case at present'. However, despite the improvements in a refurbished Press suite which was opened in 1990, it still falls far short of these requirements.

Its general service, nonetheless, is better than anywhere else in Whitehall for answering factual queries. However much policies are wrapped in secrecy, spokesmen are readily available for supplying facts and figures. The Foreign Office is the only department which enables the Press to have direct access by telephone to a spokesman twenty-four hours a day seven days a week. Other ministries have spokesmen available until 7 p.m. or 7.30 p.m. on weekdays but thereafter callers have to rely on being put through to a home telephone number by an operator. Foreign Office spokesmen with portable telephones can be contacted about a coup or a hijack at any hour right through the night. They take all calls, not just from journalists in Britain, but from anywhere. Comments made by telephone on trains and buses by the Foreign Office spokesmen get into print in the next edition while some ministries advise callers to 'try again in the morning'.

Where the Foreign Office was slow to modernize was in maintaining the pattern of selective briefings which characterized the elitist approach of the Foreign Office to the Press for the first twenty-five years after the Second World War. It was only abandoned when Tom McCaffrey, the first Head of News Department, who came from outside the Diplomatic Service as James Callaghan's spokesman, streamlined the system and brought it up to date. Until then the *Times* correspondent had a separate briefing and was often allowed to go into a room on his own and read the telegrams from ambassadors, although not always understanding them. On one occasion his article contained a section of a telegram including a phrase which had been garbled in transmission and came out in a jumble of letters. At 5 p.m. the *Daily Telegraph* also had a briefing on its own – but without a bundle of telegrams to read. The Three O'Clock Group, known as 'The Trusties', comprised the *Manchester Guardian*, BBC radio, BBC World Service, the now defunct *News Chronicle*, and the *Birmingham Post*. Each day at 3.30 p.m. there was a meeting of the popular news-papers – the *Daily Mail*, the *Daily Express*, the *Daily Mirror*, and the *Sun*. It was known as the Home Group because it once contained Charles Douglas-Home who was Diplomatic Correspondent of the *Daily Express* when his uncle was Foreign Secretary and would ask: 'What clangers has the Foreign Secretary dropped today?' Another group was called the Circus since it had a strange mix of characters from provincial newspapers. The quality Sunday newspapers received separate briefings while the *Sunday Express*, *Sunday Mirror*, and *News of the World* were lumped together. All these sessions were off-the-record. The one on-the-record occasion was the open Press conference which is still held every day at 12.30 p.m. for British and foreign journalists. Only one afternoon briefing survives, for all British correspondents from daily or Sunday newspapers, news agencies, radio, or television.

A parallel public relations operation is directed overseas by the Information Department whose function is described as 'the pro-vision of guidance material and background briefing on matters of general concern affecting Government policies'. Much of the background material comes from the Central Office of Information which supplies radio tapes of the Foreign Secretary's Press confer-ences abroad, television film, leaflets, and commissioned articles for overseas newspapers. At times of crisis the Information Depart-ment provides a stream of material for embassies to supply to local newspapers, radio and television stations. During the Gulf crisis of 1990–91 transcripts of statements by the Prime Minister and Foreign Secretary were sent round the world immediately and some twenty television films on the Iraqi regime and the threat to the Gulf were dispatched to Moslem countries. These were carefully targeted for audiences abroad, unlike the over-enthusiasm in the 1960s which resulted in the indiscriminate projection of Britain and British Government policies throughout the world. In those days it reached ludicrous proportions in terms of staff and expenditure. Over £24m a year was being spent on information work abroad with 150 UK-based staff – some 10 per cent of the staff overseas – plus 1,200 locally engaged personnel.

The Duncan Committee were amazed to find in 1969 that the Information section of the British High Commission in New Delhi had a staff of 117, including 6 UK-based staff, and that the Deputy High Commission at Calcutta had a staff of 36, including 2 UK-based staff, on information services. While it acknowledged the need for vigorous export promotion, the Duncan Report called for the information staff overseas to be cut down to half its size. More drastic cuts were urged by the Berrill Report in 1977. It came to the conclusion that the information services abroad did not produce results 'commensurate with the resources committed'. Although it recognized a case for projecting Britain in the Communist world and other 'closed societies', it recommended abandoning the traditional information activity in most of the Third World 'except for a few rich or influential countries'. Severe pruning followed so that by 1990 much of the information work abroad was done on a part-time basis along with other functions in embassies. If it were calculated on a full-time basis, the information staff would be 47 UK-based and 329 locally engaged. The vast numbers in New Delhi were whittled down to 1 UK-based diplomat and 21 locally engaged persons. Calcutta was left with no full-time British information officer and only 2 locally engaged staff. The budget of the information services was pruned to under £20m in 1991 and that included the cost of 2,400 sponsored visitors to Britain, formerly met by the Central Office of Information.

Overseas opinion is influenced in more sophisticated ways at seminars held at the Wilton Park Conference Centre, an impressive Elizabethan country seat known as Wiston House at Steyning in West Sussex. Although independently run as an academic institution, the conference centre is sponsored by the Information

Department at a cost of over £1m a year. It brings together politicians, newspaper editors, and university lecturers from a wide range of countries. They absorb ideas in discussion groups of about fifty people, spending four days on themes such as China's Evolution after the Tiananmen Square Massacre, the US Role in a new Europe, Out of Debt and into Development, Reconciliation in Southern Africa, Political Refugees, Fighting Drugs, and the Soviet Union's Economic Problems. The subjects are chosen by the Foreign Office in collaboration with the Wilton Park Director, Geoffrey Denton. The Foreign Office often invites participants to stay in London after the seminars as guests of the Government to meet people in Whitehall.

Despite being quick off the mark in establishing a News Department for projecting policies at home and an Information Department for doing the same abroad, the Foreign Office took a long time to come to terms with public relations techniques. It was the impact of the two dominant figures on the international scene in the early 1960s through their public relations skills which convinced Downing Street that presentation was of crucial importance – John F. Kennedy in the United States and Nikita Khrushchev in the Soviet Union. With two-thirds of the adult American population watching the four one-hour television debates between Nixon and Kennedy during the presidential campaign in September and October 1960, the skill of the young senator from Massachusetts in putting his case across to the people was seen as a basic factor which took him to the White House. Khrushchev showed the same talents with a different style on two occasions in the same year. First, in Paris, following the collapse of the Big Four summit before it started because of the U-2 spy plane crisis, Khrushchev used a Press conference at the Palais Rose to communicate as no Soviet leader had ever done before to the world. Even when the power failed because of overloaded television operations, Khrushchev shouted his message to 3,000 journalists just as effectively without microphones. In New York during the United Nations summit he projected his views from the balcony of the Soviet delegation twice a day in impromptu Press conferences which won him headlines in every continent. Both men made a drama simply out of presenting foreign policy in colourful terms which ordinary people understood. The rest of the statesmen in the world had to catch up with this new technique.

For Macmillan, Selwyn Lloyd, and Lord Home this was not a political style that suited them. They were ill at ease outside their own political environment. Not Harold Wilson. He had watched Kennedy closely, copying his techniques and using his yardstick of the first 100 days for measuring the swing of the pendulum of change. Whenever he went abroad he was always aware of deadlines and thought in headlines whenever he talked to the Press. At the end of the emergency Commonwealth summit in Lagos on 12 January 1966, three correspondents were invited in the late evening to join the Prime Minister for a drink in his room. His first words were not about how narrowly he had escaped being humiliated over British policy on Rhodesia. He had won a breathing space over his prediction that UDI would be finished in weeks rather than months – simply because Albert Margai of Sierra Leone went over the top in denouncing Britain for not sending troops to quell the rebellion. Instead of expressing his relief, the Prime Minister said he was sorry that he had missed getting into the first editions since Margai had gone on talking so long. Then he turned to his personal physician, Dr Joseph Stone, munching a ham sandwich alongside him, and made his predictions: 'I can see the headlines in the last editions. The *Mirror*: Wilson Wins. The *Express*: Wilson Wins Time. The *Mail*: Wilson Wins But .... The *Manchester Guardian*: Outbreak of Bubonic Plague Delays Conference.' His forecast predicted three out of four correctly.

For all his ability in personal projection, Harold Wilson knew that that was not enough. No. 10 Downing Street required a very special type of person as spokesman. To ensure a high profile in public relations, he chose an experienced journalist as his Press Secretary so that when he was not able to talk directly to the Press there was someone whom he trusted completely to convey his thinking accurately. First, he had Sir Trevor Lloyd Hughes, a shrewd political correspondent from the *Liverpool Daily Post*. Later, he drew in the talent of Joe Haines, a dedicated party man from the *Sun*. Foreign Secretaries soon realized how essential it was for them as well to have a skilled personal spokesman in the competitive international political arena. Britain's entry into the European

Community required the Foreign Office to have the necessary expertise to ensure that its policies were fully projected in face of the barrage of criticism from the other eleven delegations. Conference 'spokesmanship' became a highly prized talent which elevated the Head of News Department to a status almost on a level with the PUS and made the Press Secretary at No. 10 as important as a Cabinet minister – and, in the days of Sir Bernard Ingham, sometimes second only to the Prime Minister.

The toughest test in 'spokesmanship' was the fourteen weeks of the Lancaster House Conference on Rhodesia in 1979 which earned Sir Nicholas Fenn the accolade of 'star of the show' from Lord Carrington. Like all Heads of News Department with two exceptions – Sir Tom McCaffrey, a member of the Home Civil Service, and Brian Mower, brought from the Home Office by Douglas Hurd when he returned to the Foreign Office in October 1989 – Sir Nicholas Fenn became a spokesman as a professional diplomat, not a public relations expert. He had a number of advantages as a career diplomat, knowing the Foreign Office team negotiating on Rhodesia, being familiar with the Foreign Office system, and having experience as a former assistant private secretary of how the power house of the Secretary of State's Private Office operates.

His biggest advantage of all was a personal commitment from the Foreign Secretary. On the first day Lord Carrington called Fenn in and told him that anything said to the Press by him as spokesman, even though it was not cleared in advance, would be upheld 100 per cent in Parliament. By contrast the Ministry of Defence spokesman at the time of the Falklands War, Ian Mac-Donald, who was often unfairly criticized for not giving more than the very minimum of information, had to operate on a very tight leash. The Defence Secretary John Nott warned him at the outset that if he said anything to the Press that had not been written down and approved by the Chiefs of Staff he would be disowned.

Officially, Sir Nicholas Fenn had two roles at Lancaster House. He was the spokesman of the chairman of the conference, Lord Carrington, and also the conference spokesman. He had a third role, which on many occasions was most important of all, that of being a key factor in the negotiating process – selling a point of view to the Press and airing suggestions as diplomatic kites flown for the Press to report. In both cases it was of great interest to Sir Antony Duff, as head of the British negotiating team, to gauge the public and private reactions of the other delegations to what appeared as a result in the Press. For correspondents caught in the middle of news management from the various delegations, it was frequently a test of judgement and professional integrity to decide what to report as fact and what as political gamesmanship.

This flexibility in the spokesman's role was not the sole prerogative of Sir Nicholas Fenn. When he gave his on-the-record briefings in the Press Centre at the old Bath Club in St James's twice a day, he usually had the two African nationalist spokesmen from the Patriotic Front delegation sitting in front of him as journalists. Robert Mugabe's spokesman, Eddison Zvobgo, and Joshua Nkomo's spokesman, Willie Musururwa, were also registered as editors of their party newspapers and could ask questions. Later they could take over the Press conference platform and give their own briefings. That enabled them to have two opportunities to comment on the British version of what was happening at the negotiations. For Sir Nicholas Fenn there was always an extra option. As the proceedings of all the Press conferences were recorded these could be played back and analysed by him. He would then report to Lord Carrington, Sir Antony Duff, and Sir Robin Renwick so that they could adjust their negotiating tactics, if necessary. The African nationalist delegations were convinced that their rooms were bugged. They claimed their proposals were known by the British before they were tabled at the conference.

Selected British correspondents were invited to a backstairs room at the Bath Club for off-the-record briefings by Sir Nicholas Fenn at the end of the day. These were occasions when subtle, and sometimes not-so-subtle, explanations were given about how difficulties had arisen and how they might be overcome by amendments to draft proposals. However much a correspondent might be inclined to dismiss background briefings as propaganda, there was always pressure to write something in case another newspaper swallowed the official line completely and carried an extensive report on a possible 'new initiative'. Foreign Office 'guidance' could be deployed in such an apparently convincing manner that it was difficult for a correspondent to swim against the tide.

One frequently employed device was to have an optimistic comment on the negotiations made by Lord Carrington to the television cameras without any detail to substantiate it. That made it awkward for newspaper correspondents to write a gloomy assessment of the prospects of the Government finding a way out of the current deadlock unless a concession were made to the African nationalists. Any negative writing risked being dismissed as misguided since newspaper executives who heard the optimistic comment on television were apt to question the judgement of the correspondent. 'It can't be right. Carrington was very upbeat on television,' was likely to be the verdict. The Foreign Office public relations practitioners realized the power of television in updating the newspaper cliché, 'The camera can't lie.' By using backstairs briefings to promote the idea that certain small concessions were the last that could possibly be drawn from the British Government, the Foreign Office sought to win over those dubious about the optimistic comments on television.

The very success of these techniques caused problems in Parliament. MPs became worried at the way a 'faceless official' was able to answer questions on Government policy towards Rhodesia without any statement having been made in the House of Commons. As Sir Nicholas Fenn was being seen in television 'bites' from Press conferences as a 'faceless official', an unnamed spokesman not accountable to Parliament, some MPs felt that they had a good constitutional point. The strength of feeling was so great that procedures were revised at the Press Centre. Questions at a Press conference which appeared to cut across the right of Parliament to be informed were carefully evaded. When a major initiative had been taken with the tabling of a new draft, Lord Carrington would make the announcement at the Press Centre at the end of the session as Conference Chairman rather than as Foreign Secretary.

Lord Carrington was so pleased at the way the public relations aspect of the Lancaster House negotiations was handled that he assigned Sir Nicholas Fenn as spokesman to Sir Christopher Soames in charge of Rhodesia as Governor in the transition to independence. Along with the two key members of the Carrington team, Sir Antony Duff and Sir Robin Renwick, he had to ensure that the political problems were kept below boiling point in terms of media coverage. On his return to the Foreign Office Sir Nicholas Fenn enjoyed a much enhanced status as Head of News Department until his departure to be Ambassador in Burma in 1982. But like every other department of the Foreign Office, News Department was under a cloud after the resignation of Lord Carrington over the Falklands war. Although that cloud lasted for a year, Mrs Thatcher's second term as Prime Minister, when she began to play a bigger part on the international stage, produced a new impetus for an enlarged public relations role on both sides of Downing Street.

It reached a peak in the second half of the 1980s with the partnership of Christopher Meyer at the Foreign Office as Sir Geoffrey Howe's spokesman and Sir Bernard Ingham at No. 10 Downing Street as Mrs Thatcher's Press Secretary. It is difficult to imagine a more unlikely public relations duo: Meyer, the product of Lancing College, Sussex, and Peterhouse, Cambridge, a smooth sophisticated diplomat fluent in French, Spanish, and Russian, who had postings to Madrid, Brussels, and Moscow; and Ingham, a rough-hewn Yorkshireman who left school at sixteen, became a journalist whose column in the *Leeds Weekly Citizen* dismissed the Conservative Prime Minister in 1964, Sir Alec Douglas-Home, as 'a political fossil', left the *Guardian* after five years, and served Barbara Castle as her Press Secretary at the Department of Employment. Yet it was the most formidable combination of public relations talents ever seen in capitals all round the world.

Meyer gave the impression of almost liking journalists on a good day. Ingham enjoyed lecturing journalists for their 'cavalier approach to facts, especially if inconvenient'. Meyer acknowledged that the Press had a right to ask questions but not necessarily a right to an answer. Ingham never hesitated to answer any question even if it were only to dismiss it as 'prejudiced bunkum'. Wherever the partnership appeared – at summits of the European Community, the Commonwealth, or the Economic Group of Seven – the British delegation briefing room attracted the biggest crowd of correspondents, often four times as many as any other delegation. It was the place where 'British sources' – since they insisted on not being identified – purveyed the views of the British Government. At least some ideas were set out, if only those which were thought to be in its best interests to disclose.

Foreign journalists regarded a British briefing as a political event in itself. For them it was fascinating to hear an Englishman dismiss reports in the language of the 1930s as 'bunkum and balderdash'. But for British journalists, no matter how abrasive it might be, 'the Ingham–Meyer show' was an occasion not to be missed. If a Ministry of National Guidance had been created, Ingham and Meyer would have been the automatic choice as ministers. When there were no hard facts and the summit sessions had not started, correspondents desperate for something to write looked to these two for 'guidance'. No one knew the minds of their leaders better. Ingham was trusted to interpret the thinking of Mrs Thatcher in a style few others would dare to, certainly not in public. She backed him to the hilt saying, on one occasion, 'Isn't he marvellous? He's great. He's the greatest.' Meyer was closer to Sir Geoffrey Howe than anyone but his PPS. Even if he had not the chance to discuss an issue with him, Meyer could indicate precisely what his reaction would be.

Each had a highly professional approach to his job which was in essence to ensure the best possible Press for their leaders. Meyer started his day at 6 a.m. in Putney listening to the BBC World Service news. Then over breakfast he read through all the main newspapers. Walking to the station, he listened on his Walkman radio to the BBC's *Today* programme and read the rest of the newspapers on the train. On his desk in the Foreign Office at 8.30 a.m. he had a file of all the cuttings from the newspapers on foreign affairs and the box of telegrams. By 9 a.m. he had compiled a list of all the items liable to affect the Foreign Secretary and had a clear view of how the Foreign Office should react. Anything urgent was cleared with the Private Office. On crisis questions the Foreign Secretary's door was always open for him.

Ingham drove from his home in Purley at 7 a.m. also listening to the BBC's *Today* programme on his way to Downing Street. On his desk at 7.45 were all twelve national newspapers and a selection of twenty to thirty telegrams sifted for him as liable to be of the most interest. He delved into the newspapers starting at the other end from Meyer, with the tabloids first. An hour later Ingham had gutted the essentials from the Press and written a précis 1,000 words long summarizing all that the Prime Minister should know about what was in the newspapers. Mrs Thatcher trusted him so completely that she rarely read the newspapers and relied almost entirely on his précis. At 9 a.m., if Ingham thought he needed approval from the Prime Minister for his line on some urgent issue, he would go to her office. His relationship was so close that it was almost routine for her to nod when he would say, 'I think we ought to be saying so and so.' Even if the Prime Minister was not available, that did not stop Ingham from putting out his line to the Press. He had no problem in having it approved by her after the event.

Since the downfall of Mrs Thatcher in 1990 and the replacement of her Press Secretary by Gus O'Donnell from the Treasury to serve John Major, there has been a barrage of criticism against Sir Bernard Ingham. Most of it was focused on the way he used the Lobby system at Westminster to denigrate ministers falling out of favour with Mrs Thatcher. There is no doubt that he made many enemies at Westminster because of his cutting comments on politicians. But abroad his pugnacious, bulldog-breed style of projecting the British view served a purpose. His objective was to put the best gloss on the Prime Minister's position regardless of whether it left some correspondents frustrated at the way it was shaded to conceal certain basic weaknesses. The role of the Ingham–Meyer partnership was to put the British Government's case. They did not believe it was their duty to explain the cases of other governments unless they were supportive of Britain's stand.

When they did carry their arguments into others' camps to the point of being accused of behaving like a 'dirty-tricks department', it was usually Ingham who was blamed as 'the thug'. However, on one occasion when a British briefing caused an international incident it was the outcome of a stratagem devised by the smooth partner of the duo. Christopher Meyer was always quick to spot trouble in advance for his minister. During a visit to Canada in the autumn of 1985, Sir Geoffrey Howe was given a rough time at his Press conference over Britain's policy towards economic sanctions against South Africa. In his preparations for the

Commonwealth summit in Vancouver in October 1987, when he suspected another attack, Meyer sought some ammunition for a pre-emptive strike. He procured the statistics for Canada's trade with South Africa. The latest annual figures available from the International Monetary Fund were for 1986 and showed a 45 per cent increase in Canadian imports from South Africa compared with 1985.

On the flight to Vancouver going over their briefing papers, Meyer, sitting alongside Ingham, highlighted the case for showing that trade with South Africa was not illegal and illustrating it with the IMF figures on Canada's trade. Ingham, never a man of great enthusiasm for the Commonwealth, was taken with the idea of exposing the 'sanctimonious posturing' of the Canadians. Meyer and Ingham agreed that the first briefing would be a good time to fire the opening salvo. It hit where it hurt. The Canadians were furious. Prime Minister Brian Mulroney was already under attack from his opposition in Parliament for seeming to have softened his policy on economic sanctions. Yet the implication from the British briefing was that, despite the decision at the Commonwealth summit in Nassau in 1985 for more sanctions, Canada's trade had increased. The Canadians angrily pointed out that the Nassau decisions had little effect on trade apart from the import of Kruger-rands. It was the seven-nation Commonwealth summit in London in August 1986 which took decisions affecting trade with South Africa. The Canadian Ministry of External Affairs sent officials to take notes at British briefings and were annoyed at subsequent Ingham–Meyer sessions with the Press repeating the 1986 figures. Canadian figures for the first six months of 1987 showed a 50 per cent drop in trade with South Africa compared with the same period in 1986. When this point was raised at later British briefings it was shrugged off on the grounds that the only annual statistics available were those of the IMF.

The row escalated to the Heads of Government. Prime Minister Bob Hawke of Australia said he was outraged at what he claimed was deliberate misinformation at the British briefings. He condemned the picture presented there as 'an abominably untrue statement'. He was supported by President Robert Mugabe of Zimbabwe who said he was 'completely disillusioned'. Mrs

Thatcher remained defiant and unrepentant, accusing the Canadians of 'going up in smoke' over the issue. As always, she stood four-square behind her spokesman: 'I think what has happened is that some people have not liked the message, and therefore have gone for the messenger.' By making the Canadians as hosts of the summit conference appear hypocritical, the British were left more isolated than ever on the South African issue. There were many at the Vancouver meeting who thought that the thrust of the British public relations operation had gone too far and caused the conference to end on a sour note with recriminations against Britain from all sides. For the first time at a Commonwealth meeting, four Heads of Government held a joint Press conference to express their distaste – India's Rajiv Gandhi, Zambia's President Kaunda, Australia's Bob Hawke, and Zimbabwe's President Mugabe.

Where the public relations machine went wrong on that occasion was that it was geared for a confrontation on the European scale. The tradition of the Commonwealth is, ideally, that everyone should be treated 'as family' – quarrels sometimes, vendettas never. Everyone at a European Community summit accepts that it is a contest – to score as many points as possible and win as much back as you can persuade, or bully, the others to give. That was the target of the policy presentations at the EC when the question of the size of the rebate on the British budget contribution dominated the summits from 1979 until the successful outcome at Fontainebleau in 1984. Sir Bernard Ingham could claim that part of the reason the British Government secured a budget rebate totalling £10 billion between 1984 and 1989 was the way briefings set out the case for what he called 'hard pounding' to get what Britain wanted. He realized he was not an economist capable of explaining the intricacies of the Treasury arguments. Whenever the questioning became complex he turned to his Foreign Office experts. But his authority was never questioned as the person best qualified to convey the Prime Minister's priorities and the mood at any meeting. People looked to him to paint the scene in its primary colours and political shading. The role of the Foreign Office was to have someone do the detailed brush work.

At summits there is the complication of mixing doorstep interviews on television and radio with the more detailed background briefings. All politicians thrive on publicity. They like to be seen talking to other important figures all over the world. They want their words to go out live to voters in their homes. Television and radio give them the chance to get a message across, but when these 'bites' are fitted into bulletins the recordings have to be cut down from five or ten minutes to less than thirty seconds. Interviews at the end of conferences allow ministers to put their own slant on the outcome. Again, in the editing some answers are lost and what finally appears is not always what the ministers thought most important. In theory, ministers look to the writing Press to convey a coherent account of a meeting from the Press conferences. But there is so much material to be drawn from so many sources in various delegations that what a British minister may think is his best line is not necessarily what the correspondent believes is the most newsworthy element in a situation.

This different appreciation based upon an alternative set of values is the reason there is a feeling on each side that the other is an adversary. In foreign policy the Government – at No. 10 and at the Foreign Office – has reached the stage where it is accepted that presentation is virtually as important as substance. They look to the spokesman to advise them on how to sell the policies. The task of the Press is to find out not just what the policies are but what is behind the presentation which is not being said. There is a clash of interests. As Iain Macleod observed as Colonial Secretary in 1960, there must always be an abrasive element in relations between politicians and the Press. Politicians are eager to have their good works and themselves projected in print or on radio or television in the best possible light. They try to narrow the area of questioning to focus on the positive aspects of the issues. Correspondents are concerned to find out what is really happening, regardless of whether the Government comes out well or badly.

Every policy meeting held in the Foreign Office is attended by the Head of News Department as the Foreign Secretary's spokesman. If he says, 'This is the wrong policy for dealing with this situation', he will not command attention. But if he says, 'This policy will be heavily criticized if it is presented as a change of direction', people will listen and accept constructive suggestions. His role is important in ensuring that the platforms for speeches are employed to their full advantage. As space in newspapers for parliamentary debates has been severely reduced, public speech-making has become an increasingly significant means of achieving coverage in the media for the presentation of policies. When James Callaghan was discussing the question of speech-making in the US with Henry Kissinger, the American Secretary of State said he had a team of speech-writers. On James Callaghan's return he summoned the PUS, Sir Michael Palliser, and said he must have a team of speech-writers too. The Foreign Office could not muster enough diplomats for a team but they detached a bright young first secretary from the Eastern European and Soviet Department, transferred him to Planning Staff, and made him speech-writer. Thus Christopher Meyer set a pattern, writing speeches for Callaghan, then Crosland, and Owen – a challenge in adapting styles if ever there was one. It continues to be followed in the Policy Planning Staff Department.

Ministers sometimes use the cocktail hour to gather correspondents in their room to give off-the-record briefings which allow them to indicate the way they see situations developing. Even then, with drinks in hand, neither side forgets they are adversaries. For the Foreign Secretary such meetings are an occasion to put something across to journalists. If his policies are running into some flak and editorials in the newspapers are becoming critical, what better way for the Foreign Secretary to disarm some of the opposition than by taking correspondents 'into his confidence'? In this cosy atmosphere he can tell them some of the difficulties that for diplomatic reasons cannot be openly explained. For the correspondents it is an opportunity to put some of the real reasons for the Government's difficulties on a particular issue to the Foreign Secretary to test how much he admits and how much he evades. It is recognized as part of the tug-o'-war in news management.

One variant to news management at the cocktail hour was Sir Geoffrey Howe's penchant for a 'working breakfast' with the Press. Selected correspondents from the twelve national newspapers, the Press Association news agency, the BBC, and Independent Television News were invited to his official residence at No. 1 Carlton Gardens, off Pall Mall, at 8 a.m. once every two months. They were invited individually, not as representatives of a particular newspaper. In case of illness no substitutes were accepted. It was an occasion, in the words of one participant, 'for the Foreign Secretary to take in a trencherman's breakfast of bacon, sausages, and eggs – and the Press as well.' It had two drawbacks for the correspondents. Unless they were close to Sir Geoffrey Howe at the breakfast table, it was difficult to catch what he was saying in his soft tones in between munching through the crisp toast. Secondly, if something of special interest dropped from his lips inadvertently, his spokesman would be alert to the danger of an indiscretion appearing in print and would have a Breakfast Briefing Phase II afterwards to make sure that everyone 'got the line right'.

In one significant respect news management in Britain is unique: the influence on presentation of foreign policy through the Lobby system. The Prime Minister's Press Secretary meets political correspondents at Westminster twice a day at 11 a.m. and at 4 p.m. under Lobby terms which enable Government policy to be expounded without any sourcing to him, without even the admission officially that the questions had been asked and answers given. In most other Western democracies the chief government spokesman takes questions on-the-record and is quoted for comments on government foreign policy. There is a person on the rostrum at briefings who is identified. President Bush had Marlin Fitzwater. President Gorbachev had Gennady Gerasimov. At Westminster Sir Bernard Ingham did not exist officially at briefings. Abroad, he was an anonymous 'British source'. None of his briefings could be televised. Only when he appeared alongside Mrs Thatcher at a televised Press conference was his existence official. Yet his influence went far beyond that enjoyed by the spokesmen of other governments whose existence was never disguised.

The system of non-attribution was not of his making. It is the way the majority of the correspondents at Westminster want it. They were perturbed when Wilson's Press Secretary Joe Haines turned against the Lobby system in 1975 and issued on-the-record statements. It was a relief to them that Sir Tom McCaffrey restored the Lobby briefings system on its old basis when he became James Callaghan's Press Secretary at No. 10 in March 1976. Ten years later the system came close to being abandoned when Andreas Whittam Smith, launching the *Independent*, demonstrated its independence by refusing to have his Political Editor Anthony Bevins attend Lobby briefings under the non-attribution rules. Ingham's old newspaper the *Guardian* also withdrew its correspondents. If *The Times* and the *Daily Telegraph* had joined the boycott of the system, that would have been the end of it. They could not be persuaded. A ballot among members of the Lobby in October 1986 enabled Sir Bernard Ingham to continue as 'Government sources' at home but only by a margin of twelve votes: 67 to 55. It left a legacy of bitterness right to the end of the Ingham regime in 1990. Political correspondents of the *Independent*, the *Guardian*, and the *Scotsman* remained outcast, not even allowed to fly in the RAF VC 10 with the Prime Minister on her travels.

Abroad, there was not the same animosity. At a summit conference political correspondents acknowledged that an Ingham briefing abroad was invaluable when it dealt with Mrs Thatcher's interventions. He was the only source able to supply a comprehensive account of what she said. Moreover, he knew what she would say before she spoke. If the Prime Minister's place in the order of speaking was too late for the first editions of national newspapers, Sir Bernard Ingham could feed the Press the line from her speaking notes. On one occasion at a Luxembourg summit the agenda was delayed so long over the first item that Mrs Thatcher did not have the chance to make her speech on the controversy over agricultural subsidies. But the briefing had been given and all the first editions of national newspapers had front-page reports on the 'Battle of the Green £' – a battle that never took place.

Dependence on Ingham briefings had other, more sinister dangers. If political correspondents relied upon Sir Bernard for the main theme of their report of a summit meeting, it could leave them with a very unbalanced perspective of events. At Westminster they had many ways of off-setting the Downing Street assessment against other sources of information. Abroad, many of them were at a disadvantage without the contacts to take soundings of the views of other delegations. Aware of this vulnerability, Sir Bernard Ingham was shrewd enough to play up everything that seemed to be going Mrs Thatcher's way and to be dismissive of the importance of what was not. Views of other heads of government at European Community meetings or Commonwealth conferences had relevance for him only when they threatened to diminish the chance of Mrs Thatcher getting the main headlines. Then he would do his best to pour scorn on them.

In the course of ten years at the centre of the Government machine, Sir Bernard Ingham came to the conclusion that the Prime Minister's Office was the primary guardian of truth, the main repository of wisdom, and the stoutest defender of the country's best interests. He was by no means alone in Downing Street in these views, nor the first to hold them. The steady accretion of power in the hands of the Prime Minister has been a major political phenomenon of the past three decades. It required every department to be wary about how its policies were enunciated and the way they were implemented in case they caused trouble for the Minister. This awareness of the risk of incurring the wrath of the Prime Minister became a factor of increasing importance in the assessment of issues in all departments, most of all at the Foreign Office during the Thatcher era. The interaction of the two sides of Downing Street on the approach to European union and a wide range of other foreign policy issues created tensions which undermined the authority of the Foreign Office and the Foreign Secretary at a crucial period in international affairs.

XII

Downing Street Diplomacy: No. 10 and the FO

A certain degree of irritation, actual or potential, between the Prime Minister and the Foreign Secretary is the normal law of Whitehall.

Sir Nicholas Henderson, *The Private Office*

This relationship (between Prime Minister and Foreign Secretary) is rarely an easy one.

Lord Gore-Booth, *With Truth and Great Respect*

Margaret Thatcher evinced at times a distrust of the Foreign Office, a determined attitude that it didn't stick up for Britain and was softly conciliatory where the reverse was needed. I found that this sentiment was never far from the surface, and could erupt in impatient hostility unless ably countered – and sometimes even then.

Lord Carrington, *Reflect on Things Past*

Prime Ministers have always recognized that votes are won at home but reputations can be gained – or lost – abroad. This basic political fact explains why there are occasions, increasingly frequent in recent years, when a Prime Minister intervenes in the international arena on the grounds that foreign affairs are too important to be left solely in the hands of the Foreign Secretary.

It has taken Bagehot's constitutional definition that the Prime Minister is just *primus inter pares* somewhat beyond its original limits. But Gladstone acknowledged the difference between rights and realities in 1878: 'The Prime Minister has no title to override any one of his colleagues in any one of the departments. So far as he governs them, unless it is done by trick, which is not to be supposed, he governs them by influence only. But upon the whole, nowhere in the wide world does so great a substance cast so small a shadow.' Although Mrs Thatcher amply demonstrated the impact of such a great substance as the occupant of No. 10 Downing Street, she was by no means the first in the years following the Second World War.

Churchill dominated Eden at the Foreign Office. He in turn did the same to Selwyn Lloyd. Wilson did not hesitate to take over foreign policy regardless of the resentment of both Stewart and Brown. Callaghan often treated his protégé Owen with scant respect when he felt that foreign affairs needed an experienced hand. Thatcher went her own way whenever she felt that the backbone at the Foreign Office was showing signs of softness. Once she had established her authority over the economy, she became steadily more dominant in foreign affairs from the moment Pym took over from Carrington. It was significant that the two politicians who reached No. 10 Downing Street between 1960 and 1990 without passing through the Foreign Office had the least respect for it and the least compunction about overriding it. Home, Heath, Callaghan, and Major, who all served at the Foreign Office, had a high regard for its professionalism and valued its judgement. Neither Wilson nor Thatcher, who came to the premiership without any experience of foreign affairs or even being a shadow foreign secretary, had such an opinion of the Foreign Office. Although they had a great respect for individual members of the Foreign Office who worked with them at No. 10, to neither of them was the Foreign Office 'one of us, on our side'.

The evolution of summit diplomacy enhanced the scope for the Prime Minister to play a bigger part in international affairs. In Harold Macmillan's time at No. 10, the only large summits he attended were the Commonwealth conference and the disastrous Big Four summit in Paris in 1960. Throughout the 1960s and into the 1970s, the main international events were attended by foreign ministers. Lord Home went to foreign ministers' meetings with the US, Russia, and France regularly in Geneva. When Mrs Thatcher came to Downing Street in 1979 she was frequently at international conferences. Major decisions in the European Community were taken not by foreign ministers but at heads of government meetings. As many of them were overshadowed by the Battle of the Budget, this put Mrs Thatcher where she wanted to be – in the front line. Economic policy outside the Community was again a matter for the Prime Minister at the Group of Seven summits. NATO, which held all its meetings for its first twenty-five years at foreign minister level, had three summits between March 1988 and December 1989. Policy on South Africa at EC meetings and Commonwealth conferences was planned from No. 10. Mrs Thatcher underscored her approach by ruling out any participation by Sir Geoffrey Howe in the nine-nation committee group of foreign ministers set up at the Okanagan retreat during the Commonwealth summit in Vancouver in 1987 as a pressure group against South Africa.

Although summit diplomacy was still in its infancy during his first premiership, Harold Wilson was never at a loss for a springboard into the international arena. The verdict of Cabinet colleague Denis Healey in his memoirs, *The Time of My Life*, was devastating: 'No Prime Minister ever interfered so much in the work of his colleagues as Wilson did in his first six years. His short-term opportunism, allied with a capacity for self-delusion which made Walter Mitty appear unimaginative, often plunged the government into chaos.' Wilson was obsessed with the idea of being the one statesman in the Western world able to bring peace to Vietnam. One of his wildest projects, undertaken against all the advice of the Foreign Office, was the Davies peace mission in July 1965 to Ho Chi Minh in Hanoi. It is hard to imagine any other British prime minister having the audacity to imagine that sending a junior minister to Hanoi could bridge the gap between Ho Chi Minh and President Johnson.

The emissary was Harold Davies, the 61-year-old Welsh MP for Leek, who was Joint Parliamentary Secretary at the Ministry of Pensions and National Insurance. Davies had travelled widely in Asia and was as familiar with communes there as with pit shafts in his native Wales. He had contacted two North Vietnamese journalists in London, Nguyen Van Sao and Cu Dinh Ba. They arranged for him to be the guest in Hanoi of the Fatherland Front. Although the Foreign Office tried to dissuade Foreign Secretary Michael Stewart from approving the visit, he was in no position to resist Wilson's project. Stewart bowed to Wilson's pressure and instructed the head of South-East Asia Department to send his No. 2, Donald Murray, recently returned from South Vietnam, with Harold Davies. The first setback was the refusal of the Vietnamese to give Murray a visa. He was left behind in Laos when Davies flew from Vientiane to Hanoi on 8 July. The next setback was fatal. That same day the *Daily Mail* had a front-page exclusive report under the banner headline: 'Wilson's Secret Peace Move'. With the mission exposed for the gimmick it was, Ho Chi Minh refused to see Davies. He got no further than Tran Troy Quat, head of the Foreign Ministry's Western Department. After four days Davies flew back from Hanoi to report on the failure of his mission.

Wilson was incandescent with rage. He was ridiculed in the House of Commons. Liberal leader Jo Grimond pressed for clarification: 'Was this an official invitation from Hanoi? Did it specify Mr Davies or was he suggested by the British Government?' Shadow Foreign Secretary Reginald Maudling observed: 'It seems quite astonishing that a member of the Government with no connection with foreign affairs should, at his own request, visit Hanoi at this moment.' Wilson never forgave the *Daily Mail* for disclosing his hare-brained scheme. Six years later Wilson, still fuming, wrote in his book *The Labour Government: 1964–70* that it was all the newspaper's fault: 'Whatever hopes the Davies visit might have justified were dashed by a serious, indeed disastrous leak in London, while he was on his way.'

The Davies mission was the second intervention by Wilson on Vietnam in a month over the heads of the Foreign Secretary and the Foreign Office. Wilson decided that the Commonwealth Conference in London in June 1965 would be an ideal launching pad for a Vietnam peace initiative. There was the added advantage that it would divert attention from Britain's failure to produce any new ideas for solving the Rhodesia crisis. The Wilson plan was for four heads of government – from Britain, Nigeria, Ghana, and Trinidad – to undertake a Vietnam peace mission, visiting Washington, Moscow, Peking, Hanoi, and Saigon. He kept his Foreign Secretary, Michael Stewart, in the dark until the last minute. Worse still, he leaked the idea to the London *Evening Standard* before the plan was formally put to the Commonwealth Conference.

When delegates came back from lunch to the first business session at Marlborough House in Pall Mall on 17 June 1965, they were staring in amazement at the *Standard*'s front-page story stating that the Commonwealth would be sending a mission to Vietnam. Several African leaders resented Wilson jumping the gun and assuming his plan would be accepted as it stood. To rub in the point, Jo Murumbi, Kenya's Vice-President who had lived in exile in London for many years and knew all about the leak system, suggested it would be better to have a more objective leader for the mission than Wilson and proposed Canada's Lester Pearson. Although Wilson won the leadership of the mission, the project was blocked by Russia, China, and North Vietnam refusing to meet it. China's leading newspaper, the Peking *People's Daily*, administered the final put-down, dismissing Wilson as a 'nitwit'.

Throughout the fourteen years of the crisis after UDI, Rhodesia was a persistent problem which kept cropping up on the Cabinet agenda. Heath had little interest in Africa and left it to his Foreign Secretary, Sir Alec Douglas-Home, to negotiate with Premier Ian Smith in 1971. James Callaghan shrewdly calculated there was not much chance of success and was content to let David Owen expend much time and energy on it to little purpose. Mrs Thatcher was engrossed in the economy and had no enthusiasm for Africa. She was relieved to have Carrington wrestle with it for fourteen weeks and grateful he reached an agreement without any need for her to intervene. The one prime minister who could not resist meddling in the Rhodesia crisis was Harold Wilson. During his first premiership there were two major attempts at a settlement. He took the minister in charge, Commonwealth Relations Secretary Herbert Bowden, with him to the HMS *Tiger* talks in December 1966. But he did all the talking to Smith. Two years later he tried again. On his own initiative, Wilson took soundings through two special envoys to Rhodesia, Sir Max Aitken and Lord Goodman. Then he went to Gibraltar for talks on board HMS *Fearless* in October 1968. The Commonwealth Relations Secretary, George Thomson, went with him. The talking, as ever, was done by Wilson.

On only two occasions did James Callaghan make a personal intervention on the Rhodesia problem as Prime Minister and that was somewhat out of character. He took everyone by surprise with a burst of Wilson-style instant diplomacy, jetting off in the RAF VC 10 on 22 September 1978 to meet President Kuanda half-way between Britain and Zambia at Kano in northern Nigeria. It was an attempt to mollify Kaunda over the disclosure that Shell and British Petroleum had circumvented the Rhodesian oil sanctions since 1965. Although Wilson claimed he had been hoodwinked, Lord Thomson revealed that as Commonwealth Secretary he had informed the Prime Minister of the transactions in writing in 1968. These, he added, had continued for ten years afterwards – covering the time of Callaghan's premiership. Kaunda accused Government ministers in London of cheating in what he described as 'an Oilgate worse than Watergate'. Callaghan felt he could not pass it all over to Owen. Although he took his Foreign Secretary with him, Callaghan decided it was a time for personal diplomacy.

His second intervention was two months later when he sent Cledwyn Hughes, chairman of the Parliamentary Labour Party and a former Commonwealth Office minister, on a mission to the various Rhodesian leaders. Callaghan had ambitions to preside over a Rhodesia summit after the fashion of President Carter's success at Camp David in getting an agreement between President Sadat of Egypt and Prime Minister Begin of Israel. But the bleak report brought back by Cledwyn Hughes ended that pipedream.

Tensions between the two sides of Downing Street tend to be explained in terms of personalities. The personal chemistry between the Prime Minister and the Foreign Secretary is often an important factor in determining how much policy will be formulated at the Foreign Office and how much will be initiated from No. 10. Of almost as much importance at times is the status of advisers on foreign policy at No. 10. In the latter half of Mrs Thatcher's eleven-year premiership, the emergence of her Private Secretary for Overseas Affairs, Sir Charles Powell, as a figure of significant influence was regarded in some quarters as an alarming new phenomenon. The way his power increased over the years caused some consternation, but the position of trust he acquired under Mrs Thatcher was by no means unprecedented.

If Powell had required a role model, he could have justified his status by citing the example of Sir Philip de Zulueta who served for nine years at No. 10 as Private Secretary to Eden, Macmillan, and Home. Picked out by Eden as a resident clerk at the Foreign Office, de Zulueta was praised by Macmillan in the terms Mrs Thatcher later used of Powell: 'He understands the way my mind works. I don't have to explain everything to him.' Despite his origins – his grandfather was a diplomat in the Spanish Embassy in London – de Zulueta had the bearing of an English aristocrat, a style that pleased Macmillan. Unlike Powell, he kept a low profile and was rarely seen alongside the Prime Minister on television. Macmillan relied on de Zulueta's judgement, calling him 'my chief adviser' to the irritation of the Foreign Office. His importance was underlined when Macmillan went to Rambouillet in December 1962 for talks with de Gaulle which subsequently became the subject of controversy over Britain's nuclear options after the cancellation of Skybolt. Although two Cabinet ministers went to France with him – Lord Home and Peter Thorneycroft – Macmillan had only one person with him at the talks: de Zulueta.

When Sir Philip de Zulueta left the Service in 1964 for a distinguished career in merchant banking, a succession of rising stars from the Foreign Office were assigned to No. 10. Sir Oliver Wright, who later became Ambassador in Washington, served both Home and Wilson. He was sent by Wilson in July 1966 to take soundings in Rhodesia. Two other up-and-coming diplomats who served Wilson as Private Secretaries became PUS: Sir Michael Palliser and Sir Patrick Wright. In the Thatcher era the traditional Private Secretary from the Foreign Office was supplemented by other advisers on foreign affairs. The first of these was Sir Michael Palliser, who was taken on for a second tour of duty at No. 10 when he went to say farewell to Mrs Thatcher on retiring as PUS. It was five days after the Argentine invasion of the Falklands. Mrs Thatcher was inundated with problems and mounds of paper about them. She turned to Macmillan for advice. His recommendation was one practical suggestion: Get yourself a sort of chief-of-staff as Churchill had in 'Pug' (Lord) Ismay during the war.

Mrs Thatcher realized she needed someone to keep an eye on all the strands of the Falklands operations, making sure nothing was overlooked. That was the role given to Sir Michael, the watchman over all that was happening. He was the one person at No. 10 who had the time to read all the telegrams and all the submissions from the various departments. At the daily War Cabinet, Sir Michael was the one to ask the awkward questions: Who is taking charge of procuring X, Y, or Z and will there be enough available in time?

His function proved so useful at No. 10 that when he left Mrs Thatcher looked for another extra adviser on foreign affairs in the autumn of 1982. Various names were proposed: Sir Nicholas Henderson, brought out of retirement to be Ambassador in Washington where he played a vital role during the Falklands war, Sir Antony Duff, Deputy Cabinet Secretary, and Sir Frank Cooper, PUS at the Ministry of Defence. Instead, she picked another of her Falklands favourites, admired for his service as Ambassador to the UN, Sir Anthony Parsons, as the first Special Adviser to the Prime Minister. It was a typically British arrangement. There was no proper definition of his job, no research assistants, not even a personal secretary. He had to share one with Mrs Thatcher's economic adviser, Sir Alan Walters. It was a part-time job, four days a week, with a full-time commitment.

Mrs Thatcher saw it as an alternative system of assessing foreign policy questions. Sir Anthony, as a good Foreign Office man, refused to be a competitor to the FO, trying to catch them out. He saw his mandate as spotting problems on the way to becoming crises and stopping them from reaching the explosive stage. Whenever he sent an assessment of a situation to the Prime Minister he always sent a copy to the Foreign Office to avoid people there thinking he was working behind their backs.

On Sir Anthony's departure after a year, Sir Percy Cradock, the Mandarin-speaking former Ambassador to China who played a major part in the negotiations over Hong Kong, became Foreign Affairs Adviser. His main activity, which occupied 80 per cent of his time, was focused on national security as Chairman of the Joint

Intelligence Committee. His foreign policy brief was largely to identify trends some six or nine months ahead. With less regular access than Sir Anthony Parsons, who saw the Prime Minister almost every day, Sir Percy did not have the chance to wield a powerful influence on foreign policy at No. 10. Once Sir Charles Powell arrived in June 1984, the opportunity had gone for ever. Within a few months he had established himself in a position of immense authority.

As a former head boy at Canterbury Choir School who gained a First in History at New College, Oxford, Powell arrived with an incisive mind and an impressive diplomatic record at No. 10. With four foreign languages – Finnish, Italian, French, and German – he had served as Private Secretary to Lord Cromer at the Washington Embassy, been part of the Carrington team at the Rhodesia negotiations, and served in Brussels, Bonn, and Helsinki. A phenomenally hard worker, Powell often put in a fifteen-hour day seven days a week. It began with a stroll through the park from his Kensington mews home to be at his desk at 6.30 a.m. He read quickly and could get through all twelve national newspapers in an hour, ready for his first meeting of the day with Press Secretary Bernard Ingham.

Each respected the other's professionalism but there was a wide cultural gap between them, which Ingham was frequently made to feel. Throughout the day Powell kept in touch with the flow of telegrams and was constantly on the telephone to the Foreign Office – at least twenty times a day, often double that – discussing how he saw developments with Stephen Wall, the PPS to the Foreign Secretary who eventually succeeded Powell at No. 10. He played a key part in preparing the Prime Minister for Question Time in the House of Commons on Tuesdays and Thursdays. By being with Mrs Thatcher more than anyone else at Downing Street or even her Cabinet ministers, travelling with her abroad, and staying with her at Chequers at weekends, Charles Powell acquired extraordinary influence as a political guru on foreign affairs. He determined what she should read. He sifted through sometimes as many as 200 Foreign Office telegrams a day, knew instinctively what would interest her, and selected about four or five for her attention. Longer analyses in the form of reporting telegrams from particularly highly regarded ambassadors he would allocate to her overnight boxes. He decided where telegrams and submissions went: either into her Action Box or her Information Box.

As a voracious reader he selected articles for her to read from American publications such as *Foreign Affairs* or *Aviation and Space Weekly*, marked passages for her in specialist journals, and gave her digests of lectures delivered to the Royal Institute of International Affairs. She lapped up everything he sent her on defence and the maintenance of a balance of arms. He was usually the first person she met in her office at the start of the day and often the last, late in the evening. There was always a place for him – and his vivacious Italian-born wife Carla – at official dinners at No. 10. Because of the time-lag of Washington being five hours behind London, Powell and the Prime Minister frequently had half an hour at the end of dinners to discuss developments together.

He decided which British ambassadors it was worth her while to meet. Immediately before a European Community summit, he would arrange for Sir David Hannay – and subsequently his successor Sir John Kerr – to come over from Brussels and spend an hour talking over the main items on the agenda and the problems the Prime Minister would face from other leaders. He was supplied with a list of ambassadors coming home on leave so that he could select the most suitable envoys to discuss matters with Mrs Thatcher. Top of his list were Sir Antony Acland from Washington, Sir Crispin Tickell from New York, Sir Rodric Braithwaite from Moscow, Sir Robin Renwick from Pretoria, and Sir Christopher Mallaby from Bonn. As her political doorkeeper he could determine who from outside that special inner circle was allowed time with her. Sometimes he would find a gap in her programme and decide that it would be useful to have her mind diverted to problems she rarely had time to study.

As the one person Mrs Thatcher trusted above all, he was at her side in talks with President Gorbachev when no other officials were present. When she went to Germany for talks with Chancellor Helmut Kohl it was Charles Powell who remained with her as the doors closed on the others. Even when Sir Geoffrey Howe had his weekly 'private' meeting with the Prime Minister he was there too. It was usually no more than half an hour in a brief run-through of four or five issues. At the end she would spend more time with Powell going over the ground in detail. When the Foreign Office was putting together ideas for a course of action, he would telephone the Department and head them off some options with the advice: the PM would never go along with that.

Powell's status was recognized in Washington. He had a direct telephone to the National Security Council. In times of crisis he would go straight to General Colin Powell, Chairman of the Joint Chiefs of Staff, or Brent Scowcroft, the National Security Adviser. He listened in to all conversations between the American President and the Prime Minister as he was the official note-taker. That continued after Mrs Thatcher's premiership. The decision to launch the land war against Saddam Hussein in Kuwait on 16 January 1991 was taken by President Bush just twenty-four hours before the attack. For a time only two people in Britain were in on the secret: Prime Minister John Major and his note-taker Charles Powell. Immediately after the Bush–Major consultation only two others were informed: the Foreign Secretary Douglas Hurd and the Defence Secretary Tom King. Other Cabinet members were only told an hour before the assault.

Although he had a distaste for ordinary public relations techniques, Sir Charles was as much an image-maker for Mrs Thatcher as his younger brother Christopher was for Labour leader Neil Kinnock. Sir Charles, though officially detached from party politics, inspired many of Mrs Thatcher's most telling broadsides. He was credited as the inspiration for her comment in her speech to the Conservative Party conference in October 1986: 'A Labour Britain would be a neutralist Britain.'

His influence over foreign policy had another important dimension as the organizer of seminars to work out an assessment of trends and their implications for Britain. In September 1989, he arranged an all-day teach-in at Chequers on the consequences of conventional force reductions for NATO strategy. He circulated the discussion paper setting out the six main areas to be discussed by the twenty participants alongside the Prime Minister – Chancellor Lawson, Foreign Secretary Major, Defence Secretary Tom King, Defence Procurement Minister Alan Clark plus military top brass, academics, and three Americans. Only one Foreign Office mandarin was invited: Political Director John Weston. Other seminars were held on the Soviet Union, on southern Africa, on NATO, and on Eastern Europe.

A leak to the Press of Powell's 3,000-word summary at the end of a seminar on Germany on 24 March 1990 ruffled Anglo-German relations considerably, even though its conclusion was: 'We should be nice to the Germans.' There were embarrassing revelations of the discussions involving Mrs Thatcher, Douglas Hurd, Lord Dacre, Professor Norman Stone, American professors Fritz Stern and Gordon Craig, George Urban, former research director at Radio Free Europe, and the journalist Timothy Garton Ash. They listed some abiding aspects of the German character as 'angst, aggressiveness, assertiveness, bullying, egotism, inferiority complex and sentimentality'. Despite concern at the German tendency to 'overdo things, to kick over the traces', the Prime Minister and her seminar guests took comfort from one conviction: 'The more assertive Germany became, the easier it ought to become to construct alliances against Germany on specific issues in the Community.' While it aroused interest that so much traditional prejudice still existed, observers in Bonn were concerned at the way the confidential memorandum reaffirmed the back-stage influence exerted by Charles Powell on Mrs Thatcher.

The interventions of Mrs Thatcher in foreign affairs were not confined to European Community matters or economic policy towards South Africa. One of the most damaging divisions in Downing Street occurred over a request from President Reagan in April 1986 for American F-111 bombers to fly from bases in Britain to bomb Libya. Mrs Thatcher was opposed not only by her Foreign Secretary, Sir Geoffrey Howe, but by virtually her entire Cabinet. Three months earlier, addressing the Association of American Correspondents in London, she had enunciated an agreed Cabinet policy on the use of force against Libya: 'I must warn you that I do not believe in retaliatory strikes that are against the law. Once you start going across borders, I don't see an end to it.'

President Reagan had been itching to launch a punitive strike against Colonel Gaddafi for months. Public pressure reached a peak in April when the Libyans were blamed for a bomb attack on a West Berlin disco which killed an American and injured 230 others, including 79 Americans. To seek support, Reagan sent his UN Ambassador Vernon Walters round the European capitals. President Mitterrand responded by banning American planes from flying over France. After Walters's visit to London, Mrs Thatcher was almost alone in the Cabinet in wanting to honour the 'special relationship'. Only Lord Hailsham, the Lord Chancellor, appeared to side with her. Sir Geoffrey Howe was bawled out as a 'fair-weather friend' for suggesting that Article 51 of the UN Charter, cited by Mrs Thatcher as a cover for Reagan's action, was concerned with the right of self-defence, not offensive action.

The specific request to use British bases arrived at No. 10 in the middle of an official dinner for President Chun Doo Hwan of South Korea on 8 April. Charles Powell passed it to Mrs Thatcher as the guests were leaving and she asked Sir Geoffrey Howe and Defence Secretary George Younger to stay behind. They sat in her study – with Powell as always in attendance – to consider how to answer Reagan. Sir Geoffrey told the Prime Minister it was impossible to give Reagan a blank cheque for offensive action from British soil. Younger agreed with Sir Geoffrey. Foreign Office anxieties about arousing the anger of Britain's friends in the Arab world cut no ice with Mrs Thatcher. She was determined to stand by Reagan 100 per cent. Howe and Younger argued for demanding justification from Washington that Reagan could make a case under international law. She brushed these arguments aside and fired off some questions on the direct teleprinter to Washington about guarantees that no civilian targets would be hit and assurances about the accuracy of the military targeting.

When the question came up again before ministers on 10 April, Mrs Thatcher still found herself without solid support for backing the American raid. She sought further clarification about the targets and left a final decision until the morning. No reply had arrived by 7 a.m., however, and Mrs Thatcher did not want to wait any longer. Significantly, she contacted Charles Powell, not Sir Geoffrey Howe, and told him to send a message to General Colin Powell at the National Security Council giving the go-ahead on the use of the bases. It was one of her most unpopular decisions – polls registered public opinion 70 per cent opposed to it. There was obvious unease on the Conservative backbenches as Labour leader Neil Kinnock accused Mrs Thatcher of putting the lives of British citizens in jeopardy from Arab retaliation. Liberal leader Sir David Steel lambasted her for turning 'the British bulldog into a Reagan poodle'. Mrs Thatcher admitted: 'Decisions like this are never easy.' Her denial that it was done off her own bat – 'I pondered with the ministers most closely concerned' – did not carry much conviction. Sir Geoffrey made it clear that in his absence at a foreign ministers' meeting in The Hague he had not been informed of decisions either in Washington or in London. 'For my part, I had no confirmation of the President's decision to authorize the raids . . . still less of any decision to authorize them that night until I came back to London and met the Prime Minister.'

For once Mrs Thatcher appeared chastened by the experience of putting her friendship with Reagan before the principle of Cabinet solidarity. At first she tried to bluff her way out by claiming it was inconceivable that she should have rejected the Reagan request. 'If you fail to take action because there might be some risks incurred, you are saying that you should never tackle or take any action to reduce State-sponsored terrorism. You would have to cringe before Colonel Gaddafi.' But she drew back from any open-ended commitment to the Americans. 'I reserved the position of the United Kingdom on any question of further action,' she told the House. Any regrets were very temporary, however. She felt vindicated when she saw that Gaddafi was much cowed after the raid.

Mrs Thatcher's interventions on the international stage resulted in her becoming the most extensive foreign traveller of any prime minister. In her eleven years she made over 170 visits abroad to 54 different countries. But when Alan Williams, Labour MP for Swansea West, complained of the amount of time she spent abroad and asked whether the British taxpayer was getting value for money, Mrs Thatcher proved that she was more thrifty than most world statesmen. The total bill for her foreign travel from taking office in May 1979 until July 1990, four months before leaving office, was £4,300,000. In the first full year, 1980, the cost of her travels was only £133,206. By 1988 it had risen to £637,096. She always travelled light with a small staff. Unlike others before her, she never took a doctor and rarely had her Parliamentary Private Secretary with her. Sometimes her husband, Denis, travelled with her, attending Commonwealth conferences and other special visits, but he was a guest of the host government.

Much of her travelling was to summits: 33 to the European Community, 6 Commonwealth conferences, and 10 Group of Seven economic summits. European capitals were the most frequent destinations: 24 visits to France, 16 to Germany, and 14 to Belgium. Most of them were programmed to keep her totally immersed in politics – no time for art galleries or concerts; no sightseeing except for sludge-pump factories. On one tour she made eleven speeches. In December 1984 she arrived back at Heathrow just before Christmas having completed a 26,000-mile round trip to Peking, Hong Kong, Guam, Honolulu, and Washington in six days. She eschewed the temptation of de luxe travel by Concorde, preferring the old-fashioned comforts of the RAF VC 10 at a slower speed. Compared with President Bush her costs were modest. Everywhere he went there were four massive planes – his own Air Force One, plus a spare in case of engine problems, a third to carry his bullet-proof limousine, and a fourth to take his personal helicopters.

Abroad, Mrs Thatcher often relied heavily on members of the Diplomatic Service. Despite her strong reservations about the Foreign Office as an institution, there was a small number of its members she liked to have with her as a team of experts. She used them for what she called the 'nitty-gritty' of working out agreements. They were the mandarins, steeped in their subjects, whom she could trust to take up any challenge and turn the argument against whoever stood in her way. One of the most skilful of the 'golden pens', as Mrs Thatcher once hailed her scribes during negotiations with the Americans at Camp David, was Sir John Kerr, at that time a counsellor in the Embassy in Washington. His ability to interpret her mind and set out her requirements in such a way as to be acceptable to the Americans on the complexities of nuclear deterrence was invaluable to her on two occasions. Significantly, Mrs Thatcher did not deem it necessary to have her Foreign Secretary at her side although President Reagan fielded his full team. She took on the Americans single-handed – and pulled off a diplomatic coup on both occasions.

The first encounter at Camp David was the result of an increasing concern about the unbridled American enthusiasm for the Star Wars project, the Strategic Defence Initiative. After her talks with Gorbachev at Chequers in December 1984, Mrs Thatcher realized there was a danger of Russia copying SDI and with the two superpowers locked into it Britain's nuclear deterrent would be meaningless. At stake was the entire concept of nuclear deterrence which was the one pillar of British foreign policy which successive governments believed had kept the peace for forty years. Mrs Thatcher knew she could not bulldoze her way into Camp David demanding that Reagan recast his whole concept of Star Wars. Her ploy was to pledge Britain's fulsome support for SDI with certain restraints on deployment to allay Soviet fears about the Anti-Ballistic Missile Treaty of 1972 and to preserve nuclear deterrence – with, of course, the British nuclear deterrent.

On her way to Washington from China and Hong Kong, she did without sleep in order to rehearse all her arguments on SDI with Charles Powell. At the refuelling stop in Hawaii she insisted on going across from Hickham Air Base at 3 a.m. to have a look at Pearl Harbor where 2,300 Americans died in the Japanese attack on 7 December 1941. Even when she arrived at the British Embassy in Washington at 11 p.m., Mrs Thatcher had a further briefing session to prepare for the Camp David talks. As they sat down for the first plenary session, the British side seemed outgunned. On the other side were President Reagan, Vice-President Bush, Secretary of State George Shultz, National Security Adviser Robert McFarlane, and US London Ambassador Charles Price. Facing them were Mrs Thatcher, Sir Oliver Wright, the Ambassador, Robin Butler, her PPS, Charles Powell, and John Kerr. Mrs Thatcher was not someone easily overwhelmed, however.

After Reagan's short opening statement it was Thatcher all the way for over an hour – 'almost like a lecture', an American observed. As the discussion on details progressed, Kerr passed a note to Mrs Thatcher saying there were enough points of agreement to get a joint statement and suggesting he put them into communiqué language in case they were clouded over in prolonged debate. The Prime Minister persuaded Reagan they had done well enough to adjourn for lunch and gave the nod to Kerr to start drafting. He disappeared with Powell, found a secretary's room empty, and sat Nigel Sheinwald, a first secretary from the Embassy, down at a typewriter. Once Charles Powell saw the shape the draft was taking, he went off to the lunch leaving Kerr to carry on composing on his own.

Half an hour later Kerr signalled Powell that he had completed the famous Camp David accord. It received Powell's seal of approval as meeting Mrs Thatcher's requirements and it was passed to her. She chose her moment to produce it in traditional fashion from her handbag. Reagan smiled at the 'handbag trick' and handed it over for McFarlane and Richard Burt, Assistant Secretary of State, to review it with Powell and Kerr. Only two words were changed to delete a reference to testing in the same context as SDI deployment. This historic agreement, compressed into sixty-one words in less time than it takes to have lunch, became a model for diplomats to study. The document was a classic for its simplicity, and its breadth of application:

1. The United States and Western aim is not to achieve superiority but to maintain balance, taking account of Soviet developments.
2. SDI-related deployments would, in view of treaty obligations, have to be a matter of negotiations.
3. The overall aim is to enhance and not undermine deterrence.
4. East–West negotiation should aim to achieve security, with reduced levels of offensive systems on both sides.

For Mrs Thatcher it was not just the reassurance she wanted over deterrence. It allayed some of the fears of her European partners that America's Star Wars programme could block East–West disarmament negotiations. Although testing and deployment were not covered, Point 2 recognized concerns about the spirit of the 1972 ABM treaty being violated. While it enabled Mrs Thatcher to appear fully in support of SDI, the Camp David accord in effect confined Star Wars to the research laboratory. If anyone doubted the achievement, it was confirmed by the angry reaction of the SDI lobby who felt that Reagan had been bounced into it by Mrs Thatcher and her drafters. The American Defense Secretary Caspar Weinberger, who was not at Camp David because Mrs Thatcher gave no advance notice of her intention to raise SDI, did not conceal his annoyance. He insisted on the White House issuing a statement that the accord did not mean Russia had a veto over SDI deployment.

The second venture by Mrs Thatcher into direct diplomacy at Camp David over the head of the Foreign Office was an attempt to rescue the Western alliance from chaos in the wake of the Reagan–Gorbachev summit in Reykjavik on 12 October 1986. At first there had been deep disappointment that the smiles at the end of the summit as the two leaders left Hovde House in the Icelandic capital meant nothing. But within a few days the feelings turned to immense relief that a last-minute deadlock over SDI had saved Reagan from being beguiled into plunging headlong down the road to a non-nuclear world dominated by Soviet conventional forces. The confusion over the superpowers negotiating on sweeping disarmament proposals without consulting the Europeans required a public restatement of Western security objectives.

Mrs Thatcher set off for Washington on Friday, 14 November 1986, with Charles Powell. Again, she left Sir Geoffrey Howe behind even though she knew Secretary of State George Shultz would be with Reagan at Camp David. But there was no question this time of manoeuvring the Americans into accepting a piece of paper which she just happened to have in her handbag. It had to be a very carefully drafted document worked out jointly. Whatever else it said, there had to be a specific reaffirmation of NATO's policy of flexible response with a mixture of conventional and nuclear forces.

This was the mandate for the 'golden pens'. While Mrs Thatcher talked over dinner at the British Ambassador's residence with George Shultz and Caspar Weinberger, the drafting team of Kerr, Powell, and Stephen Band, a first secretary from the Embassy, began working in Ambassador Wright's office. As Powell was going in and out of the Thatcher talks, it fell to Kerr to start negotiating the framework of a statement with the US Assistant

Secretary of State, Rozanne Ridgway, who had been in Reagan's team at Reykjavik. When Roz Ridgway departed late that night they had not come within sight of an agreed text, but Kerr had a fairly good idea from her as to what was likely to be acceptable to Reagan and what would not be.

It was left to Kerr to find the final form of words since the document was to be a British statement read out by Mrs Thatcher at her Press conference. After working long after midnight drafting within the parameters set out by Roz Ridgway, he settled on a text to put to Mrs Thatcher. But he held it back until she had completed her breakfast television interviews, knowing she would be in a more relaxed mood then. When she read the final draft she was full of praise for the 'golden pens'.

At the helicopter pad before taking off for the Catoctin Mountains in Maryland, Kerr handed that approved text to Roz Ridgway. It appeared to cover the amendments she had sought to the original draft but it had to be passed by National Security Adviser John Poindexter. During the flight to Camp David he scrutinized every word. When Reagan took Mrs Thatcher off in a golf cart for talks on their own – leaving Charles Powell very obviously put out at being for once excluded as a note-taker – Roz Ridgway reported back to Kerr that one further 'small amendment' was demanded by Poindexter. He insisted on a comma being inserted in a sentence so that it read: 'We also agreed on the need to press ahead with the SDI research programme, which is permitted by the ABM Treaty.' As a Scot born at Grantown on Spey and brought up as a stickler for accurate punctuation and parsing, Kerr said the British side could not accept a comma there. To do so would mean Britain accepting that all SDI research was permissible under the 1972 treaty. He held out for excluding the comma. So did Mrs Thatcher.

The American side bowed to their visitors having the final say on punctuation since they were issuing it from the British Embassy. In return, Mrs Thatcher gave Reagan an unqualified vote of confidence at her Press conference over the looming Irangate scandal involving arms supplies for hostages: 'I believe in the President's total integrity on that subject.' Ironically, however, a typing error at the Embassy went unnoticed and the statement was handed out to correspondents with the comma included in the SDI sentence. Although that affected the reporting of the meeting in the Press, the mistake was put right later and the authentic record tabled in the House of Commons had no comma.

Despite that confusion Mrs Thatcher left Washington well pleased with her intervention to salvage the *status quo* from the turmoil of Reykjavik. The final statement reaffirmed NATO strategy with 'effective nuclear deterrents based upon a mix of systems'. Disarmament objectives were set out as priority for an intermediate nuclear force agreement and a 50 per cent reduction in strategic weapons. These were endorsed at the next NATO foreign ministers' meeting. Mrs Thatcher also secured the President's support for 'arrangements made to modernize Britain's independent nuclear deterrent with Trident'. As a bonus she got a private pledge from Reagan that he would block any American arms sales to Argentina.

Over the years Mrs Thatcher's interventions in European Community questions became more and more abrasive as the issue of economic and monetary union came to dominate the agenda at Common Market summits. Her involvement at summits became increasingly acrimonious, particularly over the cost of the Common Agricultural Policy and the reluctance of her partners to take drastic action against surpluses for fear of losing the farmers' votes. Opposition to most of the social policies coming out of the EC Commission widened the gulf between Mrs Thatcher and the others. It led many in Europe to doubt Britain's commitment to a more integrated Community. Against this background, therefore, it was decided to set out what she conceived to be the sort of Europe Britain hoped to help build. As she had accepted an invitation in April 1988 to deliver an address to the College of Europe at Bruges in Belgium, the date of 20 September was pencilled into her diary as the occasion for proclaiming her vision of Europe.

Until then Mrs Thatcher's speeches had not attracted more than passing interest. But by some strange alchemy the Bruges speech became a classic, almost in the historic category of Macmillan's 'Wind of Change' speech in Cape Town in 1960. It was the most controversial speech of her premiership. The mood as much as the substance aroused passionate argument at home and abroad. It was not just a one-day event. The speech had a sustained political life long afterwards among right-wing Conservatives with the formation of the Bruges Group. As a summation of Thatcherite philosophy on Europe it was assumed to have been entirely inspired by Charles Powell, his work from beginning to end as the one person who knew her mind best. In fact, it was the result of co-operation and ultimately conflict between two of her 'golden pens' from Camp David days: Powell and Kerr. The origins of the speech were at the Foreign Office, not No. 10.

As assistant under-secretary of state responsible for European affairs in 1988, John Kerr was the natural choice for drafting an important speech on Europe. He started work on it ten weeks before it was due to be delivered. The first draft went over to No. 10 before the end of July. Like all major submissions, it was approved by Sir Geoffrey Howe before it left the Foreign Office. It did not go directly to Mrs Thatcher. It was stopped by her other 'golden pen', Charles Powell. He tore it apart and rewrote it, changing the structure and the substance. Some of the original draft survived but the tone was toughened up. The revised version was sent back not just to the Foreign Office but to the other relevant departments in Whitehall. Copies went to the Treasury, Ministry of Defence, Trade and Industry, Transport, and Environment. They added amendments which were sent to the Foreign Office to be collated in a new draft. Some of those in Whitehall who read the revised version from Powell suggested that the more florid passages should be cut.

At the beginning of September John Kerr worked on a new draft eliminating the historical flights of fancy. Although most of Charles Powell's themes were retained, they were toned down from their original pugnacious terms. The draft went back to Sir Geoffrey Howe for his approval – and the inevitable addition from him of a few subordinate clauses. At that stage the Foreign Office hoped Mrs Thatcher would accept that it would be more appropriate for her to sound moderate rather than strident at the College of Europe. But Charles Powell took the view that the purpose of making the speech was not to please the burghers of Bruges but to make them think. His second rewrite was a far harsher exposition of the Thatcherite views on Europe. When that arrived back at the Foreign Office there was no time for a big debate. In any case Charles Powell was not to be deflected from a frontal attack on the federalists. Sir Geoffrey Howe had given up the struggle and gone off to Africa. All the Foreign Office could do was to get John Kerr to insert about twenty textual modifications for less offensive terms and these were accepted at No. 10. About 40 per cent of the Foreign Office contribution remained in the final version, but what was described in the rest of Whitehall as the 'knuckle-duster stuff' was pure Thatcher.

In retrospect, after the upheavals in Eastern Europe in 1990, much of the 3,300-word speech had a realistic perspective. It was ahead of its time in seeking to keep the door open to Warsaw, Prague, and Budapest 'as great European cities'. The Germans acknowledged the perceptiveness of the passage: 'We must never forget that East of the Iron Curtain peoples who once enjoyed a full share of European culture, freedom and identity have been cut off from their roots.' But the instant impact came from Powell's carefully burnished phrases like the warning about the folly of creating 'some sort of identikit European personality'. Thatcher's attack on the Brussels bureaucrats was an arrow at the heart of Commission President Jacques Delors: 'We have not successfully rolled back the frontiers of the state in Britain, only to see them re-imposed at a European level, with a European super-state exercising a new dominance from Brussels.' Many of her arguments were acknowledged to be sound, as when she said: 'We certainly do not need new regulations which raise the cost of employment and make Europe's labour market less flexible and less competitive with overseas suppliers.'

One reason that the speech had such an impact was the way it was put over to the British public. There were fresh stirrings of nationalism in Europe and the Prime Minister touched a chord of patriotism in Britain. She talked about the pride of being British and emphasized: 'We in Britain are rightly proud of the way in which, since Magna Carta in 1215, we have pioneered and developed representative institutions to stand as bastions of freedom.' This was the sort of jingoism Sir Bernard Ingham enjoyed highlighting, knowing it would annoy the people he called Europhiles. Although he had no part in the drafting, he knew from discussing the speech with Charles Powell that it would be in tune to stress that the Community was not an end in itself and underline the rider in the text: 'Nor is it an institutional device to be constantly modified according to the dictates of some abstract intellectual concept.'

Despite the deluge of criticism from many European capitals, Mrs Thatcher was unrepentant a month later at an Anglo-Italian summit beside Lake Maggiore. Ignoring the opposition to her arguments from her host Ciriaco de Mita, she said: 'The speech at Bruges had to be made. It caused quite a stir in some quarters and an avalanche of support from many others.' She used the occasion to attack the proposal for a European central bank on the grounds that it would mean surrendering the direction of national economic policy to the dictates of the bank's board. Mrs Thatcher brooked no second thoughts from any other member of the Government: 'I neither want nor expect ever to see such a bank in my lifetime. Nor, if I'm twanging a harp, for quite a long time afterwards.'

The clash between No. 10 and the Foreign Office over the Bruges speech triggered off fresh speculation about how to resolve the constant tug-o'-war over foreign policy between the two sides of Downing Street. One solution from the extreme right of the Conservative Party called for the creation of an independent Foreign Affairs Unit serving the Prime Minister directly. A six-page pamphlet entitled *The Case for Reform* by David Hart of the Committee for a Free Britain published in October 1988 – a month after the Bruges speech – argued that such a unit was the only way to stop the Foreign Office going to great lengths to 'frustrate government policy'. The Foreign Office was not only too ready to compromise but lacking in strategic vision, Hart argued. Its basic weakness was due to the fact that it was 'one of the last of the great institutions that have escaped the refreshing breath of Thatcherism'. The new unit, under the Prime Minister's 'National Security Adviser', was to be staffed by seconded civil servants and recruits from the private sector. Its mandate was to 'determine a global strategy for Britain'.

Normally, demands for the 'introduction of competition in foreign policy advice' would have been scoffed out of debate very quickly. But *The Times* gave a new impetus to it a month later by publishing a main article from David Hart elaborating his theme. It provoked an instant reply from Sir Geoffrey Howe in a letter to *The Times* ridiculing the suggestion that the Foreign Office was a bureaucracy with a policy of its own which it sought to perpetuate regardless of the government: 'The reality is that it is ministers, not officials, who take the decisions.' Eventually Sir Anthony Kershaw, former Minister of State and the first chairman of the House of Commons Select Committee on Foreign Affairs, came to the rescue of the FO. His letter to *The Times* stated: 'Anyone who believes that the FO is staffed by an idle clique of Champagne Charlies, of doubtful patriotism or expertise, will believe anything. They do not need another down-market, amateur government department to act as some sort of watchdog to see they do their job properly.'

There was no enthusiasm at No. 10 for a mini-Foreign Office. One reason was that by that stage in her premiership Mrs Thatcher was spending 80 per cent of her time on foreign affairs. As someone who had been continuously in office for longer than almost all her contemporaries she believed she had enough experience of international issues not to need the advice of a Foreign Policy Unit inside No. 10. At that moment of seemingly unshakeable self-confidence, however, the pendulum was starting to swing against Mrs Thatcher's confrontational policy on Europe. Her ability to hold out against the combined weight of the Foreign Office and the Treasury was being steadily eroded.

The first signal came in June 1989 from the elections to the European Parliament which resulted in a humiliating defeat for the Conservatives. They gained only 34 per cent of the vote, their lowest figure ever in a national election. Later that month, joint pressure from Chancellor Lawson and Sir Geoffrey Howe forced Mrs Thatcher to make major concessions to her European partners at the Madrid summit. Threats of resignation from her two most senior Cabinet ministers cornered her into specifying the terms for Britain joining the Exchange Rate Mechanism of the European Monetary System. Instead of the tedious repetition of being ready to join 'when the time is right', she had to commit the Government to joining when the gap between Britain's rate of inflation and the other members had come down 'significantly' and when others lifted restrictions on capital movements. She also bowed to demands for an early start on economic and monetary union from 1 July 1990.

This pressure cost Sir Geoffrey Howe his job at the Foreign Office. He was replaced in a Cabinet reshuffle a month after the Madrid summit. It also cost Mrs Thatcher her position of total dominance in foreign affairs which had previously enabled her to intervene when she chose. The final row between Nigel Lawson and Mrs Thatcher's economic adviser, Sir Alan Walters, led to John Major becoming Chancellor after three months at the Foreign Office and handing over to Douglas Hurd in October 1989. When Major and Hurd agreed on the need to join the Exchange Rate Mechanism, Mrs Thatcher was in no position to hold out against them. It was merely a question of choosing the right date in October 1990.

In her last year at No. 10 Mrs Thatcher's tones were moderated. While she defended what she saw as Britain's interests at Community summits with undiminished vigour, she was less inclined to act on her own across the board on foreign affairs. As the third Foreign Secretary she had at the Cabinet table in three months, Douglas Hurd was in a much stronger position than his two predecessors. He knew he could not be ousted in another reshuffle before the general election. With his experience of the Middle East from his days as a minister at the Foreign Office, he established his authority to handle the Gulf crisis from the moment Iraq invaded Kuwait on 2 August 1990.

Hurd operated on the basis that both sides of Downing Street had a veto: the Prime Minister could block a decision by the Foreign Secretary but equally if the Prime Minister wanted something done by the Foreign Secretary he could say 'No'. At one stage Mrs Thatcher demanded that an embassy should be closed. Hurd said he did not agree. The embassy stayed open. As the Prime Minister had to approve the appointments of senior ambassadors, she had the right to reject a nomination – which she did twice in her last twelve months in office. But she could not impose a nomination of her own. That could be vetoed by Hurd. It was acknowledged as a businesslike relationship in which Hurd knew how to handle the tricky elements. Even though there was little ideological affinity, they both accepted that they had good reason to get on with each other.

After Mrs Thatcher's resignation, the balance between the two sides of Downing Street in terms of influence and decision-making swung back to the Foreign Office. As Prime Minister John Major wanted to establish himself as his own man despite his strong Thatcherite background. Sir Bernard Ingham left with his leader, his gruff Yorkshire tones replaced by the silken style of Gus O'Donnell in the Press Office. Although Sir Charles Powell stayed until the end of the Gulf War, his power base was never the same as it had been in the Thatcher era. His successor, Stephen Wall, had served in the Private Office with Owen, Howe, Major, and Hurd, all of whom valued his judgement and skill in setting down the essentials of a meeting. But what pleased the Foreign Office most about his appointment to No. 10 was that he was such a dedicated mandarin there were no fears of his going native and turning against them.

It was more than just a change of style at No. 10 that accounted for a smoother relationship between the Prime Minister and the Foreign Secretary. In his baptism of fire on the international stage during the Gulf War and its aftermath, John Major quickly realized the value of Douglas Hurd's experience and judgement. Unlike Thatcher, who travelled as a loner abroad except at international summits, Major felt more comfortable with Foreign Office expertise at his side. If it had been Mrs Thatcher going to Moscow in September 1991 for the first time after the Kremlin coup, and on to Peking as the first Western leader after the Tiananmen Square massacre of June 1989, she would have gone on her own without the Foreign Secretary. When Major embarked on these visits of crucial importance not just to Britain but to the West he had Hurd with him in the Kremlin and in the Peking talks before the signing of the Anglo-Chinese agreement on the new Hong Kong airport. Another sign of the changed relationship between No. 10 and the Foreign Office was the increased influence accorded by John Major to his FO guru in the Cabinet Office, Sir Percy Cradock. He was not only the *éminence grise* who conducted the successful negotiations on the Hong Kong airport agreement. He had a key role in handling the complex issues of the disintegrating Soviet empire after the Kremlin coup.

This close co-operation between the two sides of Downing Street was the dividend of a deal struck by the two men when they both stood as candidates to succeed Mrs Thatcher and bar Michael Heseltine from becoming leader of the Conservative Party. Although Hurd, who attended the European Security summit in Paris with Mrs Thatcher in November 1989, was with her in the residence of the Ambassador Sir Ewen Fergusson when the results of the first ballot in the party leadership contest were announced, he stayed in a separate room as the figures came through from London. His first reaction was to telephone John Major, who was recovering from a dental operation. It was only after comparing assessments that Hurd went into the room to see Mrs Thatcher. The traumatic days which led to the downfall of Mrs Thatcher left their mark on John Major and Douglas Hurd. For both of them they were a stern warning of what happens when a dominant political leader loses touch with the grassroots of the party and fails to listen to the views of others. It was a classic demonstration of a basic political lesson that no one can ignore the pressures in Parliament and the strength of feeling among other influential groups.

XIII

Pressures on Policy-Making

> *Foreign policy is not a hermetically sealed world.*
>
> Sir Geoffrey Howe,
> *The Times*, 7 November 1988

> *Foreign policy is not an idol to be hidden in the temple, untouched by profane hands.*
>
> Lord Callaghan,
> Diplomatic and Commonwealth Writers Association,
> 10 April 1974

> *I found myself very much the target for pressure, attacks, even abuse, on the floor of the House and in Committees, both official and unofficial, which abound in the Commons and are assiduously 'looked after' by outside lobbyists.*
>
> Lord George-Brown, *In My Way*

No Foreign Secretary ever starts with a clean slate. He inherits a legacy of precedents and pressures which have to be taken into consideration whenever a decision on policy is made. History and geography apply their pressures in shaping the mould for policies. It is a gradual process of evolution since 90 per cent of the time foreign policy is, as Henry Kissinger put it, 'a trend, not a hot item'. Treaty obligations cannot be abandoned. Lesser commitments undertaken by one government cannot be lightly set aside by its successor. Being a member of international organizations requires a government to keep paying its dues, political and financial. Membership of the European Community, the Commonwealth, NATO, and the United Nations exerts a constant variety of political pressures from outside. Budgetary costs of membership also come into the calculations of the Government. United Nations contributions keep rising as agencies expand their activities and as peace-keeping operations are extended. Only in exceptional circumstances does a government renege, as happened on 31 December 1985 when the Thatcher Government withdrew from UNESCO because of the way it was being run.

Alongside the external pressures there are internal ones emanating in varying strengths from four sources: inside the party, inside Parliament, from high-powered institutions, and from organized lobby groups. As politicians, concerned with staying in office, ministers give priority to pressures from inside their own party. The extent to which they may have to bow to some of these pressures, or at least appear to take account of them, depends upon the size of the majority the party enjoys in Parliament. Labour prime ministers and foreign secretaries have always had to look over their shoulders to their backbench party support much more than Conservative ministers. All Conservative governments in the three decades 1960–90 had comfortable working majorities in Parliament. When Harold Wilson came to power in October 1964, he had an overall majority of only four seats. It was only when he went to the country again in the general election of March 1966 that he secured freedom to manoeuvre with an overall majority of 97 seats. But when the Labour Party returned to power in February 1974, they formed a minority government which suffered 29 defeats in the Commons in the two months before the summer recess. They scraped back to power with a majority of three seats in October 1974 and remained in that perilous position until the 1979 general election brought the Conservatives to office with Mrs Thatcher with a 43-seat majority. That majority was strengthened in 1983 to 144 seats and in 1987 was 102.

Both major parties have their radical wings, which ministers have to be careful not to upset unnecessarily. On the Labour left there was always concern in the 1960s and early 1970s about distancing Britain from the US on Vietnam. Labour's left-wingers had strong views about getting rid of nuclear weapons and American bases in Britain. They were highly critical of any moves which appeared to soften the stance against the apartheid system in South Africa. An added complication for any Labour Government, until the issue was finally resolved in 1975, was the division within the party over membership of the European Community. It not only split the Labour Party but caused disunity in the Cabinet. Both Wilson and Callaghan handled the Common Market issue with considerable skill inside and outside the Cabinet. They rode the storm at a special party conference, which voted against accepting the renegotiated terms of membership, until their campaign was vindicated in the referendum of 5 June 1975 by 17,378,581 votes to 8,470,073.

Labour ministers had a much tougher time from their radicals in that period. The backbenchers never hesitated to criticize their prime minister or foreign secretary even when the Government majority was fragile. Conservative radicals rarely let their opposition weaken the Government. Strong criticism welled up over Rhodesia, immigration, Falklands leaseback proposals, and Hong Kong, but party loyalty in the end reined it in before any serious damage was caused. On two occasions, however, it was the party, not the electorate, which enforced changes. What made Lord Carrington resign when Argentina invaded the Falklands was not the shouts of 'betrayal' in the emergency debate in the Commons on Saturday, 3 April 1982. It was the hostility from the backbenchers of the party when he went along afterwards with the Defence Secretary, John Nott, to the 1922 Committee. They were looking for a scapegoat and Lord Carrington fitted the bill. He admitted afterwards that it was 'a fairly disagreeable meeting'. The second time the action of the party, not the electorate or a vote of no confidence in the Commons, brought a resignation was when Mrs Thatcher failed to get re-elected as Conservative leader in November 1990.

Party manifestos and party conference resolutions have often been used to pressure foreign secretaries. But their impact lacked a cutting edge, except occasionally during the days of Labour Governments in the 1960s and 1970s. Resolutions at Labour Party conferences deploring American bombing of Vietnam were used to harry Wilson and Stewart. Even in the run-up to the 1966 general election, when it was touch-and-go for Labour, the left wing tried to pin down the Government to total dissociation from the Americans over the resumption of bombing. The radicals were angry at a Foreign Office statement issued on Michael Stewart's authority acknowledging that the US had no option but to resume after its bombing pause brought no response from Vietnam. Some ninety Labour MPs sent a message of support to Senator William Fulbright for his criticism of President Johnson.

The Labour Government's support for the Federal Nigerian Government in the civil war which broke out in July 1967 aroused deep resentment within the Parliamentary Party. Biafra's case won sympathizers at all levels including former front-bench men like Jim Griffiths who had been Colonial Secretary. Even with a substantial working majority, the Wilson Government had to fend off repeated angry attacks about supporting 'genocide'. The Biafran struggle was boosted by letters from twenty-six bishops and a resolution from the General Assembly of the Church of Scotland. But despite the moral indignation, the Government did not make any change in policy.

Conservative Governments also faced pressures from their back-benches over their African policy but these were usually more vocal than influential. In the Macmillan era the right-wing Monday Club, claiming about 1,000 members nationally, was active in trying to hold back the Wind of Change in Africa. They rallied support for Duncan Sandys as Commonwealth Secretary in his clashes with Iain Macleod who was accelerating the evolution to independence as Colonial Secretary. But by the time Lord Carrington was completing the decolonization process at the Rhodesia conference in 1979, the Monday Club had run out of steam, unable to threaten him with anything but rhetoric.

Backbench pressure for tighter immigration controls has always been treated with great circumspection by Conservative ministers. Party managers arranged for the issue to be left off the agenda of the annual conference at Scarborough in 1960. But Rab Butler had to bow to the continuing pressure the following year and made the unfortunately phrased admission that the restrictions under the Commonwealth Immigrants Bill would not be based upon 'colour prejudice alone'. The strong feelings in the party ensured that in election manifestos during the Thatcher years there was a commitment not to allow any substantial increase in immigration. That commitment was invoked for one of the most serious challenges ever mounted from the right wing of the Conservative Party, against Douglas Hurd as Foreign Secretary.

The revolt was staged just before Hurd flew to Hong Kong in January 1990 with assurances for the colony that the Government would stand by them despite the anxieties created by the Peking Government in the aftermath of the Tiananmen Square massacre of June 1989. It was Hurd's pledge to guarantee 50,000 families the right of abode in Britain under the Nationality (Hong Kong) Bill which brought a backlash. Opposition was expected from Peking. The Chinese Government warned that if the British Government did not withdraw the proposals they would have to 'bear a series of consequences'. Peking regarded it as a violation of the Joint Declaration of 1984 for the handover of Hong Kong in 1997. Opposition from inside the Conservative Party was mounted on a much more serious scale than had been anticipated. It was led by former Cabinet minister and one-time party chairman Norman Tebbit with an army of outraged Tories behind him estimated to number at least eighty ready to vote against the Government.

Tebbit tried to corner Hurd into admitting that the plan to give 225,000 people from 50,000 families passports to enter Britain was a breach of the party's election manifesto which pledged that there would be no large-scale immigration. Hurd, recalling his experience as Home Secretary, snapped back: 'I don't need any education on the importance of strict immigration control.' He insisted it was not possible 'just to close our eyes and wait for the clock to tick on until 1997'. It was necessary to balance the need for immigration limitations with obligations towards Crown civil servants and businessmen whose enterprise was vital for the continued prosperity of Hong Kong.

As the Foreign Secretary who negotiated the handover terms

with China, Sir Geoffrey Howe was wheeled out in an attempt to calm the anxieties of backbench Tories fearing a wave of 225,000 immigrants. He insisted that the object of the Bill was to encourage the people to stay in Hong Kong with a safety net of a British passport. 'What we are telling them is: You may become citizens of the United Kingdom but you do not need to come here to achieve that.' That failed to silence the critics on the Tory backbenches. Three days before going to Hong Kong Douglas Hurd appeared before the Conservative Foreign Affairs Committee to urge them to see it as part of Britain's obligation to the colony. Even if the worst scenario materialized, he emphasized, the immigrants were the sort of people with skills who would not be a burden on the British taxpayer.

The Committee chairman, Sir Peter Blaker, a former Foreign Office minister well-known in Hong Kong, accepted the argument that the passport offer was intended to make people stay in the colony. But the right-wing vice-chairman, George Gardiner, told the Foreign Secretary to warn the people in the colony that there were deep objections to the legislation and that its passage through Parliament could not be taken as a foregone conclusion. In the end, party loyalty undermined the backbench rebellion. The Bill was passed on its second reading on 19 April 1990 by 313 votes to 216 with only 44 Tories rebelling. Nonetheless, it was a reminder to the Foreign Secretary not to ignore backbench MPs over foreign policy issues which could have an impact upon constituencies.

Inside Parliament, foreign policy can be influenced in various ways. Question Time enables over 50,000 questions to be raised in a session, with just under a fifth of them answered orally. But less than one in four of the 650 MPs take an active interest in foreign policy. As a result only a small percentage of the questions asked relate to international affairs. Unless a situation has a direct bearing upon a constituency, for example with local jobs affected by a foreign contract, MPs realize there are few votes involved in foreign policy questions. At times of crisis the Prime Minister's Question Time on Tuesdays and Thursdays can be dominated by international issues. When the Foreign Secretary faces questions he normally cuts out all engagements prior to going to the House of Commons so that he can study the latest developments in the situations on which he is to be questioned. It is extremely rare, however, for a question in the House to change the direction of foreign policy.

All-party committees have been established in Parliament to look after the interests of a large number of countries and causes. Registered all-party groups are required to have at least five members from the Government party and five from the Opposition with a minimum of three from the main Opposition. Parliamentary groups are those which admit people who are not MPs but which have the same requisite parliamentary membership as all-party groups. Some groups are formed for special emergencies such as the Gulf Families Group formed under the chairmanship of the Labour MP Jack Ashley in 1990 to help relatives of British citizens affected by Iraq's invasion of Kuwait. The biggest single-issue group is the Parliamentary Group for the Release of Soviet Jewry under the chairmanship of the Labour QC Peter Archer. Another well-organized group, which attracts MPs who are lawyers, is the War Crimes Parliamentary Group.

All-party groups concerned with promoting good relations with a particular country increased from 68 in 1972 to 108 in 1991. They range from the largest, the British-American Parliamentary Group with the Prime Minister as chairman, to small groups such as the Anglo-Albanian Group and the Anglo-Luxembourg Group. Some of them are very active, such as the British-Hong Kong Parliamentary Group which has focused attention on the problems which have arisen in the colony's transition to a Special Administrative Region of China in 1997. Some are highly competitive on controversial issues, such as the British-Cyprus All-Party Group and the Friends of Northern Cyprus All-Party Group. A vigorous Israeli Parliamentary Group is matched by fourteen groups sympathetic to the Arabs. Most of the other groups concentrate mainly on spreading an awareness of the benefits of better relations with various countries. They arrange meetings with visiting dignitaries and receptions for delegations.

None of them could genuinely claim to have exercised a direct influence on policy-making. The only committee which could make such a claim is the Select Committee on Foreign Affairs, one of fourteen departmental committees set up in 1979 by Lord St John of Fawsley as Norman St John-Stevas, then Leader of the House. Under the chairmanship first of Sir Anthony Kershaw, former Foreign Office minister, and later of David Howell, former Energy Secretary, the Committee of eleven members has steadily acquired a reputation for thorough probing into situations. With the Conservatives in power the balance was struck at six Conservative members and five Labour members. During the 1989-90 session they undertook seven investigations: developments in the Horn of Africa, the situation in Eastern Europe and the Soviet Union, Hong Kong, UK policy on UNESCO, the Single European Act, German unification, and Foreign Office and Overseas Development Administration expenditure.

The budget of £114,283 was more than twice the average of all other select committees. Most of it was spent on travel – £92,439 – but there was £4,853 for the fees of two specialist advisers. Apart from travelling to Hong Kong, the Committee has spent time in South Africa, the Soviet Union, Cyprus, and Eastern European countries. Formal evidence at public hearings is taken only at Westminster or in a colony. Elsewhere the sessions are informal. Written evidence is submitted in bulky volumes, sometimes the size of telephone directories. The Foreign Affairs Committee was the first select committee to have live coverage of its hearings broadcast by the BBC when Michael Heseltine was questioned as Defence Secretary on 7 November 1984.

Every time there is a European Community summit the Committee has a session three weeks beforehand to question the Foreign Secretary about Government policy on the issues expected to be discussed. He is also invited to appear before the Committee on major investigations concerning British policy on Hong Kong or East–West relations. The Committee has the right to summon any minister, although that is rarely exercised. When Lord Carrington was Foreign Secretary and unable as a peer to take part in the activities of the Chamber of the House of Commons, he agreed to be questioned by the Foreign Affairs Committee in the Commons Committee Rooms.

Since hearings are now frequently televised, sometimes live, the occasion can be used by ministers to set out their policies to a wider audience than they normally have at Press conferences. Douglas Hurd has been skilful at taking the opportunity to project Government policy with a smoothness which subtly scores many party political points. Whenever expenditure is under investigation, the Permanent Under-Secretary of State is usually summoned to face a grilling. When the Committee reports are delivered, the Foreign Office is expected to make a response, but it usually takes its time to produce a bland answer.

Despite the commitment of MPs on the Committee, who can spend three or four days a week on working with it during peak periods, there are few occasions when their questioning or their recommendations have affected Government policy. Their questioning of Lord Maclehose, a former Governor of Hong Kong, highlighted the case for a Bill of Rights for the colony. On visa policy the Committee could claim it prodded the Government towards ending the requirement of visas for Czechs and Hungarians visiting Britain. The Committee's visit to Eastern Europe drew attention to the need for the Government to take the problems of the political and economic transformation there more seriously.

The Committee's one signal achievement was the way it handled a highly controversial request from the Canadian Government in 1980 for the British Government to amend the British North America Act of 1867 so that the power of amendment passed to the Ottawa Parliament. Complex legal arguments were presented at hearings of the Committee which drew upon the expertise of Dr John Finnis, Reader in Commonwealth Law at Oxford University. Because of the delicacy of the issue, involving the Queen as sovereign of both countries, sessions required extremely careful chairmanship from Sir Anthony Kershaw. After protracted study the Committee delivered its verdict recommending the rejection of the request from Pierre Trudeau's Government on the grounds that it was not supported by an overwhelming majority of the ten Canadian provinces. Eventually the Ottawa Government amended its proposals in such a way that Parliament passed the enabling legislation for the Constitution to be formally patriated to Canada on 17 April 1982.

Despite that success, there is increasing dissatisfaction with the limitation of the Committee's power. Because of this lack of political clout some MPs like Peter Temple-Morris have withdrawn from the Committee. Many parliamentarians in all parties would like to have more authority vested in the Committee to give it some of the prestige which the American Senate Foreign Relations Committee has on Capitol Hill. Over the years the Senate Foreign Relations Committee has established a powerful influence with its right to recommend the approval or rejection of treaties and appointments. Its strength also comes from its right to draft the bill which authorizes the amount of economic and military aid to be given each year by the US to other countries. In the 1960s and early 1970s, televised sessions of the Senate Foreign Relations Committee under the chairmanship of Senator William Fulbright, a strong critic of President Johnson's Vietnam policy, had a powerful impact on policy. In the 1980s liberal opponents of President Reagan used the power of the Committee to block confirmation of nominations put forward by him. The US Government's policies towards South Africa and the Philippines had to take account of the view of the Committee.

The organization of the eighteen-member Committee into sub-committees is a model that many people at Westminster consider worth copying. The Senators operate in seven sub-committees: African affairs; East Asian and Pacific affairs; European affairs; International economic policy; Near Eastern and South Asian affairs; Terrorism, narcotics and international operations; and Western Hemisphere and Peace Corps affairs. Although the Select Committee on Foreign Affairs was one of three in the fourteen permitted to have one sub-committee, it only exercised that right in the 1979–83 Parliament. It appointed an Overseas Development Sub-Committee to monitor aid programmes, but that was discontinued when the new full Committee took over from the first one in December 1983. While MPs would not expect to be given the full panoply of powers of the American Committee, including the power to reject treaties, as the Senate has done on twenty occasions, many think the Foreign Affairs Select Committee should have the right to have its reports and recommendations debated on the floor of the House.

Outside Parliament there are several prestigious institutions where seminars, lectures, and discussion groups produce ideas and proposals which carry considerable weight among opinion-formers. It is refreshing for those engaged in what Metternich called 'the daily application of politics' to have the longer vision projected before them by academics with the time to study situations in great detail. Senior members of the Foreign Office often attend lectures and discussion groups. These contacts and the conclusions of research undertaken by the institutes have an influence upon the thinking of ministers and senior officials at the Foreign Office. Whether it goes beyond that, however, to the point of exerting sufficient pressure to affect Government policy is extremely questionable.

In defence and security matters two organizations in particular command great respect: the Royal United Services Institute and the International Institute for Strategic Studies. Their research and study programmes are followed closely by officials at the Foreign Office and Ministry of Defence who are concerned with analysing policy options. The RUSI Soviet Forum, started in 1986, led to interesting East–West contacts including a visit to the Institute by General Petr Lushev as Warsaw Treaty Commander-in-Chief. Seminars with King's College London and the London School of Economics supplied new insights in the analysis of trends in Eastern Europe. Informal meetings at RUSI with members of staff colleges focused attention on controversial themes such as the use of the armed forces in disaster relief operations.

By far the most influential of all the outside organizations is the Royal Institute of International Affairs. Chatham House, as it is known from its location, was founded in 1920 to 'bring together people from government, politics, industry, finance, the academic world and the media, from Britain and many other countries, to examine and develop the ideas which shape policy'. It has become a prestigious forum for world statesmen, attracting President Gorbachev and President Havel among the 113 speakers in the 1989–90 meetings programme. A research staff of thirty-four, including academics from China, Germany, Japan, and Korea, cover political, economic, and environmental issues of topical interest. Although it is independent of Government, the Institute's research project income of around £1m includes £50,000 from the Foreign Office. Its 1991 membership list of 3,407 has the Foreign Office among its 26 major corporate members paying an annual subscription of £3,000. Corporate membership is also held by 351 companies and organizations.

Although anxious not to be seen automatically doing the bidding of the Foreign Office, the Institute often responds to suggestions from Downing Street. One of its most productive enterprises, the annual Anglo-Soviet Round Table, sprang from a suggestion of James Callaghan as Foreign Secretary in 1975. Working with the Institute of Economy and International Relations of the Soviet Union, the Round Table provides a valuable discussion forum alternating between London and Moscow for academic and political figures. At the request of the Foreign Office in 1986 and 1988 the Institute organized round tables with the East Germans and in 1988 with the Yugoslavs.

One unusual innovation is a discussion forum with study groups analysing issues while books about them, which have been commissioned to be published by Chatham House, are in the process of being written. Groups of twenty-five experts sit down with the author exchanging ideas and at the end the author goes away to revise his manuscript in the light of new information. The Institute established a reputation as one of the leading research centres on environmental policy following a report on the Greenhouse Effect by Dr Michael Grubb, director of its energy and environmental programme. That led to a special study, *Environmental Issues in International Relations: The Next 25 Years*, being commissioned for publication.

Lobbying has a long pedigree in Britain going back to the campaigning of the Anti-Corn Law League in 1838 and the Anti-Slavery Society for the Protection of Human Rights, which was founded in 1839 and is still active today. In the last three decades pressure groups have proliferated in all sectors. *The Guardian Directory of Pressure Groups* has a list of over 350. That is minuscule compared with the pressure groups in the USA where over 7,000 individuals register each year in Washington as lobbyists under the Federal Regulation of Lobbying Act – and there are so many loopholes that hundreds more operate without registration. The

US Congress is open house for lobbyists, or 'rainmakers' as they are sometimes known, since the First Amendment to the Constitution provides for the right of the people to 'petition the government for the redress of grievances'.

Professional lobbyists are not held in such esteem at Westminster, although it is a fast-growing industry with over forty companies operating as parliamentary consultants with fees estimated at over £10m a year. A brochure issued by Lloyd-Hughes Associates, a company founded by the former Downing Street Press Secretary, stated that it could organize private meetings 'with eminent personalities, including Cabinet ministers, the Queen's Private Secretary, and men at the very top of the UK Diplomatic and Home Civil Service'. Evidence collated for the Register of Members' Interests shows that one out of every three MPs is used as a parliamentary consultant by a professional or commercial organization. Although the normal system is a retainer fee with sometimes substantial bonuses for a successful intervention, an MP who is prepared to ask a question in the House could be paid £200.

During his time as Home Secretary, Douglas Hurd expressed concern that the operations of pressure groups could get in the way of good government. He sounded a warning about 'their increased dominance of the media and the deference with which politicians regard them' in a lecture to the Royal Institute of Public Administration in September 1986: 'The weight of these groups, almost all of them pursuing a legitimate cause, has very substantially increased in recent years and adds greatly not just to the volume of work, but to the difficulty of achieving decisions in the general interest.' He argued that pressure groups and interest groups interposed themselves between the executive on the one hand and Parliament and the electorate on the other: 'If freedom of information simply means freedom for pressure groups to extract from the system only those pieces of information which buttress their own cause, then conceivably the result might be greater confusion.'

The argument against such confusion is made by Friends of the Earth, one of the more influential pressure groups, founded in 1970, in a leaflet saying: 'We have learned how to get our facts right, how to use the law, and, where necessary, how to change the law.' The importance of establishing credibility through the supply of accurate information has been demonstrated by the Anti-Apartheid Movement. As an effective communicator, it can claim to have played a significant part in marshalling opinion against sporting contacts with South Africa and in sustaining the pressures for economic sanctions against the Pretoria Government. Claims by supporters of the Campaign for Nuclear Disarmament, which brought tens of thousands into protest marches since 1958, are more difficult to justify. Although CND and the Greenham Common women's campaign against the deployment of Cruise missiles achieved much publicity and influenced Labour Party conference resolutions, it is hard to detect any achievement in changing government policy.

Intense competition between groups of lobbyists is frequently demonstrated by supporters of the Israelis and the Arabs trying to focus the attention of politicians and the Press on their side of the argument. The Jewish lobby is very active through its MPs at Westminster who could argue that they have to be at their maximum effect there to counter what they regard as the Arabist inclinations of so many Foreign Office diplomats. More MPs have been to Israel than to any other country outside Europe. The Labour Friends of Israel have Lord Wilson, who wrote a book about Israel, as its Honorary President. The Finchley Friends of Israel have Mrs Thatcher as President. Among the twenty support groups is the influential Board of Deputies of British Jews.

The best record for achieving results is probably held by one of the smallest Jewish pressure groups, the Women's Campaign for Soviet Jewry. Every time a British minister went to Moscow they built up pressure for the release of Jewish dissidents from prison and for exit visas for 'Refuseniks'. Appeals to the Foreign Office were linked with a very professional information service to the Press. Hundreds of Jews reached Israel because of their efforts. When he was Minister of State at the Foreign Office, William Waldegrave saluted the Campaign in March 1990 over the increased freedoms for Jews in the Soviet Union 'which both you and we have fought hard for'.

Arab lobbyists are more numerous but in many cases much less sophisticated than their pro-Israeli competitors. The one who stands out from the rest is Claud Morris, whose company publishes the influential *Voice of the Arab World*. He organizes discussion groups on Palestine which have had an impact on senior Foreign Office officials and MPs. But the Palestinian groups in London often fail to get a coherent case across to MPs and the Press. Only rarely do any of the fourteen parliamentary groups dealing with the interests of Arab countries focus the attention of the Government on a topical aspect of Anglo-Arab relations. Where the Arab lobbyists have a recognized authoritative influence is in the trade associations, the Arab-British Chamber of Commerce and the Middle East Association. Both played an important role in easing the British Government back into better relations with Saudi Arabia in 1980 after the scandal caused by the television documentary *Death of a Princess*. Lord Carrington sent a signal to the Saudis expressing his regret at the incident in a televised speech at the Middle East Association. The Association's impact has been further strengthened by having a very effective lobbyist as its President, the former British Ambassador in Syria and Saudi Arabia, Sir James Craig.

Lobbyists for relief agencies such as Oxfam, Save the Children Fund, the British Refugee Council, Christian Aid, and CARE often find it hard to command attention at the Foreign Office. As effective distributors of emergency aid, the Non-Governmental Organizations – numbering over 100 – receive about £60m from Government funds. But although they keep trying to alert the Government to impending disasters it is often only when a catastrophe is seen on television screens that they get a response. Special interest groups require immense reserves of patience to convince the Foreign Office of the need to initiate a new course of action. The Friends of John McCarthy led by Jill Morrell won widespread admiration for their persistence in keeping the public and the Foreign Office aware of the campaign to secure the release of the television journalist held hostage in the Lebanon.

Successive Foreign Secretaries took a consistently firm line that there could be no deals or ransoms for Britons held hostage since yielding to terrorists' demands would put other British citizens at risk. After back-stage arrangements were made to get French and German hostages released, new pressure was mounted for extra efforts by the British Government. But the relatives of John McCarthy, Terry Waite, and Jackie Mann were left to accept assurances that everything possible was being done. The Foreign Office hoped that resuming diplomatic relations with Iran and Syria in 1990 would have cleared the obstacles to their release. It was a cruel game, with everyone waiting for someone else to take action, and the logjam was not broken until the autumn of 1991 with the release first of John McCarthy and then of Jackie Mann.

The difficulty for all pressure groups is the gulf separating them from the secret chambers where the influences on policy options are assessed. Even when access is given to someone to see a minister, he enters as a petitioner presenting a case which has to compete against many other claims for attention. Senior advisers supply the minister with a list of other considerations which are weighed against those of the petitioner once his plea is heard. It is this internal scale of priorities, which is never disclosed even under questioning in the House of Commons, that keeps the vast majority of those who wish to influence policy at a distance. Bowing to outside pressure is anathema for the elite who have been trained to believe that they are the natural interpreters of the best options in any situation. Thus the atmosphere of a secret society run by the mandarins is preserved against those who are presumptuous enough to think that sometimes people outside the Foreign Office are more aware of what will best serve the interests of Britain abroad.

XIV

Diplomacy in the Next Three Decades

> *It would be internationally harmful if professional diplomats were to lose their sense of vocation through being constantly outflanked by their political masters.*
>
> Abba Eban, *The New Diplomacy*, p. 364

> *Whatever changes take place in diplomacy, the professional ambassador is the loser on all fronts.*
>
> Abba Eban, *The New Diplomacy*, p. 369

> *Is summit diplomacy compatible with, or does it even require, the plenipotentiary status which an ambassador has always enjoyed, and required?*
>
> Sir Geoffrey Jackson, *Concorde Diplomacy*

Until over half-way through the twentieth century the Foreign Office was much the same as it had been in the nineteenth. Over the past three decades, however, there have been enormous changes. The map of the world has been transformed with new names for new countries. The Foreign Office has undergone a transformation in how it is run, how policy is formulated, how relationships are handled, and what priorities determine the pattern of Britain's interests abroad. When the 1960s began the British Empire looked almost the same as it did in the geography schoolbooks at the beginning of the century with the same areas marked in red, with two exceptions. The Indian subcontinent was divided in 1947 into two independent countries, India and Pakistan; and the Gold Coast had become Ghana in 1957 as the first of the British colonies in Africa to secure independence.

The Commonwealth at the beginning of 1960 had only 9 members. By 1990 it had 50 members. The end of Empire meant the end of the Colonial Office. The last relics, the remaining fifteen Dependent Territories with a total population of 5.5 million (of which 5.3m are in Hong Kong), were placed under the jurisdiction of the Foreign Office. Three decades ago there were fewer than 100 British ambassadors serving abroad. Today there are over 170. Some used to take several weeks to get to their post. Nowadays an ambassador can fly to most capitals in the world in twenty-four hours. In the satellite communication age ambassadors are rarely first with the news to the Foreign Office. Decisions which in the past had to be taken on the spot by envoys are almost always taken these days in Downing Street. In his first eighteen months as Foreign Secretary Lord Home did not set foot in Brussels. At present the Foreign Secretary has meetings there at least twice a month.

Membership of the European Community has completely changed the framework and terms of reference for Britain's foreign policy. A vast range of issues which used to be tackled bilaterally or at separate inter-governmental organizations are now handled multilaterally among the Twelve in Brussels. This has resulted in many home civil servants commuting to Brussels or being seconded to the UK Delegation to the Communities. Members of the Diplomatic Service have had to acquire a much wider range of economic, financial, and environmental expertise than the diplomats of the 1960s. Political co-operation has required a much greater degree of co-ordination of policies towards other areas of the world. Economic co-operation has compelled Britain to take account of her partners' interests much more than ever before.

From the end of the Second World War until 1960, summit meetings were rare events. The verdict of Sir Harold Nicolson in 1919 on the Versailles Conference was a warning heeded by many prime ministers: 'Nothing could be more fatal than the habit (the at present fatal and pernicious habit) of personal contact between the statesmen of the world . . . Personal contact breeds, inevitably, personal acquaintance and that, in its turn, leads in many cases to friendliness: there is nothing more damaging to precision in international relations than friendliness between contracting parties.' The only regular summit in the 1960s was the Commonwealth Conference, which was always held in London until 1971 when the first full-scale summit was held at Singapore and thereafter rotated round the capitals of the Commonwealth. It lasts for five or six days, the only lengthy conference for heads of government and foreign ministers. They have time for genuine debate instead of making and listening to set speeches. There is a useful pause half-way through the conference when prime ministers can escape to a retreat outside the capital city and sit down together to exchange ideas in a relaxing environment.

Summits really came into fashion in the 1970s. In most cases they do not last for more than forty-eight hours. There is an annual summit of the leading industrialized nations, the Group of Seven, which rotates round the member countries. Occasional 34-nation summit meetings are held by the signatories of the Helsinki Act on European security and co-operation. NATO's foreign ministers meet twice a year, but in the first forty years of its existence there were only eight summits. Nowadays the most frequently convened summits are those held by the European Community. There is one every six months in the country of the rotating Presidency of the Council plus at least one further summit in Brussels. On top of that, EC summits have been convened for special issues for one day only in Paris, Dublin, Rome, and Luxembourg. Transatlantic relations have gone through several phases. The 1960s saw the so-called special relationship between Britain and the US flourish in the avuncular warmth of Macmillan with the young President Kennedy. Differences over Vietnam caused a marked cooling between Johnson and Wilson. Although some of the warmth returned in the 1970s, it was not until the Reagan–Thatcher years that the transatlantic friendship regained such a dominant influence on British foreign policy. The emergence of a powerful unified Germany in 1990 changed the priorities in Washington under the Bush administration. Nonetheless, two factors – one political, the other economic – argued strongly for careful tending of relations between Britain and the US.

Keeping a strong US military commitment to Europe became an even more important pillar of British policy after a series of arms control agreements. The Intermediate Nuclear Forces Treaty signed by Reagan and Gorbachev in December 1987 started the first substantial arms reduction since the Cold War with the withdrawal of American Cruise and Pershing missiles from Europe to match the removal of Soviet SS20s from Eastern Europe. The next step was an agreement by twenty-two members of NATO and the Warsaw Pact cutting conventional forces in Europe. Thereafter, for political reasons as well as defence calculations on the need to have American back-up for Britain's nuclear deterrent, the Government set great store on keeping the US involved with both conventional and nuclear forces in Europe.

Despite the steadily increasing economic links with its European partners since joining the Community in 1973, Britain has still looked to the US for its largest positive trade balance with any country. Even more important to British economic planning were the investment flows and the significant role played by the overseas earnings of Britain's insurance and banking services which expanded in the 1970s and 1980s by an average of over 20 per cent a year. Half of all direct investment by foreign companies in Britain in that period came from North America. In international finance and investment the London–New York axis was acknowledged to be of vital importance in building up the tripod with Tokyo. No matter which way the political wind was blowing, the Thatcher Government was always aware of the economic and financial importance of keeping the transatlantic relationship in good repair.

All these elements involved in the shaping of British foreign policy in the past three decades – causing changes in the structures and the substance – will have a continuing influence in the next three decades. The vital question is: how much? Many people inside and outside the Foreign Office wonder whether the continuation of foreign policy along its present course, albeit with different priorities, is inevitable or even desirable. They also wonder whether the conduct of foreign policy is pursued with the best use of resources in the Foreign Office. The Foreign Office system itself, which was the subject of three investigative reports in 1964, 1969, and 1977, may well come under close scrutiny again. Rumblings at Westminster indicate that a fresh look at the Foreign Office cannot be long delayed. MPs worried by signs of strain in the system towards the end of the twentieth century believe it may require reshaping and reorienting in order to cope with the problems of the twenty-first.

Whatever else happens, one basic feature will be the growing European dimension in Britain's foreign policy. With the completion of the Single European Act in 1992, Britain geared itself to benefit from the effectiveness of the Community as a generator of wealth in the decades ahead. Once the objective of economic and monetary union had been established for the European Community, there was nothing any British Government could do to stop it. Realists accepted that Britain's own best interests were to be served by working to achieve integration with the least dislocation of Britain's economy. The goals of free and open markets require a monetary policy which ensures that there are no wild fluctuations in prices. Britain's policy of gradualism towards economic convergence in the past seemed to its partners to be due more to foot-dragging for domestic political reasons than to anything else. While some voices urged Britain to settle for delayed entry into full economic and monetary union until the country's economy was strong enough to adjust to the changes, others argued that delaying tactics could put Britain initially at a disadvantage in what appeared to be a two-tier system. Those urging full commitment sooner rather than later recalled the problems created by Britain's late entry into the Exchange Rate Mechanism. They cited the warning from the resignation speech of Sir Geoffrey Howe on 13 November 1990: 'The real tragedy is that we did not join the Exchange Rate Mechanism five years ago.'

The European dimension will be expanded as never before with the evolution of new relationships between the Community and the new democracies which emerged from forty years of Communist control in Eastern Europe. Countries struggling with the problems of economic and political reform look to Britain for know-how, support, and encouragement. The response from Britain will help to determine the progress of Eastern European countries through individually-tailored association agreements to ultimate membership of the Community. The thinking of many concerned with the stability of the continent is that the Europe which was originally envisaged by Jean Monnet should not be an inward-looking community centred on Western Europe but genuinely all-European. It was not intended as a Western fortress which would pull up the drawbridge against countries from Eastern Europe. There are powerful arguments for seeing the next three decades as providing stepping-stones for the new democracies, first to become healthy free-market economies and then full partners with their Western European neighbours.

This expanding European process will be fused in due course with new relationships negotiated with members of the six-nation European Free Trade Association. There should be an acceptance by Britain that it has a special obligation towards the Association, which it helped to establish in 1960 and which it left in 1972 to join the European Community on 1 January 1973. As natural partners the EFTA countries, and in particular Austria, which imports over £500m worth of goods from Britain each year, will be looking to the British to tighten the bonds with the Community.

How soon the countries outside the Community in EFTA or on their own, such as Turkey, will become members depends on how fast their economies reach the stage to qualify and the rate at which they can be absorbed. Inevitably, there will be some dilution of the Community as it existed among the twelve that signed the Single European Act with the obligation to 'transform relations as a whole among their states into a European Union'. A new European Community eventually embracing eighteen, twenty-two, or twenty-four members each with 'vital national interests' protected in certain circumstances by a veto cannot be as tightly knit as twelve. It cannot be as cohesive a European Union. But the spread of the Community from West to East will offer Britain and its partners the chance to have a much bigger influence in the new global diplomacy of the twenty-first century.

In the next few years closer European political integration among the Twelve will be an inescapable consequence of moving towards economic and monetary union. While no objections in principle have been voiced in Downing Street, it could raise practical difficulties for British Governments such as having to wait until policy is endorsed by all Twelve. That was a problem highlighted by the Gulf crisis in 1990. Britain's decision to stand side by side with the Americans in military confrontation leading to war was not matched as quickly or as wholeheartedly by many other EC members. At times there was sharp criticism of Belgium for refusing to supply ammunition for British tanks and guns in the Gulf. If Britain had been obliged to wait for endorsement of its military commitment from the rest of the EC, the coalition forces ranged against Iraq would not have been ready for action when they were. British Governments will not allow themselves to be held back awaiting approval from their partners when issues of vital national interest are at stake.

This attitude is likely to prevail through the coming decades, particularly when it is a case of transatlantic co-operation. However strong European union becomes, no British Government will allow the Anglo-American dimension of certain global concerns to be totally submerged. Britain and the US have always worked closely together in seeking ways of ensuring stability in the Middle East. Although Britain played a leading role in getting the European Community to recognize Palestinian rights to self-determination in statements such as the Venice Declaration in 1980, it also retained a separate, direct interest. During the Gulf crisis the European minister who visited the Middle East more than any other in the wake of US Secretary of State James Baker was Douglas Hurd. Britain's long-standing interest in a Middle East settlement to resolve some of the problems stemming from the Balfour Declaration of 1917 makes it inevitable that there will be a continuing involvement alongside the Americans both separately and collectively with other European countries.

Together with the economic and political changes brought about by the transformation of Europe, one of the biggest challenges of the decades ahead will come from social changes. An enlargement of the European Community to the extent of almost doubling its current size is liable to produce greater social fluidity. In turn that could bring immigration problems for Britain on an unprecedented scale. Waves of migrants moving westward from Eastern Europe and the western republics of the Soviet Union could change the traditional social patterns in Britain, France, and Germany. Standards in health services, education, social security services, and the basic issue of law and order could be seriously affected. Foreign Office expertise in handling situations created by mass migration could well be one of the priority requirements for the next generation of diplomats.

The level of aid required to cope with the environmental catastrophes threatening to befall the poorer communities in Africa and Asia will present serious problems for Britain and her Western partners in the years ahead. The scale of disasters by famine or flood is approaching the point where the parameters of foreign policy will become increasingly enmeshed with domestic economic priorities. Governments will be challenged more and more on the cost of foreign policy even when there are good humanitarian reasons for the expenditure. The Foreign Office will face anguished arguments in trying to justify retaining political influence in certain areas when the cost of the aid programme to ensure stability could eat into funds required for social services in Britain. The costs of aid and of military intervention to reverse aggression are liable to be questioned in much greater detail in future.

The Commonwealth connection is bound to be scrutinized in an increasingly critical light. While a Gallup poll taken in 1983 showed that 83 per cent of British people wanted to see a closer relationship with the Commonwealth – more than those wanting closer ties with Europe – the interest of the public and the Government has declined in recent years. When the Rhodesia problem was removed from the Commonwealth Conference agenda in 1980 with the independence of Zimbabwe, only the controversy over how to end apartheid in South Africa kept the international focus on the Commonwealth. On the retirement of Sir Sonny Ramphal in 1990 after fifteen years as Commonwealth Secretary-General, the organization lost a dynamic high-profile publicist. His Nigerian successor, Chief Emeka Anyaoku, kept the machinery ticking over smoothly but without putting the Commonwealth into the headlines.

As the ties of history are seen by many to depend more and more on nostalgia, there has been more questioning of the role of Britain in the Commonwealth. In a pamphlet from the Institute for Defence and Strategic Studies in October 1990, Dr Christopher Coker of the London School of Economics argued that the case for the Commonwealth was fast disappearing: 'The truth is that Britain's interests and those of its Commonwealth partners are not only unlikely to converge; they are beginning to diverge significantly.' However, withdrawing from the Commonwealth would be a difficult decision for any British Government, especially since the Queen takes great pride in being Head of the Commonwealth and the monarch of eighteen of its fifty countries. If Britain were to pull out, the Commonwealth would be unlikely to survive. Winding down the British commitment and abandoning regular summits could be a compromise. But it would deprive many small countries of the advantage of tapping into the experience of Britain and its ministers and, almost as important, deny British ministers the opportunity to understand global issues from the perspective of other continents.

While Commonwealth conferences may disappear from the record books in the not so distant future, there is no threat to the other summits in the diplomatic calendar. World leaders recognize that summits are the only satisfactory means of meeting the demand for public diplomacy in the era of satellite communications. The idealism of the first objective of Woodrow Wilson's 14 Points in 1919 was quickly shown to be impracticable: 'Open covenants openly arrived at, after which there should be no private international understandings of any kind, but diplomacy shall proceed always frankly and in the public view.' For any experienced politician it was a contradiction to be both frank and open. But the increasing invasion of the conference chambers by the television cameras resulted in the public suspecting that what went on behind closed doors was conspiratorial and not in the public interest.

What has taken place, therefore, is an updating of the means which Walter Bagehot believed were employed by Lord Palmerston in the 1860s to ensure a successful political career: 'He was profoundly aware that the common mass of plain sense is the great administrative agency of the world; and that if you keep yourself in sympathy with this you win, and if not you will fail.' At European Community summits ministers spend almost as much time in front of television cameras and radio microphones as in the conference itself. They use television and radio interviews as if they were party political broadcasts to assure the electorate that all their interests are being sturdily defended in the international arena. The entire summit scene has become a television show, with all the leaders aware of each other's need to be seen on national screens working to achieve a better standard of living for everyone. Television cameras zoom in on 'working breakfasts' between heads of government. Other TV crews await the doorstep interview on the way out. More comments are timed for the lunchtime TV news. Then there are televised Press conferences at the end of the session followed by the Prime Minister having as many as eight separate interviews.

When summit meetings were rare events it was always assumed that there would be dividends from the meetings for both sides. World leaders would not normally meet unless there had been careful preparations for a successful outcome. The harsh lessons of failure were learned by President Kennedy from what he called 'a very sober two days' with Khrushchev at the Vienna summit in June 1961. The frequency of summit meetings nowadays removes the expectation that ministers will score a diplomatic triumph every time. Being seen on television screens at EC summits three or four times a year enables the Prime Minister to establish himself (or herself) as an important figure at the top table without having to announce specific battle honours. It is a refreshing escape from the rigours of domestic politics while allowing ministers the chance to demonstrate to their critics at home that their problems are only part of a larger international issue. This enables ministers to get away with deadlock on an important question since they can argue that although they had 'a useful exchange of views' the ultimate answer to the problem lies in concessions from a range of other interested parties.

This form of diplomatic shadow-boxing is destined to perpetuate the summit syndrome indefinitely. The weakness of the system is that heads of government can be confronted with highly complex questions such as production levels in agriculture which are beyond their competence to understand fully. To expect them to negotiate with any degree of skill on these matters is a dangerous delusion. At the same time the ultimate decision in the democratic system rests with the head of government. An agricultural expert or a high-tech specialist is not normally mandated to take a decision which could have widespread political consequences. Striking the proper balance between these two dilemmas will remain the challenge for the summiteers and the diplomatic sherpas preparing the path to summits in the future.

Although heads of government may well be locked into the summit system indefinitely whether they like it or not – and most of them like it – there is no binding obligation on the Foreign Secretary to be in a different capital each week, or even each day at certain times of the year. The only time a British Foreign Secretary was awarded the Nobel Peace Prize was in 1925 when it went to Sir Austen Chamberlain for his work on the Locarno Treaty settling the German borders. After the careful preparatory work the Locarno Conference required Chamberlain to be in London from 5 October until the initialling ceremony on 15 October. In recent years there have been extremely few occasions when Sir Geoffrey Howe or Douglas Hurd has been at the Foreign Office for ten consecutive days. This treadmill of travelling which adds up to an average of 130,000 miles a year has surely reached the point where it is right to enquire whether that is the best way of conducting Britain's foreign policy.

All the official inquiries into the conduct of foreign policy – Plowden, Duncan, Berrill, and the Commons Select Committee investigations – have confined themselves to the Foreign Office itself. They have not concerned themselves with the way the politician invested with the seals of office of Her Majesty's Secretary of State for Foreign and Commonwealth Affairs has discharged his duties. One observation often made was that senior officials at the Foreign Office were overworked and were not allowed time to escape from the business of the day and consider the general direction of policy. An inquiry into the working day of the Foreign Secretary would reveal an even more oppressive time-driven cycle of events.

When the Foreign Secretary is out of the country he takes on a programme beginning with breakfast meetings and progressing through formal discussions to working lunches and official dinners. Then at the end of the day he has to catch up with the flow of telegrams. No wonder that Sir Geoffrey Howe, for all his stamina, often making do with only four or five hours' sleep a night, nodded off during a discussion on factory production at Kiev. Douglas Hurd had to grab every spare moment in his official car driving him from meeting to meeting to read documents and policy submissions from his staff. He often confessed that he needed two extra days in the week. One is required simply as a day away from foreign affairs to handle the normal constituency business of an MP and then switch off from the pressures of politics. The other is for the opportunity to do some longer-term analysis with a small group at Chevening, his official residence in Kent, looking, for example, at the problem of immigration in the next ten years.

It is a basic question of finding time to think. Unless a Foreign Secretary stays still long enough to analyse where the trends of current situations are leading, his grasp of foreign policy is liable to become a mere synthesis of snatched impressions in between airports. The only way to ensure that there is enough thinking time is for the Foreign Secretary to reduce his travelling by 50 per cent and run foreign policy from the Foreign Office. It is ludicrous that anyone in charge of foreign policy should be logging the mileage of a commercial traveller. His job is not to peddle 'Great Britain Limited' round the world. Flying the flag is for others. His main responsibility is making policies, not selling them. The real value of a Foreign Secretary is as a man of ideas, galvanizing his team, not leading them onto the field every week. In times of crisis it may be necessary for the Foreign Secretary to attend emergency meetings abroad frequently. But six months before the Gulf crisis Douglas Hurd travelled 20,404 miles by air in one month, January 1990.

Cutting his travel abroad by half would enable the Foreign Secretary to have regular study sessions with experts inside and outside the Foreign Office. That would allow him to get to the heart of issues which are destined to be at the top of the international agenda before they actually get there. It would give him more time to go down the policy-pyramid beneath the deputy under-secretaries and assistant under-secretaries to the heads of department and the desk officers. These are the men and women at the diplomatic coalface who have served overseas and are back at desks in London following every strand of developments. Views at that level carried weight in the past. The first secretaries at their desks are still well worth listening to. They require encouragement. Between the ages of thirty-five and forty they can become disillusioned by the drudgery of desk work. A Foreign Secretary who is seen within the Foreign Office to be consulting them more would not only gain in the policy-formulation process but would give a significant boost to morale.

One argument against curtailing a Foreign Secretary's travel is that he has to keep pace with the other Community foreign ministers. But it is only when Britain has the rotating Presidency of the Community that the Foreign Secretary is required to chair the meetings in Brussels or Luxembourg every fortnight. That comes round only once in six years at present. At other times there is no disadvantage in having a minister of state from the Foreign Office at EC meetings, especially since the UK delegation leader, Sir John Kerr, is renowned for his sharpness in detecting political boobytraps in advance. Many of the regular Foreign Affairs Councils which are attended by foreign ministers have routine agendas which could well be left in the hands of experienced specialists in Community matters. Political directors are capable of taking a large amount of the detailed workload off ministers.

Some members of the Community have a Minister of European Affairs with Cabinet rank who can take some of the burdens off the Foreign Minister. If that were considered excessive deference to the importance of Brussels, it would be possible for the Foreign Secretary to have a No. 2, designated Deputy Foreign Secretary for European Affairs. At meetings liable to be concerned with politically sensitive issues, the Foreign Secretary could attend but otherwise he would be free to concern himself with his global responsibilities at the Foreign Office while his No. 2 deputized for him in Brussels. Visiting countries outside Europe is assumed to be an essential part of a Foreign Secretary's job. That can often be justified where it is important to nurse relations with a country over a difficult patch or symbolize a new chapter in relations. Making a visit just because there has not been a ministerial visit for a number of years is hardly a justification for being away from the nerve centre. The overriding advantage of being in direct control of events from the Foreign Office warrants a careful rationing of official visits.

With the Foreign Secretary released from many of the chores traditionally accepted, there is also a strong case for freeing the Permanent Under-Secretary of State from the managerial functions which have been loaded on to him in recent years. As 'Chairman of the Board' at the Foreign Office he should be able to operate more like the head of an international business enterprise. He should be the politico-economic supremo always on hand to advise the Foreign Secretary without being distracted by management investigations. As the person who has worked his way to the top of the Service, he has the experience to be assessing with the Foreign Secretary more than just the events of the day. He should also be regularly surveying important trends with the Foreign Secretary instead of confining himself to the current monthly meeting with deputy under-secretaries.

While the maintenance of morale among diplomats is a top priority, particularly in view of the shortcomings disclosed in the recent inquiry by Coopers & Lybrand Deloitte the main duties of the PUS as Head of the Diplomatic Service should be transferred to another member of 'the Board' at the Foreign Office. There is no reason why the Foreign Office should not follow the example of most international companies and have an executive director responsible for ensuring a cost-efficient service. That would relieve the PUS of the obligation to appear before committees on questions of staffing, budgeting, and embassy-building expenditure. Some of these duties have been shared with the Chief Clerk – a title out of tune with diplomacy in the satellite era which was reintroduced in 1970. But the time has surely come for managerial responsibility to be concentrated in one portfolio. Matters of internal discipline and other management problems should not take up the time of the PUS. Since continuity is important, the person appointed executive director should be installed for more than the usual three-year or four-year posting.

It seems ridiculously archaic that the Head of the Foreign Office should have to suspend his activities – three times a week, on occasion – to change into court regalia for ceremonial duties at Buckingham Palace at the introduction of ambassadors. To transfer that role to someone else would require royal approval but the argument for change is compelling. If the duties cannot be undertaken by the Vice-Marshal of the Diplomatic Corps for reasons of protocol, there may be a case for reviving the role of Special Representative of the Secretary of State. In November 1960 Lord Home brought Sir Nevile Bland, an old Etonian who had been Ambassador to the Netherlands, out of retirement at the age of seventy-four to be his Special Representative, fulfilling all sorts of ceremonial duties with superb aplomb.

In the coming decades the role of the Head of the Foreign Office will become increasingly significant, provided efforts are made now to siphon off duties diverting him from his primary function of ensuring that the Foreign Secretary has all the skills of the staff employed to their best advantage. This will be made easier if there is a restructuring of the upper echelons of the Diplomatic Service which have remained top-heavy since the absorption of the Commonwealth Relations Office in 1968. Instead of having 21 senior officials under the PUS – 6 deputy under-secretaries and 15 assistant under-secretaries – as at present, it should be possible to operate efficiently with a directorate of 12. That would enhance the responsibility of heads of department who usually form the intellectual spearhead of the Foreign Office.

If Foreign Secretaries cut their travel by half in the next three decades, it will enable the Diplomatic Service to revert to its traditional function of having ambassadors playing a significant role in the conduct of foreign affairs. Instead of being asked for a thumbnail sketch of the political situation by the Foreign Secretary in the beflagged car driving him from the airport, the ambassador can be the 'usual diplomatic channels' again. There are sometimes dangers of an ambassador becoming a victim of what the distinguished American diplomat Charles Thayer called 'localitis' – the belief that one's own parish is the diplomatic centre of the universe. But normally by the time a diplomat becomes an ambassador he has acquired the experience and judgement to set events in a balanced perspective. Occasionally, it can be almost as unwise to be too laid back in following the well-known advice of Talleyrand,

'*Et surtout pas trop de zèle*'. For an ambassador to get excited at times may help to expedite action in London.

In the past three decades the decline of the role of British ambassadors in the conduct of foreign affairs, with the exception of those in posts such as Moscow, Peking, Washington, Brussels, and Pretoria, has been doubly damaging. It has diminished the input from diplomatic posts in policy-making and allowed some politicians to believe that the impressions they gain during their travels or at conferences are the best guidelines for the formulation of policy. It has contributed to a devaluation of Britain's standing in many capitals. Countries and their governments often judge Britain by the ambassador sent to them. If he is a highly regarded envoy, trusted to convey important policy decisions directly to the host government and relied upon for an accurate assessment of that government's views to his own government, then his usefulness will have a significant effect upon relations between the two countries. If he is seen to be bypassed by ministers in London, much of his value will be lost.

Reversing the trend of recent years and re-establishing the traditional role of the ambassador will pay many dividends. It will enable the Foreign Secretary to have an authoritative analysis of a situation from a capital which he can take time to assess, free from the fatigue of constant travelling. The government to which the ambassador is accredited will have the confidence of knowing that events and attitudes are being intelligently reported and put in a realistic context by someone who knows the country well and is respected in London as such. Not least important will be the effect on the Diplomatic Service. Once ambassadors are convinced that they really matter and their views count in Downing Street, that will engender a new *esprit de corps* throughout the Diplomatic Service. It may even justify the elitism that maintains the mystique inside the Foreign Office.

APPENDIX I

Foreign Secretaries
1960–1992

28 July 1960	Lord Home (Conservative)
21 October 1963	R. A. Butler (Conservative)
16 October 1964	P. C. Gordon Walker (Labour)
24 January 1965	Michael Stewart (Labour)
12 August 1966	George Brown (Labour)
15 March 1968	Michael Stewart (Labour)
20 June 1970	Sir Alec Douglas-Home (Conservative)
5 March 1974	James Callaghan (Labour)
9 April 1976	Anthony Crosland (Labour)
22 February 1977	David Owen (Labour)
5 May 1979	Lord Carrington (Conservative)
5 April 1982	Francis Pym (Conservative)
11 June 1983	Sir Geoffrey Howe (Conservative)
25 July 1989	John Major (Conservative)
26 October 1989	Douglas Hurd (Conservative

APPENDIX II

Permanent Under-Secretaries of State at the Foreign Office 1957–1992

4 February 1957	Lord Inchyra (Sir Frederick Hoyer Millar)
1 January 1962	Lord Caccia (Sir Harold Caccia)
10 May 1965	Lord Gore-Booth (Sir Paul Gore-Booth)
1 February 1969	Lord Greenhill (Sir Denis Greenhill)
8 November 1973	Lord Brimelow (Sir Thomas Brimelow)
22 November 1975	Sir Michael Palliser
8 April 1982	Sir Antony Acland
23 June 1986	Sir Patrick Wright
28 June 1991	Sir David Gillmore

Bibliography

A great many volumes touch upon various aspects of the period covered in this book. Those which are particularly relevant are listed below.

Adamson, David: *The Last Empire* (London: I. B. Tauris, 1989)

Andrew, Christopher, and Gordievsky, Oleg: *KGB: The Inside Story* (London: Hodder & Stoughton, 1990)

Astrow, André: *Zimbabwe: A Revolution that Lost Its Way* (London: Zed Press, 1983)

Butler, R. A.: *The Art of the Possible* (London: Hamish Hamilton, 1971)

Callaghan, Lord: *Time and Chance* (London: Collins, 1981)

Carrington, Lord: *Reflect on Things Past* (London: Collins, 1988)

Clark, Eric: *Corps Diplomatique* (London: Allen Lane, 1973)

Commonwealth Secretariat: *Diplomatic Service* (Harlow: Longman, 1971)

Cromwell, Valerie: *Foreign Ministries of the World: The F.C.O.* (London: Times Books, 1982)

Crosland, Susan: *Tony Crosland* (London: Jonathan Cape, 1982)

Denktash, R. R.: *The Cyprus Triangle* (London: George Allen & Unwin, 1982)

Dickie, John: *The Uncommon Commoner: A Study of Sir Alec Douglas-Home* (London: Pall Mall, 1964)

Dzhirkvelov, Ilya: *Secret Servant: My Life with the KGB and the Soviet Elite* (London: Collins, 1987)

Eban, Abba: *The New Diplomacy* (London: Weidenfeld & Nicolson, 1983)

Falkender, Marcia: *Downing Street in Perspective* (London: Weidenfeld & Nicolson, 1983)

Feltham, R. G.: *Diplomatic Handbook* (Harlow: Longman, 1977)

Fox, Robert: *Antarctica and the South Atlantic* (London: BBC Books, 1985)

George-Brown, Lord: *In My Way* (London: Victor Gollancz, 1971)

Gladwyn, Lord: *Memoirs* (London: Weidenfeld & Nicolson, 1972)

Gore-Booth, Lord: *With Truth and Great Respect* (London: Constable, 1974)

Haig, Alexander M., Jr: *Caveat: Realism, Reagan and Foreign Policy* (London: Weidenfeld & Nicolson, 1984)

Haines, Joe: *The Politics of Power* (London: Jonathan Cape, 1977)

Harris, Kenneth: *David Owen Personally Speaking* (London: Weidenfeld & Nicolson, 1987)

Harris, Robert: *Good and Faithful Servant* (London: Faber & Faber, 1990)

Hastings, Max, and Jenkins, Simon: *The Battle for the Falklands* (London: Michael Joseph, 1983)

Healey, Denis: *The Time of My Life* (London: Michael Joseph, 1989)

Henderson, Sir Nicholas: *The Private Office* (London: Weidenfeld & Nicolson, 1984)

HM Stationery Office: Plowden Report (London: Cmnd 2276, 1964)
> Duncan Report (London: Cmnd 4107, 1969)
> Berrill Report (London: Cmnd 7308, 1977)

Home, Lord: *The Way the Wind Blows* (London: Collins, 1976)

Horne, Alistair: *Macmillan. Vol. 2: 1957–80* (London: Macmillan, 1989)

Howard, Anthony: *Rab: The Life of R. A. Butler* (London: Jonathan Cape, 1987)

Hudson, Miles: *Triumph or Tragedy: Rhodesia to Zimbabwe* (London: Hamish Hamilton, 1981)

Hunt, Sir David: *On the Spot* (London: Peter Davies, 1978)

Ingham, Bernard: *Kill the Messenger* (London: HarperCollins, 1991)

Jackson, Sir Geoffrey: *Concorde Diplomacy* (London: Hamish Hamilton, 1981)

Jenkins, Simon, and Sloman, Anne: *With Respect, Ambassador* (London: BBC Books, 1985)

Johnson, Lyndon Baines: *The Vantage Point: Perspectives of the Presidency 1963–69* (London: Weidenfeld & Nicolson, 1972)

Koumoulides, John T. A.: *Cyprus in Transition* (London: Trigraph, 1986)

Martin, David, and Johnson, Phyllis: *The Struggle for Zimbabwe* (London: Faber & Faber, 1981)

Moorhouse, Geoffrey: *The Diplomats* (London: Jonathan Cape, 1977)

Nkomo, Joshua: *Nkomo – The Story of My Life* (London: Methuen, 1984)

Ogden, Chris: *Maggie* (New York: Simon & Schuster, 1990)

Panteli, Stavros: *A New History of Cyprus* (London: East–West Publications, 1984)

Parsons, Sir Anthony: *The Pride and the Fall: Iran 1974–79* (London: Jonathan Cape, 1984)

Salinger, Pierre, with Laurent, Eric: *Secret Dossier: The Hidden Agenda Behind the Gulf War* (London: Penguin Books, 1991)

Satow, Sir Ernest: *Guide to Diplomatic Practice*, 5th edition, edited by Lord Gore-Booth (Harlow: Longman, 1979)

Smith, Geoffrey: *Reagan and Thatcher* (London: Bodley Head, 1990)

Smith, Hedrick: *The Power Game: How Washington Works* (London: Collins, 1989)

Stewart, Michael: *Life and Labour* (London: Sidgwick & Jackson, 1980)

Thayer, Charles: *Diplomat* (London: Michael Joseph, 1960)

Toplis, Ian: *The Foreign Office: An Architectural History* (London: Mansell, 1987)

Trevelyan, Lord: *Worlds Apart* (London: Macmillan, 1971) *Diplomatic Channels* (London: Macmillan, 1973)

Tugendhat, Christopher, and Wallace, William: *Options for British Foreign Policy in the 1990s* (London: RIIA, 1988)

Verrier, Anthony: *The Road to Zimbabwe* (London: Jonathan Cape, 1986)

Wallace, William: *The Foreign Policy Process in Britain* (London: RIIA, 1976)

The Transformation of Western Europe (London: RIIA, 1990)

Weinberger, Caspar: *Fighting for Peace* (London: Michael Joseph, 1990)

Wilson, Harold: *The Labour Government: 1964–70* (London: Weidenfeld & Nicolson, 1971)

Young, Hugo: *One of Us* (London: Macmillan, 1989)

Index